POSTCARD HISTORY SERIES

Narragansett Bay

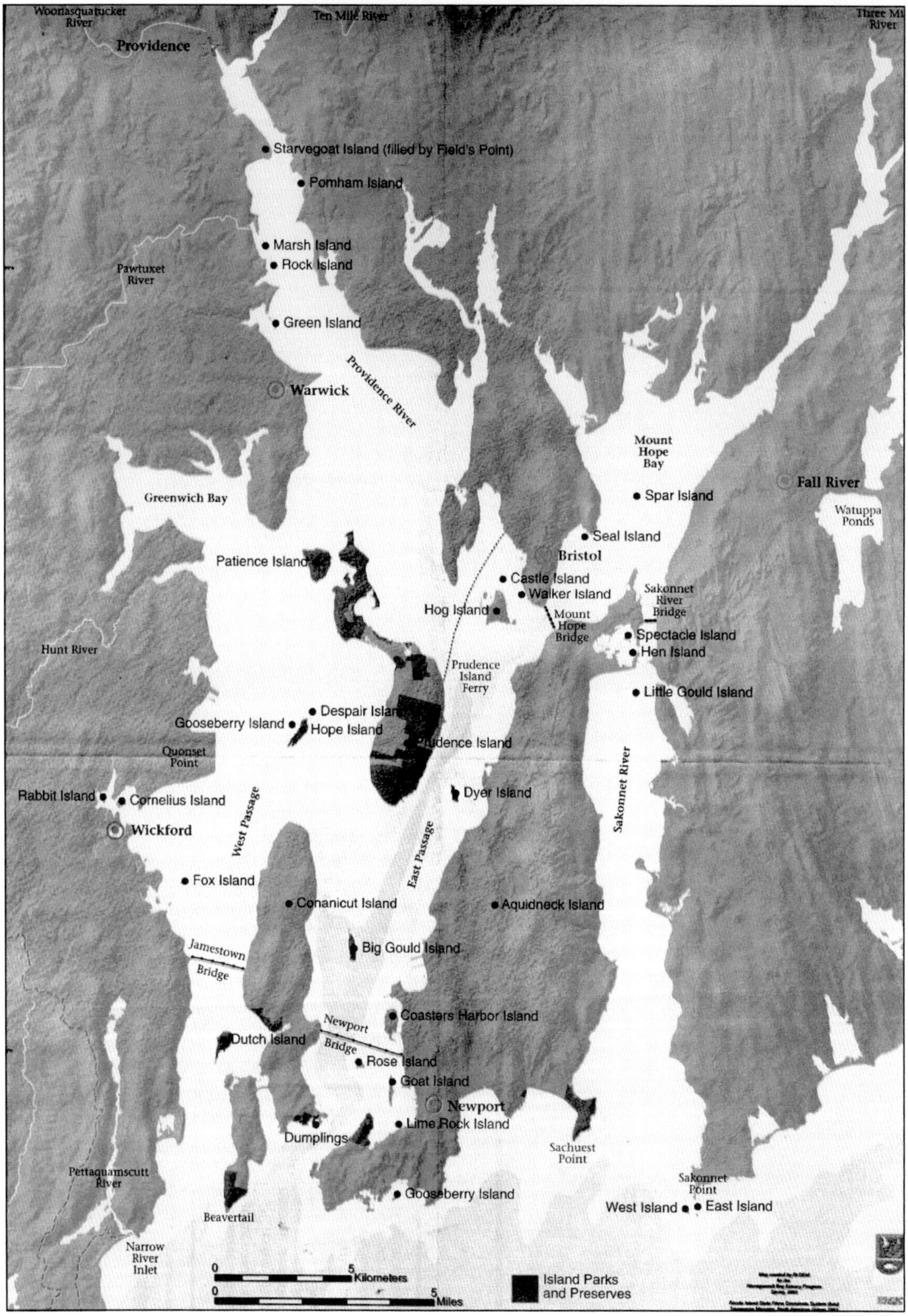

Rhode Island is "the Ocean State," and Narragansett Bay is its heart. The author supports the goals of Save The Bay.

Postcard History Series

Narragansett Bay

Richard V. Simpson

ARCADIA
PUBLISHING

ISBN 978-0-7385-4458-8

Published by Arcadia Publishing
Charleston, South Carolina

Printed in the United States of America

Library of Congress Catalog Card Number: 2005936499

For all general information contact Arcadia Publishing at:
Telephone 843-853-2070
Fax 843-853-0044
E-mail sales@arcadiapublishing.com
For customer service and orders:
Toll-Free 1-888-313-2665

Visit us on the Internet at www.arcadiapublishing.com

Other Books by Richard V. Simpson

Bristol, Rhode Island (1996)
Bristol, Rhode Island: Volume II (1998)
The America's Cup Yachts: The Rhode Island Connection (1999)
Building the Mosquito Fleet: U.S. Navy's First Torpedo Boats (2001)
Bristol: Montaup to Poppasquash (2002)
Postcard History Series: *Bristol* (2005)

Books by Richard V. Simpson and Nancy J. Devin

Portsmouth, Rhode Island (1997)
Tiverton and Little Compton (1997)
Tiverton and Little Compton: Volume II (1998)

On the cover (Front): Several steamship lines operated on the lucrative Providence to Block Island run. In this *c.* 1906 postcard image, carriages and omnibuses wait to convey ferry passengers to nearby hotels and resorts.

On the cover (Back): The steamer *Mount Hope* approaches the busy New Harbor Wharf, Block Island.

Contents

FOREWORD

Richard V. Simpson is a native Rhode Islander who, when a teenager living in the Edgewood section of Cranston, spent many summer days fishing from the docks of the Edgewood Yacht Club. When he moved to Bristol in 1960, he chose to move into a *c.* 1810 Federal-style home, only a short walk from the sweet-salt aroma of Narragansett Bay that flows into Bristol Harbor. For 28 years, Simpson commuted over the Mount Hope Bridge to his job as a graphic designer with the U.S. Navy in Newport. During his daily commute, he was treated to the sweeping vistas of Narragansett Bay, Prudence and Hog Islands, the Hog Island Shoal Light, and the passage of commercial and pleasure boats; that is when he began collecting Narragansett Bay related graphics, including the postcards that illustrate this book. This book is his 13th published title; it is his 10th title published by Arcadia. Since 1985, Simpson has authored over 65 articles on various antiques subjects for the national monthly *Antiques & Collecting Magazine.*

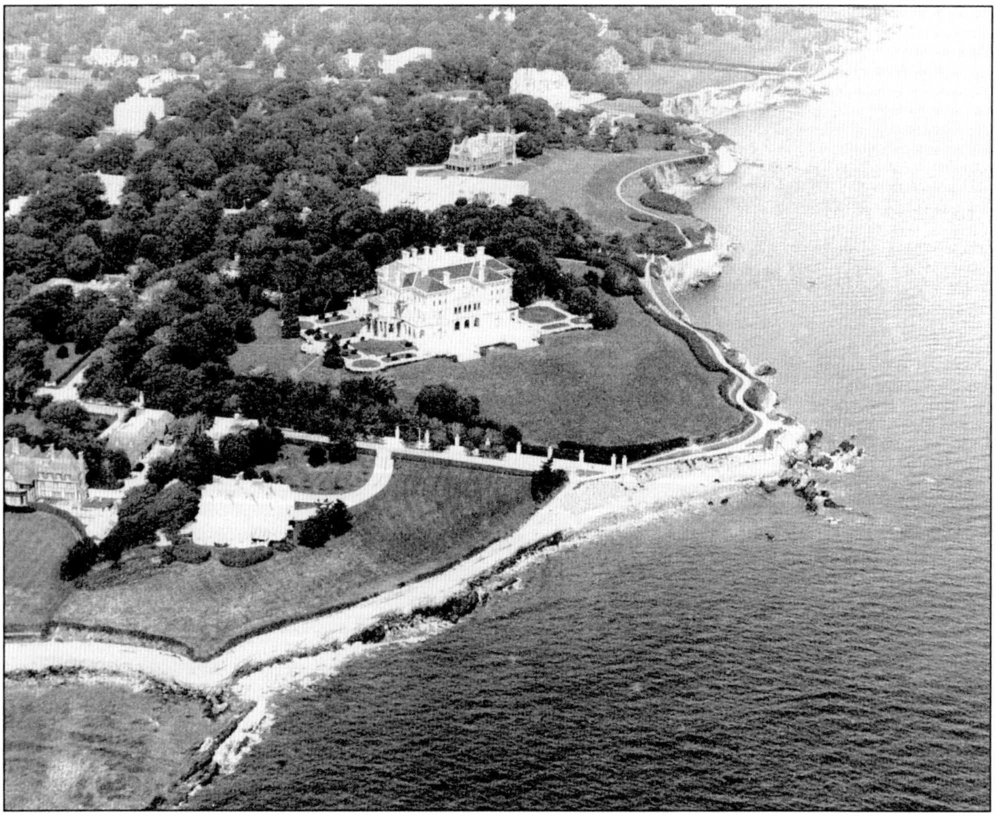

The celebrated and wealthy of the world came to the shores of Narragansett Bay to build their palatial summer "cottages." This is Cornelius Vanderbilt's flamboyant cottage called the Breakers, built overlooking the roaring Atlantic, and Newport's pedestrian shore-path Cliff Walk.

Introduction

Glaciers have advanced and retreated across North America many times during the past three million years. The glaciers are in good part responsible for the present shape and character of the land, since the ice leveled off hilltops and filled valleys with rocks, clay, and gravel. Narragansett Bay and much of Rhode Island lie in an ancient basin filled with soft sedimentary rocks. When the glacier of 18,000 years ago bulldozed its way across southern New England, it reached as far south as Long Island. One of the legacies of the glacier is the glacial drift that blankets the bedrock above most of the land and seafloor in this region. This drift, the unconsolidated layer of boulders, cobbles, gravel, sand, and clay that was moved and deposited by the ice sheet, is as much as 300 feet thick in channels scoured out by the ice and some 12 to 150 feet thick in most areas of Rhode Island and Block Island Sounds in Narragansett Bay.

Viking, explorer, trader, and pirate, men of peace, and men of war have all raised their sails high on the masts of their ships; they have come and ventured forth upon the waters of Narragansett Bay. The waters of Narragansett Bay have played host to tall warships and whaling and commercial ships of the 18th and 19th centuries, tall steel training ships from many nations in the late 20th century, and the graceful little sloops and gallant racing yachts that one sees in the fair harbors of the Rhode Island sailing fraternities' yacht clubs.

The opening date of the era of steamboats was 1817, an era that has lasted up to the present day; alas, the motive power of wood and coal has been replaced by diesel fuel. In that year, the ugly little steamer the *Firefly* made its first appearance in Narragansett Bay when it steamed from New York to Newport in about 28 hours. To those accustomed to seeing the slim and graceful lines of the tall flyers, this tiny vessel with its awkward lines and black smoke, puffing and wheezing, was a bitter disappointment. By 1821, steamboats were making a major impact on transportation on the bay. The early sound steamers, the *Fulton* and the *Connecticut*, made one round-trip each week between New York and Providence. In 1825, the *Washington* was put into service. It was 131 feet long and was the first steamer to have a pair of beam engines, each independent of the other. Two years later, a rival steamship company, owner of the *Chancellor Livingston*, took that ship off the Albany–New York route and placed it on the Providence run as an opposition boat to those who had become successful. In retaliation, in 1828, the *Benjamin Franklin* was brought to Rhode Island waters by rivals of the *Chancellor Livingston*.

In 1831, the *Chancellor Livingston* ran down and sunk the *Washington* during a dense fog in the Rhode Island Sound. To replace her, the *Boston* was built. The *Boston* was the first steamer to be built without masts and sails. As a sister ship, a new boat called the *Providence* was built by the Providence Steamboat Company.

In 1835, Cornelius Vanderbilt constructed the steamboat *Lexington* and began to take a decided interest in navigation in Narragansett Bay. The following year, Captain Comstock built the *Massachusetts*, which his brother commanded. The bay was now becoming crowded by steamers.

In 1851, a line of freighters was established. These steamers were the first to get away from the use of paddle wheels, being equipped with single screw propellers.

At the same time, there were many little steamers going up and down the bay. There were many of them from the time of the *Firefly*. About the same time, there was the *Wadsworth*, named for the man who built it. Following in the order named were the steamers *Rushlight*, *Balloon*, and the *Iolas*. These made regular trips between Providence and Newport, with side stops at Warren and Bristol, carrying passengers principally on excursions that lasted through afternoons and evenings.

Ferryboats moved passengers and supplies between coastal communities. Luxurious overnight steamers and excursion boats owned by the Fall River Line carried vacationers from Fall River, Providence, and Newport to New York and beyond. These, then, were the early days of steamboats in Narragansett Bay. With the advent of modern Narragansett Bay bridges, the need for bay commuter ferries ended.

To escape city heat, southern aristocrats and wealthy captains of industry came to Newport, Little Compton, and Bristol, to Wickford, and to Westerly to build their summer cottages, and with them came their sport of ocean sailboat racing. Later, with the emergence of an affluent middle class with disposable wealth and abundant free time, private yacht clubs began to appear in all the bay's principal harbors.

Because so many Rhode Islanders were visiting the beaches of Narragansett Bay for work (longshoremen and boatmen, shell and fin fishermen) and for recreation (to swim, sail, and sport fish), the United States Volunteer Life Saving Service (USVLSS) was formed to provide a source of rescue to all who may be seized by the wiles of the ocean.

The Rhode Island chapter of the USVLSS was formed in 1904. The goals of the USVLSS, as stated in its charter, was to provide for the saving of human life on any of the waters of the United States where no provisions is made therefore by the national government, by the organization of crews of Volunteer Life Savers fully equipped with lifesaving appliances and thoroughly qualified for every variety of lifesaving work on the water; to place lifeboats, medicine chests, life preservers, and other necessary appliances at all dangerous points on the said waters, as well as to give instruction in Red Cross and lifesaving work, and to present honor medals and certificates for all acts of heroism on the waters.

For strategic reasons, the British Navy, the Colonial Navy of Rhode Island, and the United States Navy have all had a keen interest in Narragansett Bay.

In 1764, Robert Melville, newly appointed governor of the island of Granada, conducted a three-month survey of Narragansett Bay. It was he who first reported the merits of the bay for the establishment of a naval anchorage to the British Admiralty. He considered the bay as "one of the best natural harbours [sic] in the world." Melville continued, "The vicinity of the ocean is such that in one hour a fleet may be from their anchorage to sea; or from sea to safe anchorage."

The first apparent interest expressed by the United States Navy occurred in 1798, when Newport was considered as a site for a navy shipyard. Secretary of the Navy Benjamin Stoddert, in a message to President Adams of April 1800, said that Narragansett Bay was far superior to Boston as a "principal rendezvous for the Navy in a war on our coast and as an asylum for ships damaged in action and seeking a port for repairs."

The first official move to Newport by the U.S. Navy came at the behest of Rear Admiral Stephen B. Luce, assistant commandant of the Naval Academy in Annapolis, Maryland. With action in the Civil War raging so close to the academy, it was Luce's decision to move all operations to Newport.

Things remained reasonably quiet in Newport until the time of the Civil War. Fort Wolcott, along with Fort Adams, on the southwestern shore of Newport Harbor, had fallen into disrepair in the intervening years. Tension and apprehension among coastal residents again began to rise in the mid-1800s. It became increasingly apparent that discord between the states on the subjects of slavery and state's rights would not be settled peaceably. It was on May 8, 1861, that the calm of a balmy spring afternoon was shattered by the sound of heavy cannon fire. All Newport rushed to the wharves and hills, concerned that the often-rumored rebel attack on Fort Adams had begun.

Much to their surprise, they saw that it was the frigate *Constitution*, "Old Ironsides," its guns thundering an answer to the 24-gun salute from Fort Adams. On board were 130 midshipmen from the recently evacuated Naval Academy at Annapolis. They were supposed to go to Fort Adams, but the staff took one look at the place and quickly began looking for suitable quarters in Newport, in a nicer part of town. Finding none to their satisfaction, they took residence at Fort Wolcott on Goat Island.

A few hours later, the steamer *Baltic* entered the harbor; on board were the professors, their families, and every book and piece of equipment that they could carry from the academy. The *Constitution* was soon joined by the Naval Academy school ships the *Macedonian* and the *Santee*. These tall ships soon became a familiar part of the Newport skyline.

One

The U.S. Navy's Atlantic Fleet, Naval War College, Naval Torpedo Station

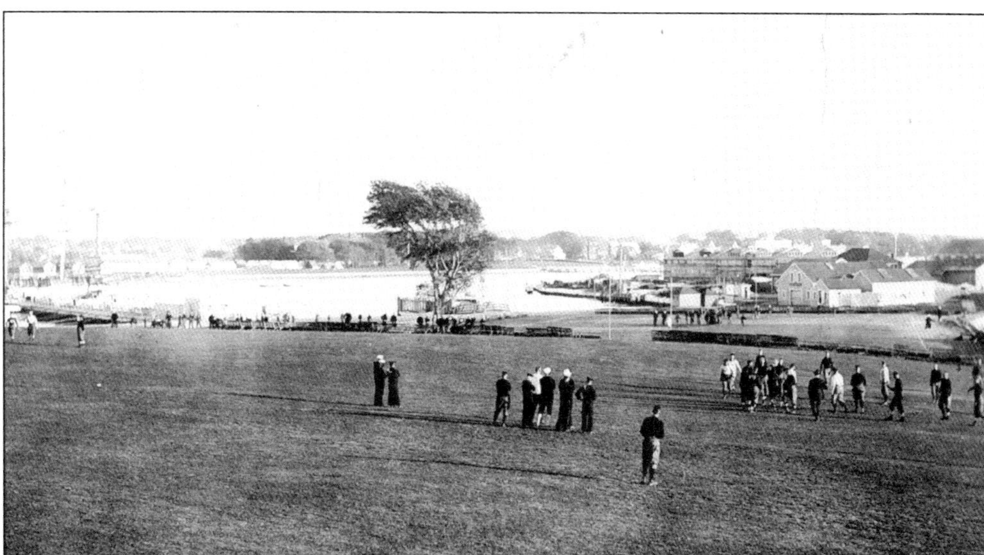

Midshipmen play football on the parade grounds of the Naval Training Station on Coasters Harbor Island. Faintly, in the left background can be seen the training ship the USS *Constellation* around 1900.

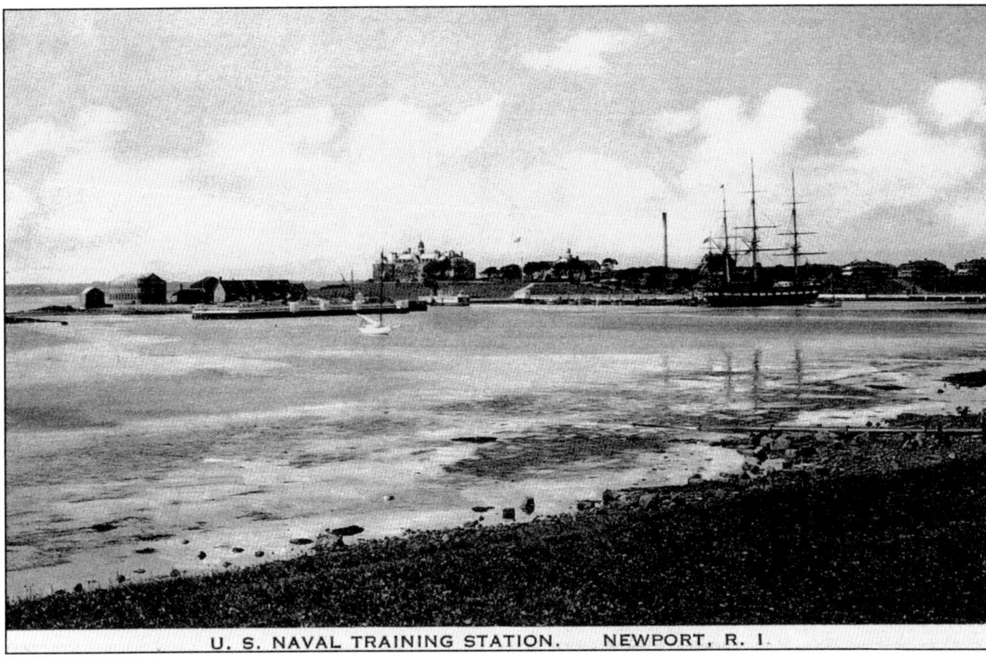

The U.S. Naval Training Station, Coasters Harbor Island, is viewed here from the Newport shore around 1903. From center right to left are the Naval War College (largest building), the administration building, the commandant's quarters, the training ship the USS *Constellation*, and the Marine barracks.

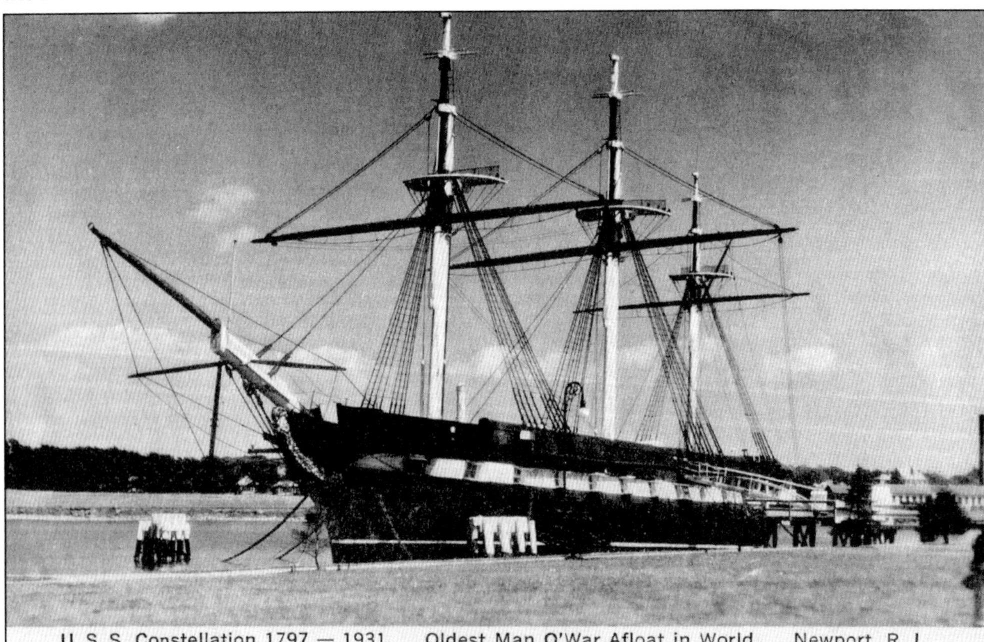

In 1894, the *Constellation* underwent conversion to a stationary training ship. Arriving under tow at Newport on May 22, 1894, it remained a permanently moored vessel at the U.S. Naval Training Center. When the Navy ended training in sail handling in July 1920, the *Constellation* remained in Newport, seeing decreased activity over the next 20 years.

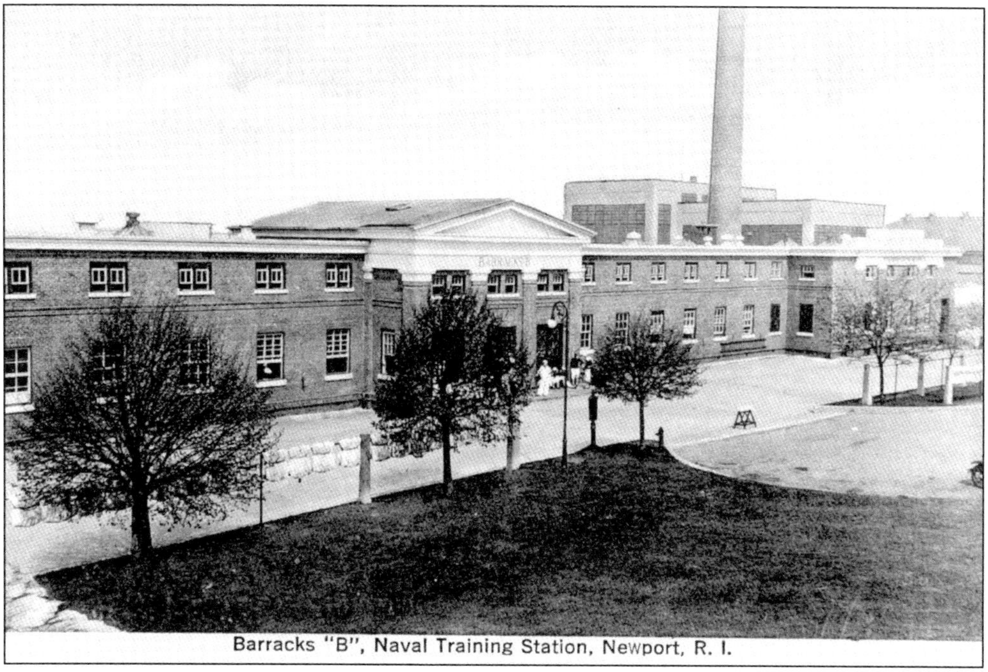

Barracks B and the power station are seen here at the Naval Training Station around 1930.

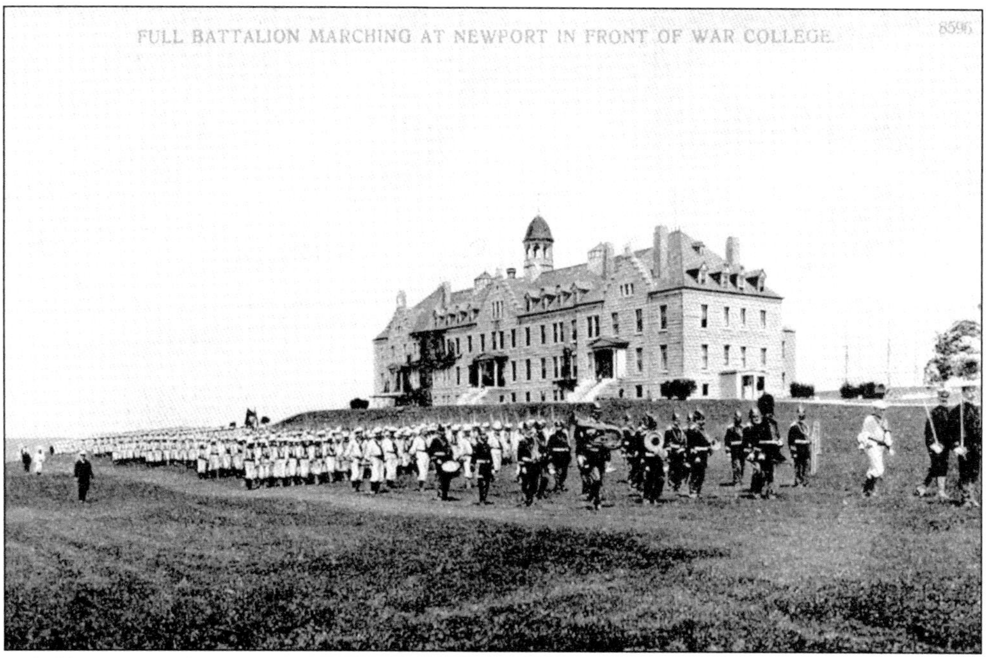

A full battalion of midshipmen pass in review on the parade in front of the Naval War College building around 1910.

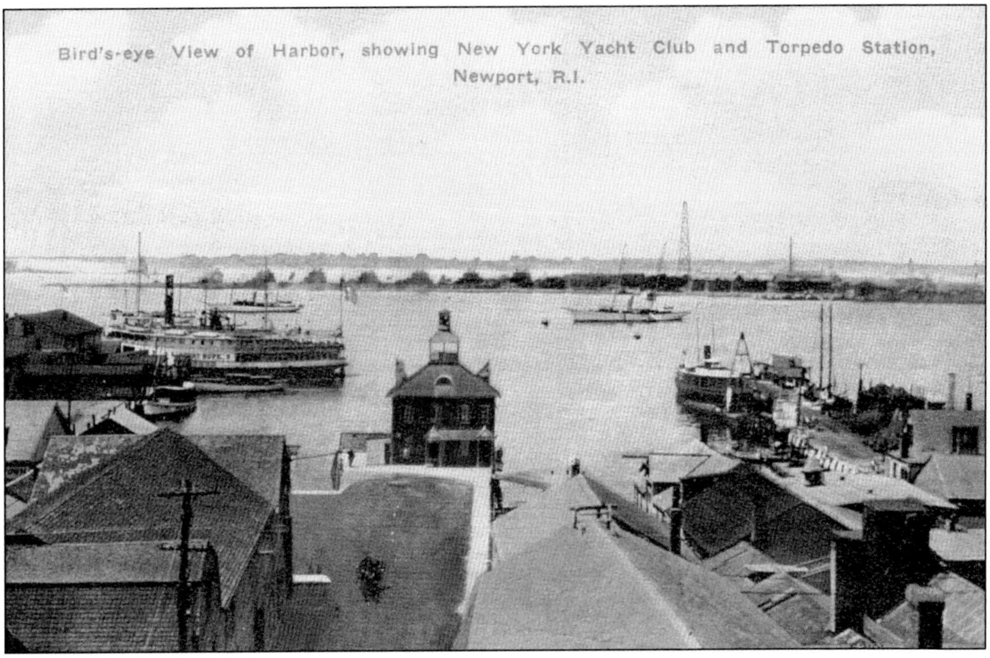

In this *c.* 1904 bird's-eye view of Newport Harbor is the docked steamer *Mount Hope* (left), the New York Yacht Club (center), and the Jamestown ferry at its slip (right), and in the background is Goat Island and the Naval Torpedo Station.

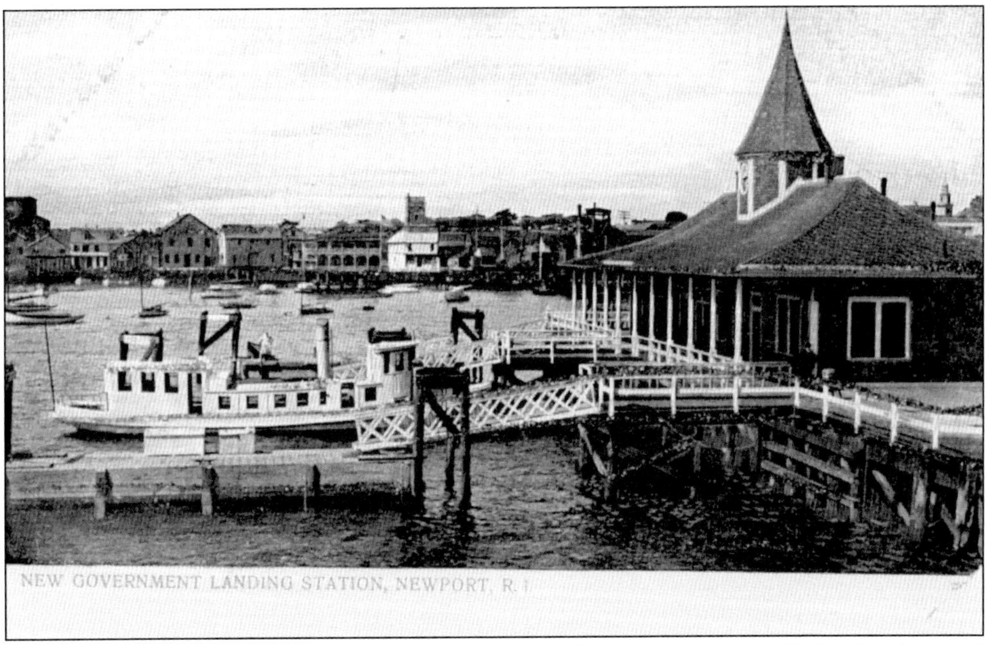

This is a view north of the new government ferry landing station around 1910. The cluster of buildings in the background is comprised of warehouses and pubs on Long Wharf.

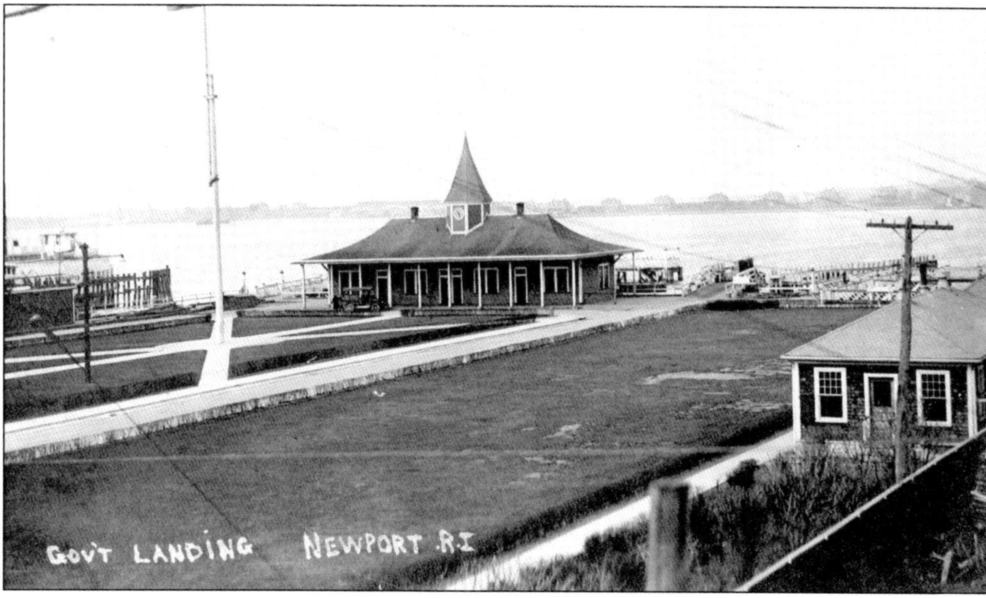

Here is a view west of the government ferry landing station with Goat Island and the Naval Torpedo Station (NTS) in the background around 1910. From this ferry landing, civilian and military personnel commuted to their jobs at NTS.

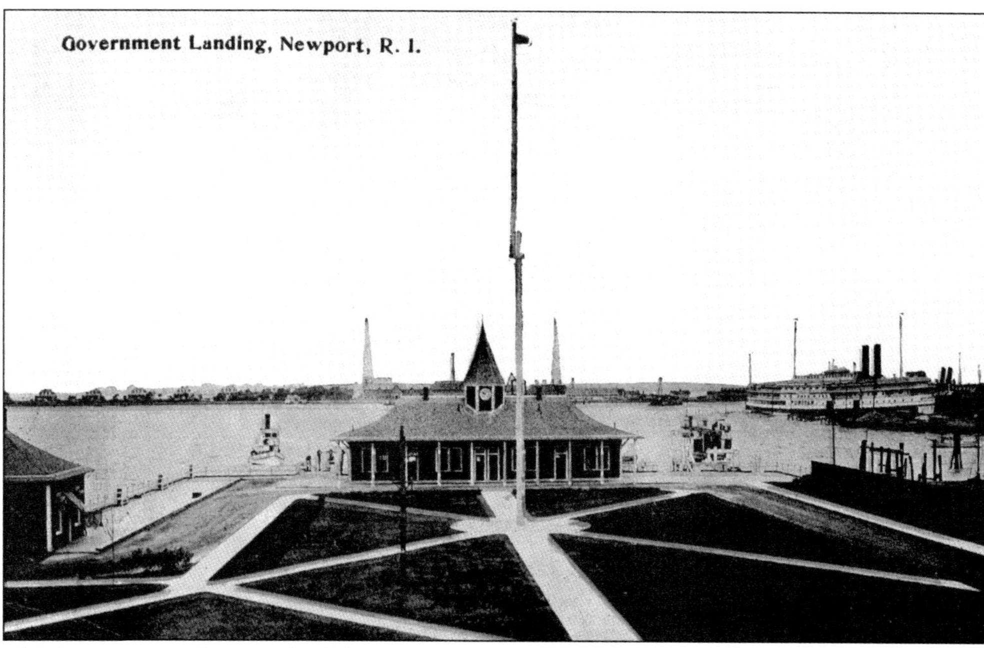

This later *c.* 1915 photograph of the government landing shows the well-manicured quadrangle. The overnight excursion steamer the *Puritan* is taking on passengers at its Long Wharf dockage.

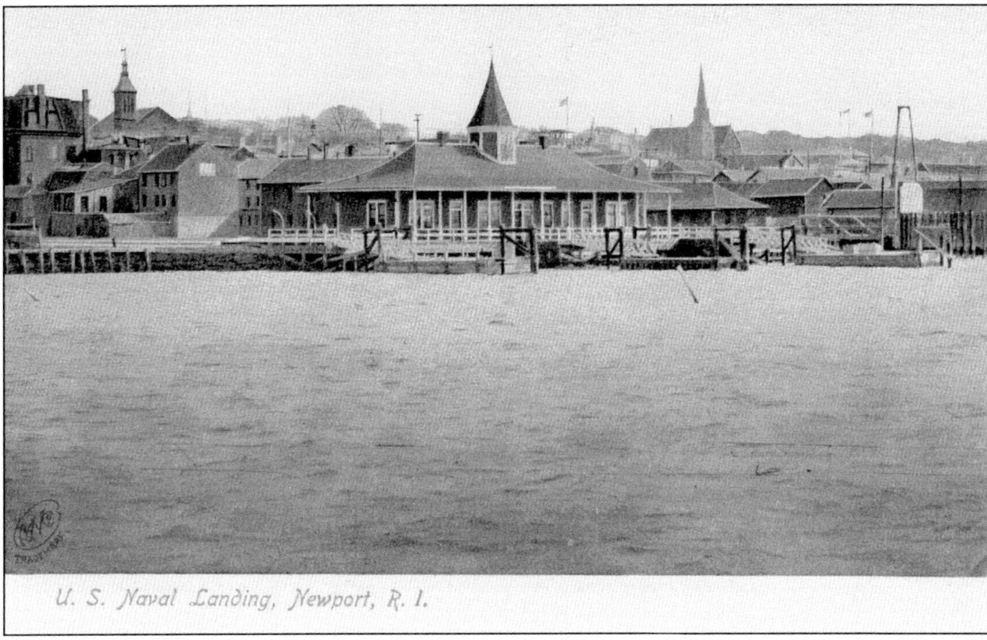

This is a view east with the government landing in the center. In the background is the tightly packed commercial center of downtown Newport; the spire of the Trinity Episcopal Church dominates the right horizon.

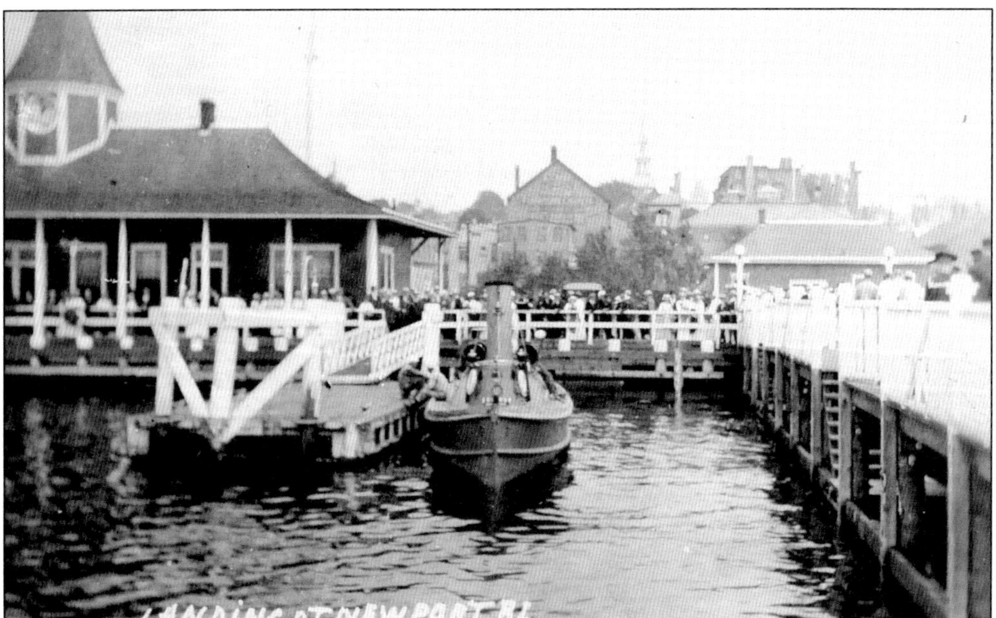

A U.S. Navy steam launch is docked at the government landing. Notice the multitude of civilians and sailors milling around the railings of the wharf; some sailors are returning from duty while others wait to depart.

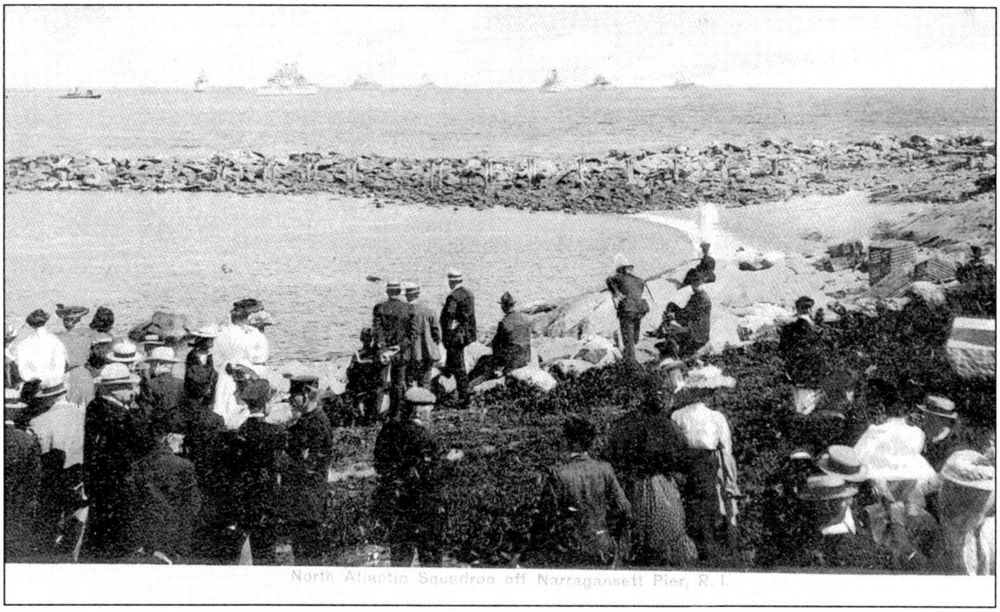

It was always a festive day when the North Atlantic Squadron was scheduled to make an appearance in Narragansett Bay. Rhode Islanders, dressed in their Sunday best, gathered at favorite viewing spots along the bay's coast to welcome the approaching fleet.

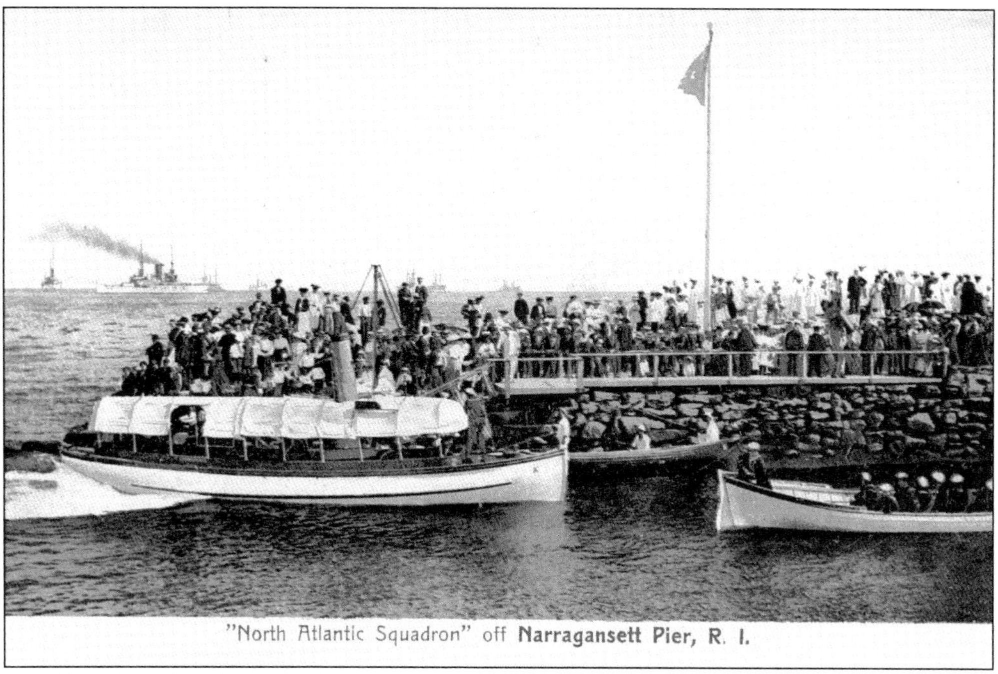

The ships' launches dispatch Blue Jackets to the welcoming arms of families and friends waiting at Narragansett Pier.

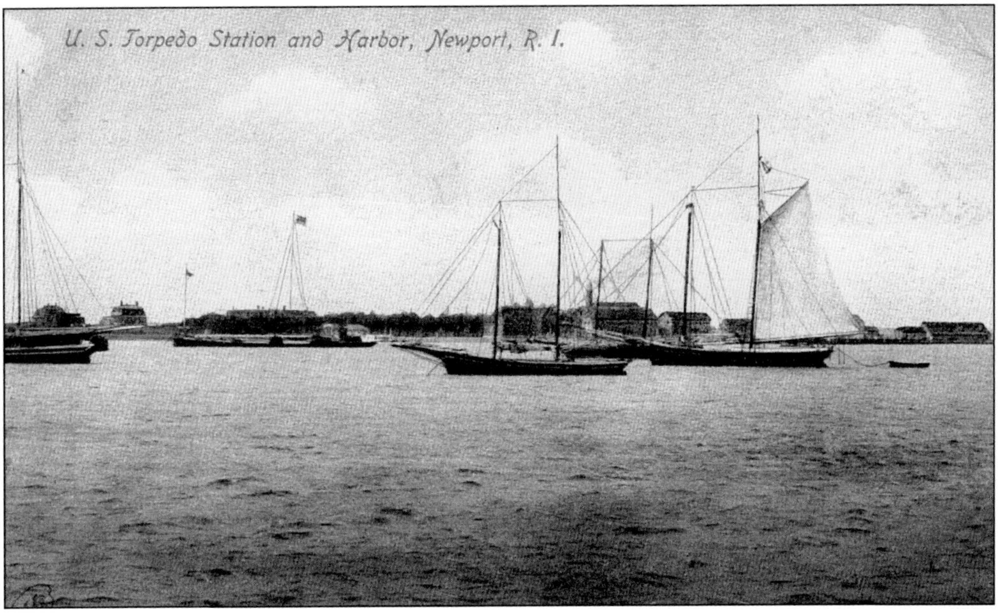

Sailboats at anchor in Newport Harbor are seen here. The Naval Torpedo Station is in background, around 1910.

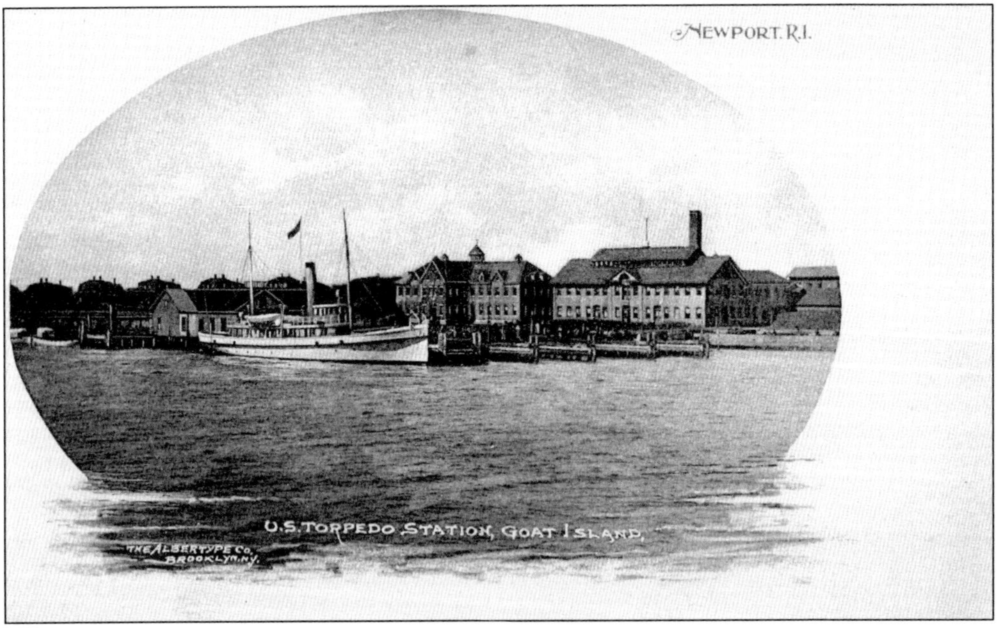

From left to right at the Naval Torpedo Station are the administration building, and the machine shop; the U.S. Navy (USN) tug *Lyden* is in the foreground, and torpedo boat slips are on the right, foreground, around 1915.

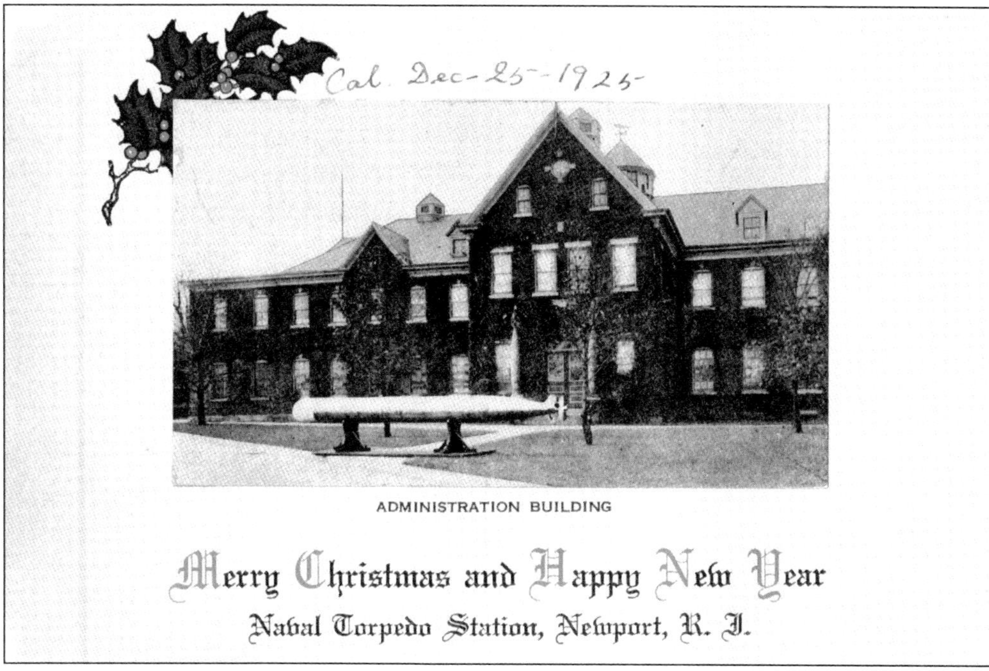

A Naval Torpedo Station (NTS) Christmas greeting postcard is dated 1925.

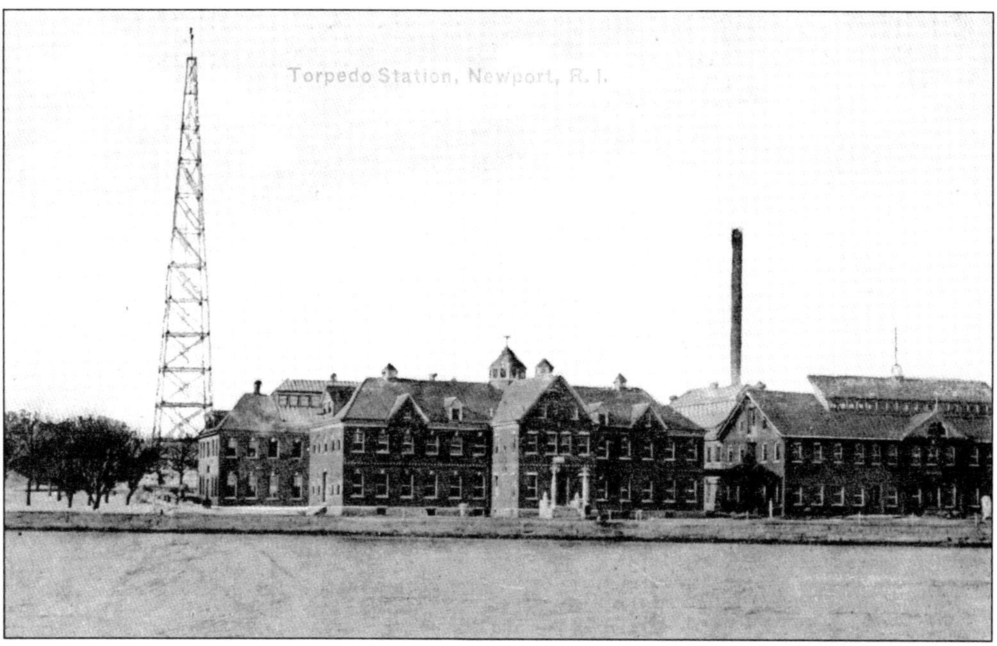

A close-up view of the torpedo station administration building and machine shop is seen here.

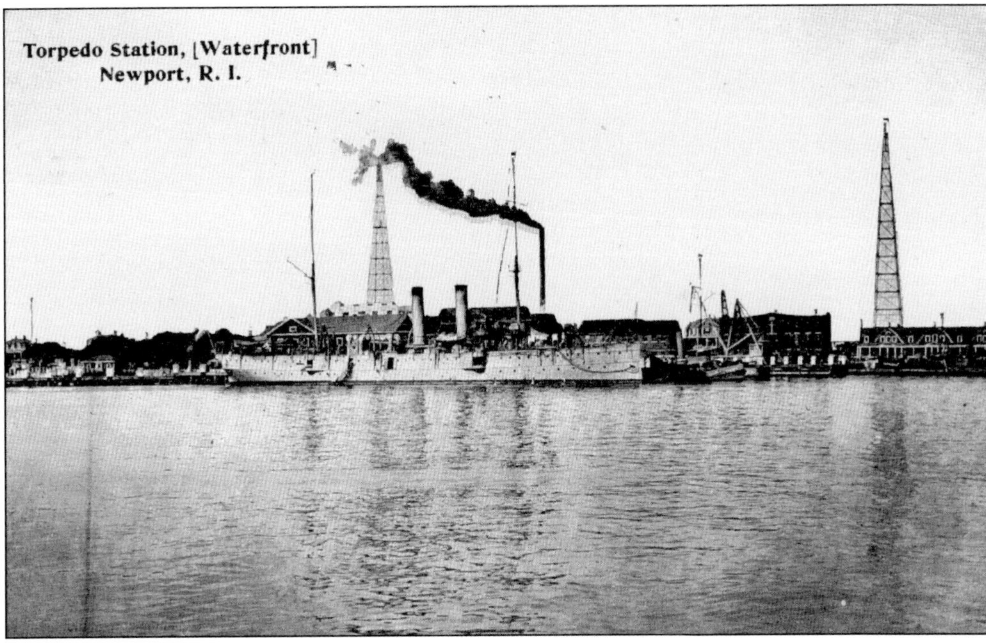

The NTS with a USN cruiser dockside is seen here, taking on torpedoes for testing on the Narragansett Bay torpedo test range around 1914.

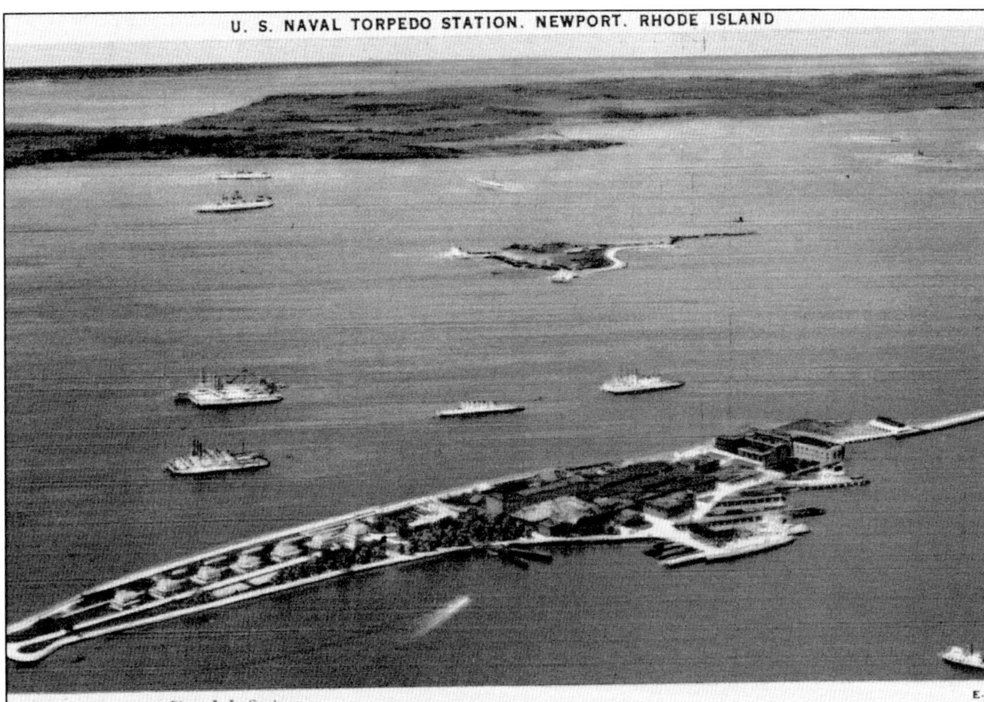

Here is a bird's-eye view of Goat Island and the NTS. In the near background is Rose Island, and in the far background is Conanicut Island (Jamestown) around 1920.

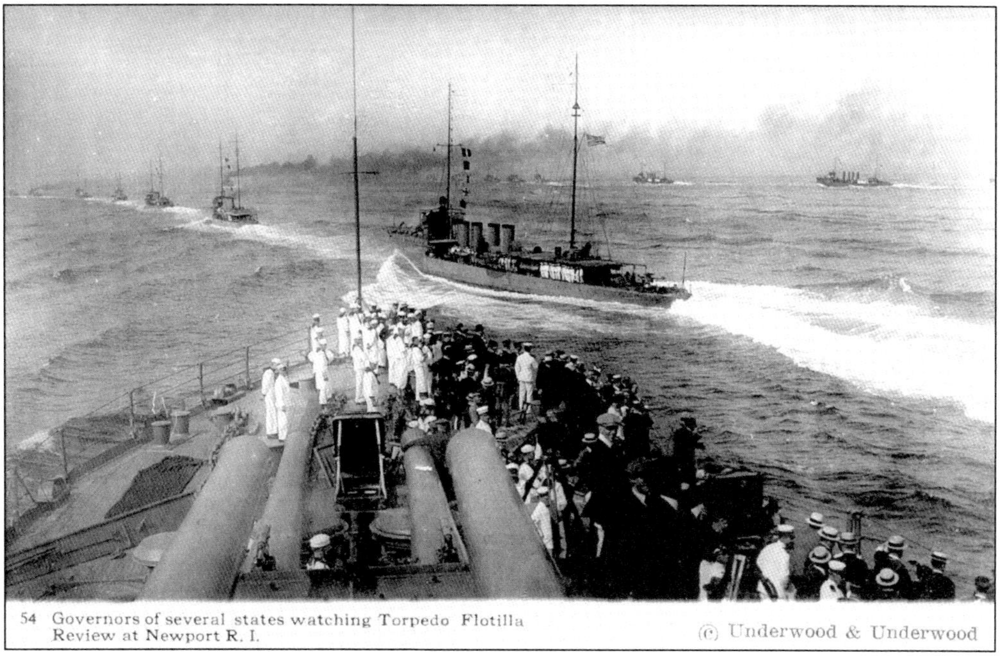

The navy's torpedo boat destroyer fleet conducts maneuvers in Narragansett Bay, reviewed by navy brass and governors of several states.

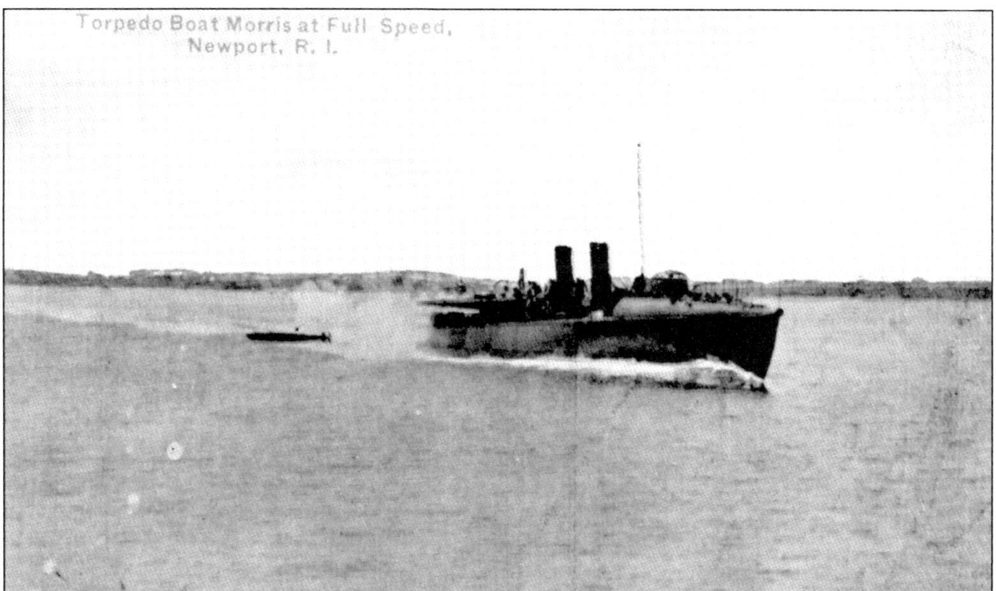

The Herreshoff-built torpedo boat *TB14 Morris* conducts a practice torpedo war shot in Narragansett Bay.

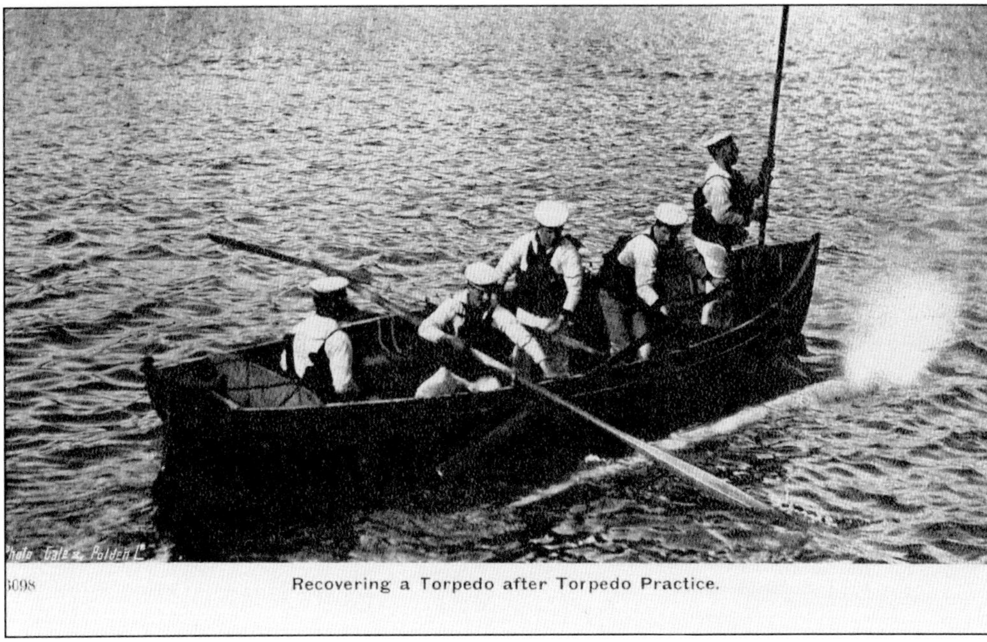

Blue Jackets from NTS retrieve a spent torpedo after a practice war shot.

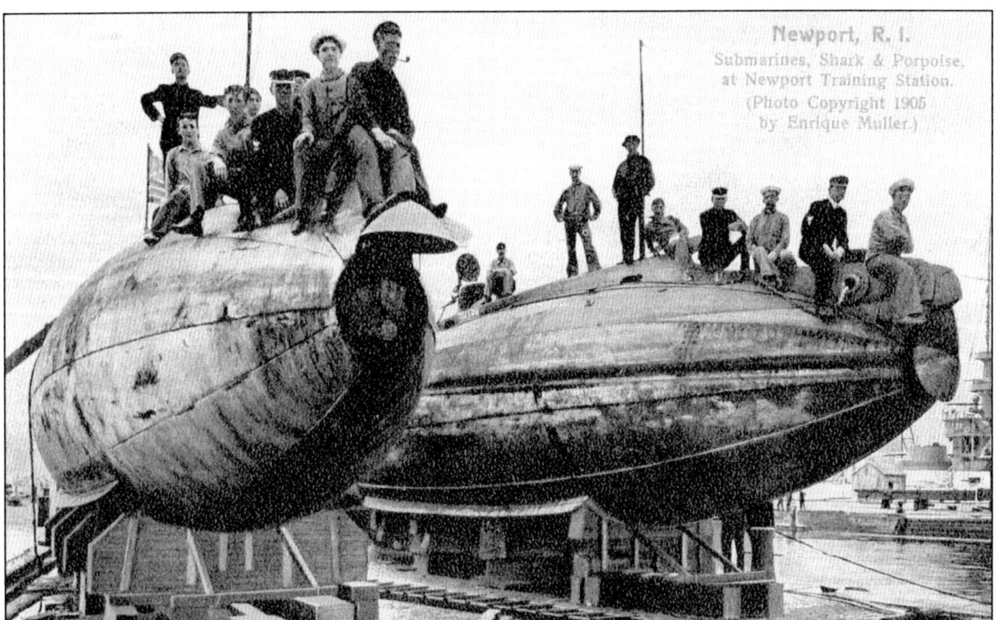

The Holland-designed submarines *Shark* and *Porpoise* were tested and evaluated in Narragansett Bay by NTS personnel around 1904.

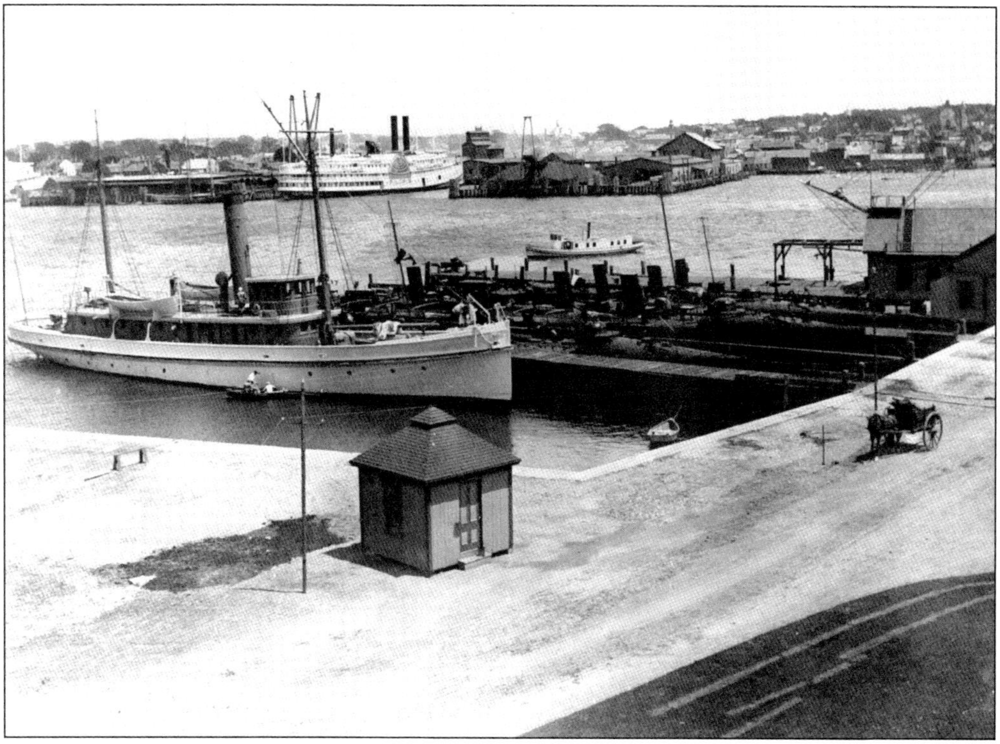

In this *c.* 1904 photograph one can see the torpedo boat slips on the east of Goat Island with the torpedo boats *Stiletto*, *Morris*, and *Porter*; the navy tug *Leyden* is at its birth. The station ferry *Wave* is approaching, and the overnight excursion steamer the *Pilgrim* is docked at its Newport wharf.

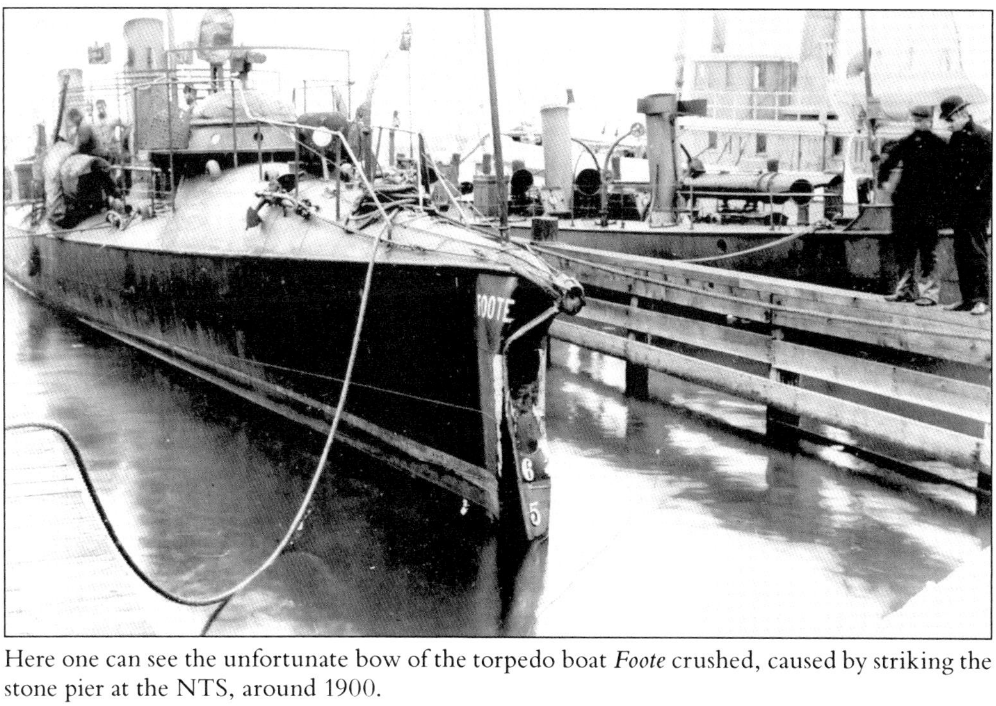

Here one can see the unfortunate bow of the torpedo boat *Foote* crushed, caused by striking the stone pier at the NTS, around 1900.

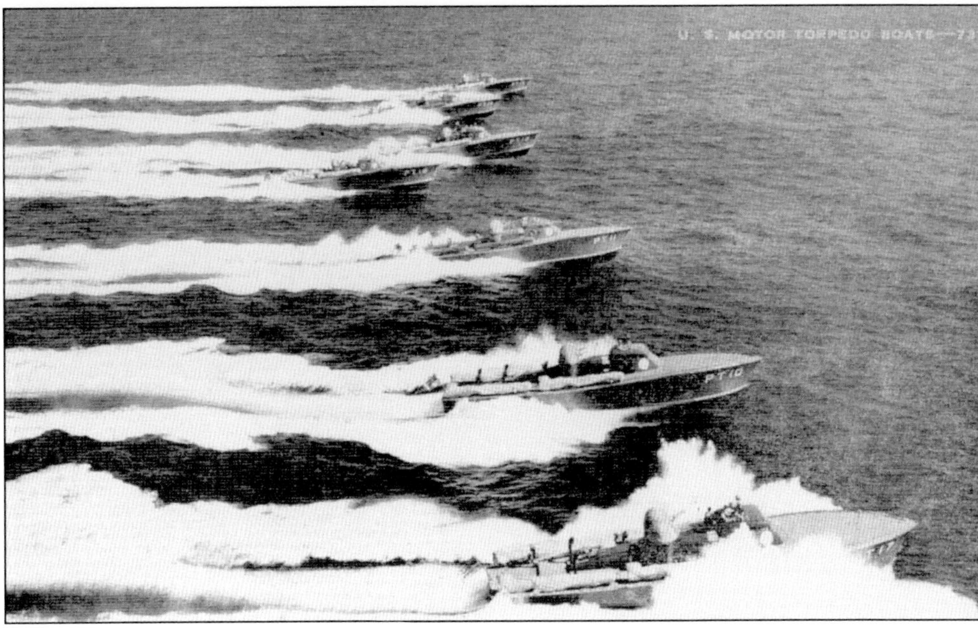

A squadron of patrol torpedo boats based at Melville, in Portsmouth, on the northern end of Aquidneck Island, goes through exercises in Narragansett Bay around 1940.

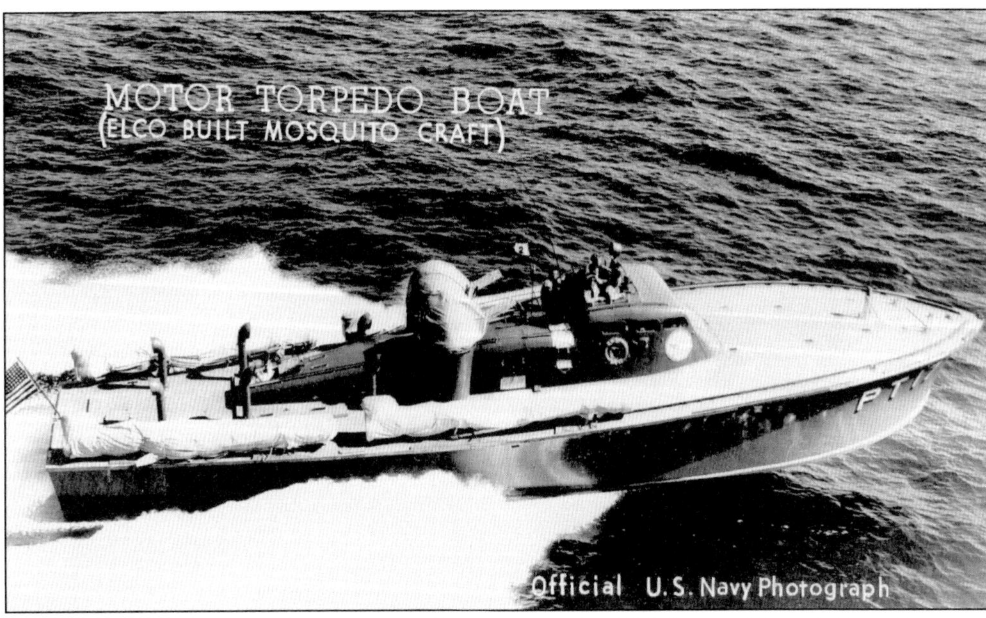

ELCO patrol torpedo (PT) boats were built at ELCO Naval Division of Electric Boat Company in Bayonne, New Jersey. Many of these swift mosquito boats were used to train crews at the Motor Torpedo Boat Squadron Training Center at Melville during World War II.

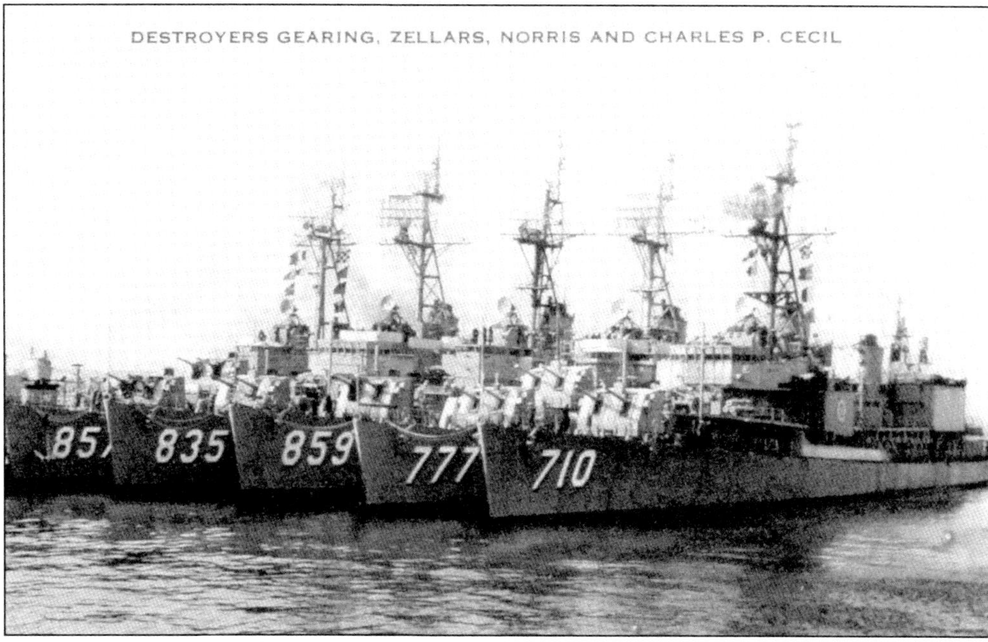

A representative view of the Atlantic Destroyer Squadron based at the Newport Naval Base is seen here around 1940.

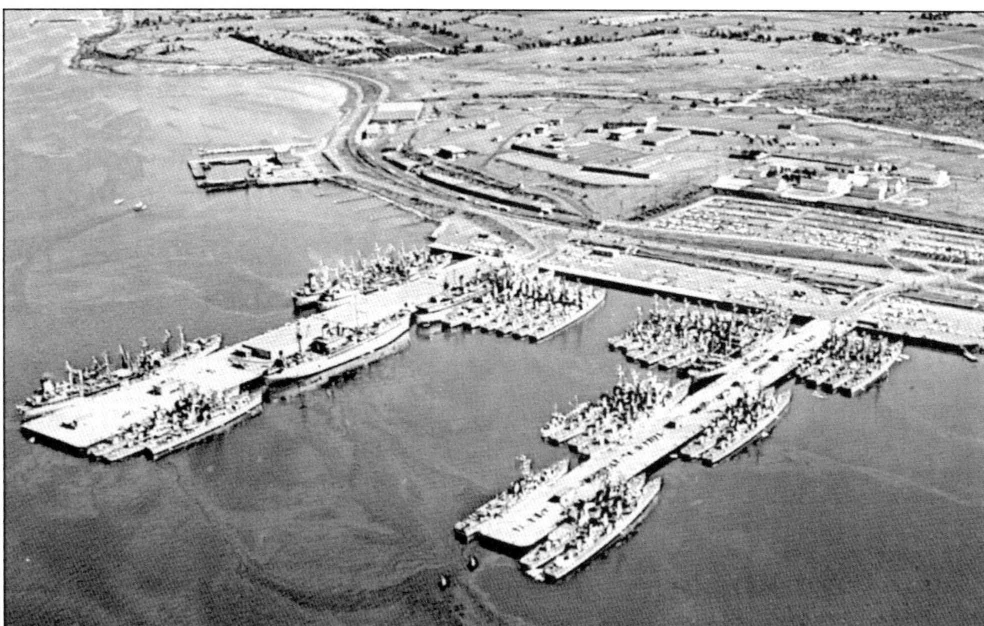
This bird's-eye view shows destroyer and cruiser piers 1 and 2 at the Newport Naval Base. In the background is the Naval Undersea Weapons Research and Engineering Station, and the small boat anchorage is in the upper-middle-left, around 1945.

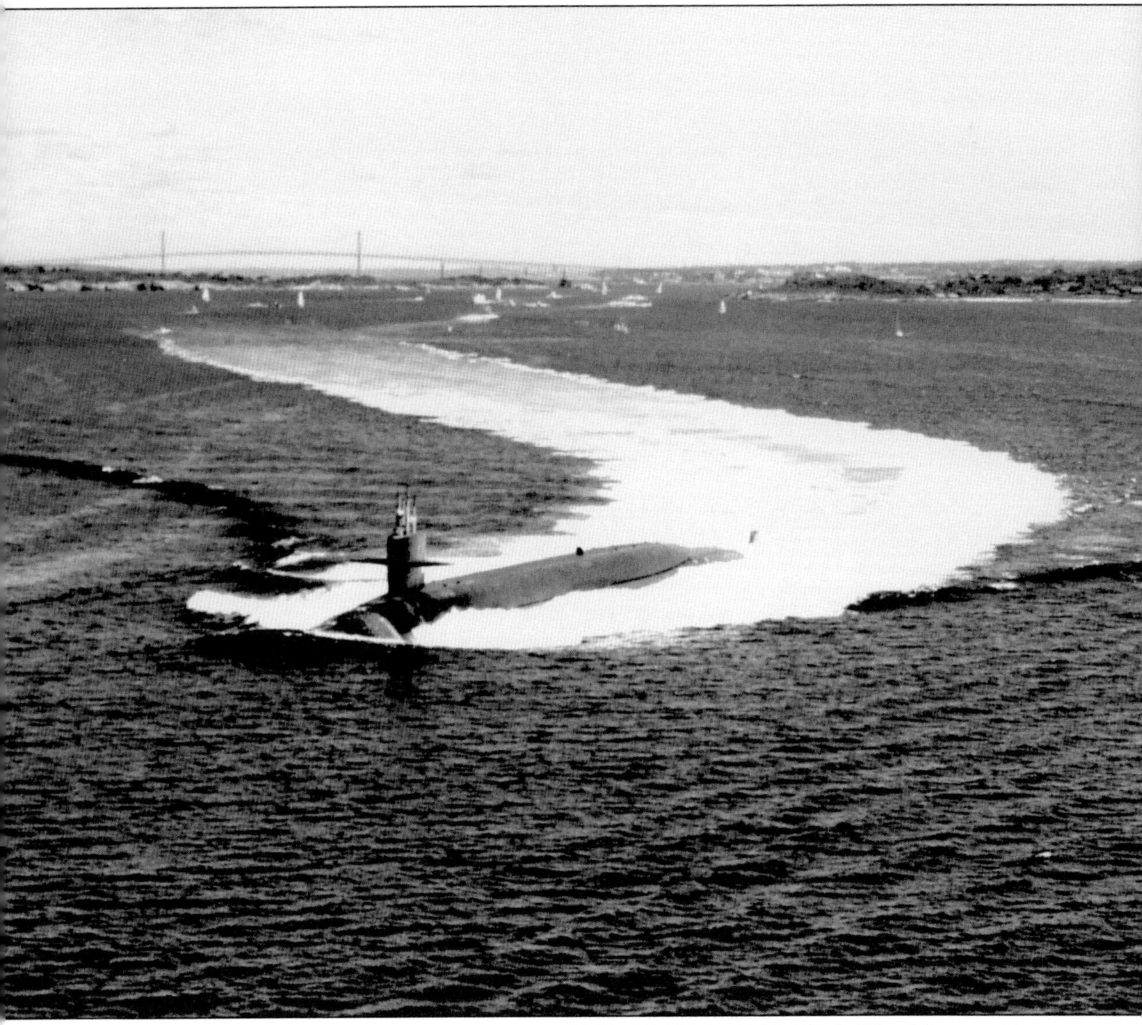

After its July 1994 commissioning ceremony, (SSBN 740) the USS *Rhode Island* departs Newport into lower Narragansett Bay and the deep Rhode Island Sound; the Newport-Pell Bridge is in the background.

Two

TALL SHIPS AND SWIFT SAILORS

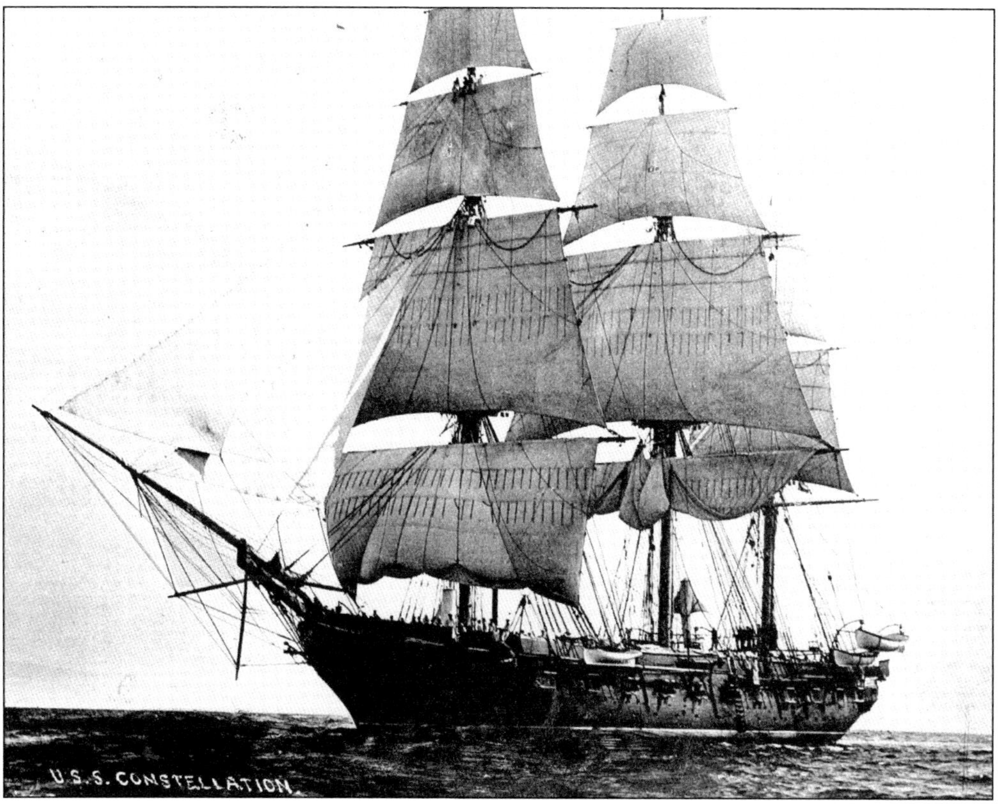

With plans completed in May and the keel laid on June 25, 1853, just before steam propulsion was adopted as auxiliary power for all new warships, *Constellation* was the last all-sail ship designed by the navy, as well as the largest sloop built to that date. As a "sloop-of-war," it was much larger than most other ships of that category. Being closer in size to a second-class frigate enabled *Constellation* to carry a heavier battery of guns than conventional sloops. Launched on August 26, 1854, at the Gosport Navy Yard in Virginia, *Constellation* was commissioned on July 28, 1855.

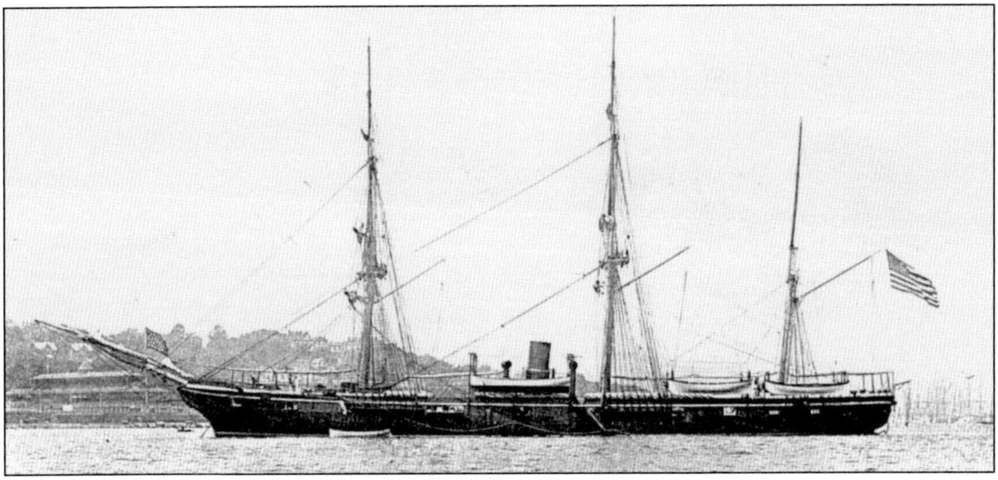

The first *Juniata* was a steam sloop-of-war launched at Philadelphia Navy Yard on March 20, 1862, and commissioned there December 4. After a cruise to the Caribbean, the *Juniata* sailed for the European Station May 6, 1874, and remained on duty there until it returned to the United States, arriving at Baltimore February 6, 1876. It decommissioned at Norfolk on September 1. It took part in the Bristol, Rhode Island, Fourth of July celebration in 1876.

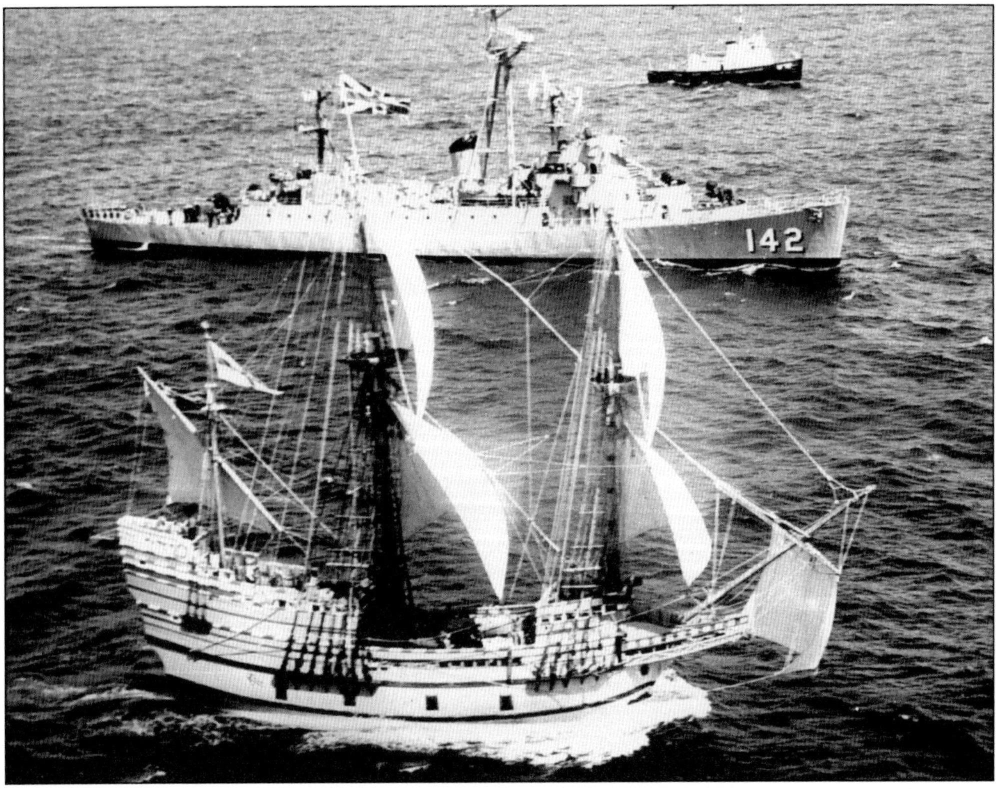

The *Mayflower II* visits Narragansett Bay on its voyage from England to its permanent home in Plymouth, Massachusetts; it is escorted by DD 142, the USS *Tarbell*. This is the only time that *Mayflower II* has sailed across the Atlantic. The replica of the *Mayflower*, the *Mayflower II* was built in 1957 by England as a gift to America.

A family of naval officers and friends enjoy the 1982 Tall Ships' Regatta and Parade of Sail from the rocky shore of Narragansett Bay. The Portuguese sail training ship *Sagres* is the large vessel in the background.

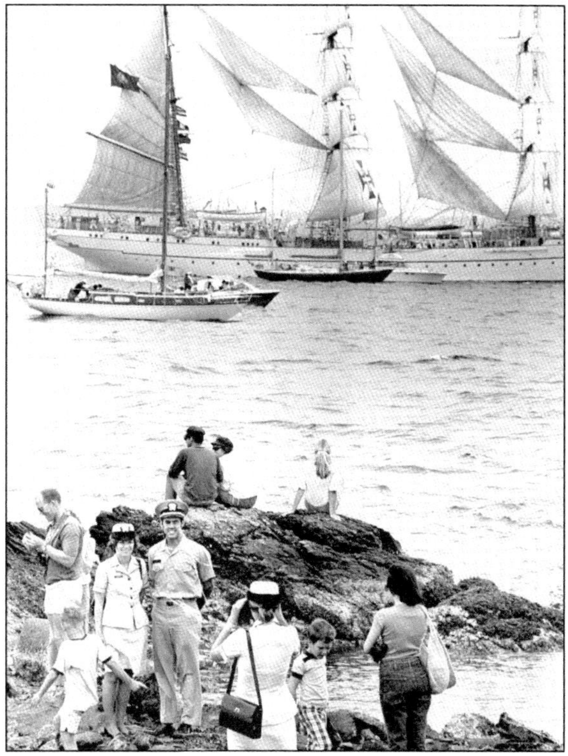

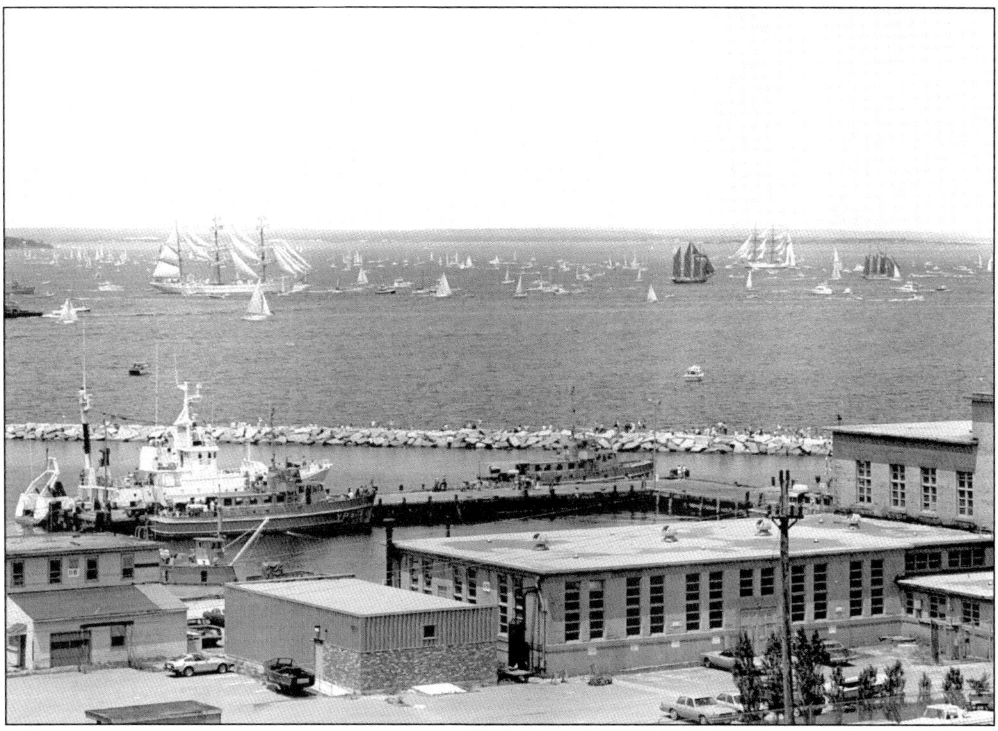

The 1982 Tall Ships' Regatta and Parade of Sail passes the small boat anchorage called Still Water Basin accompanied by a flotilla of small sailing craft.

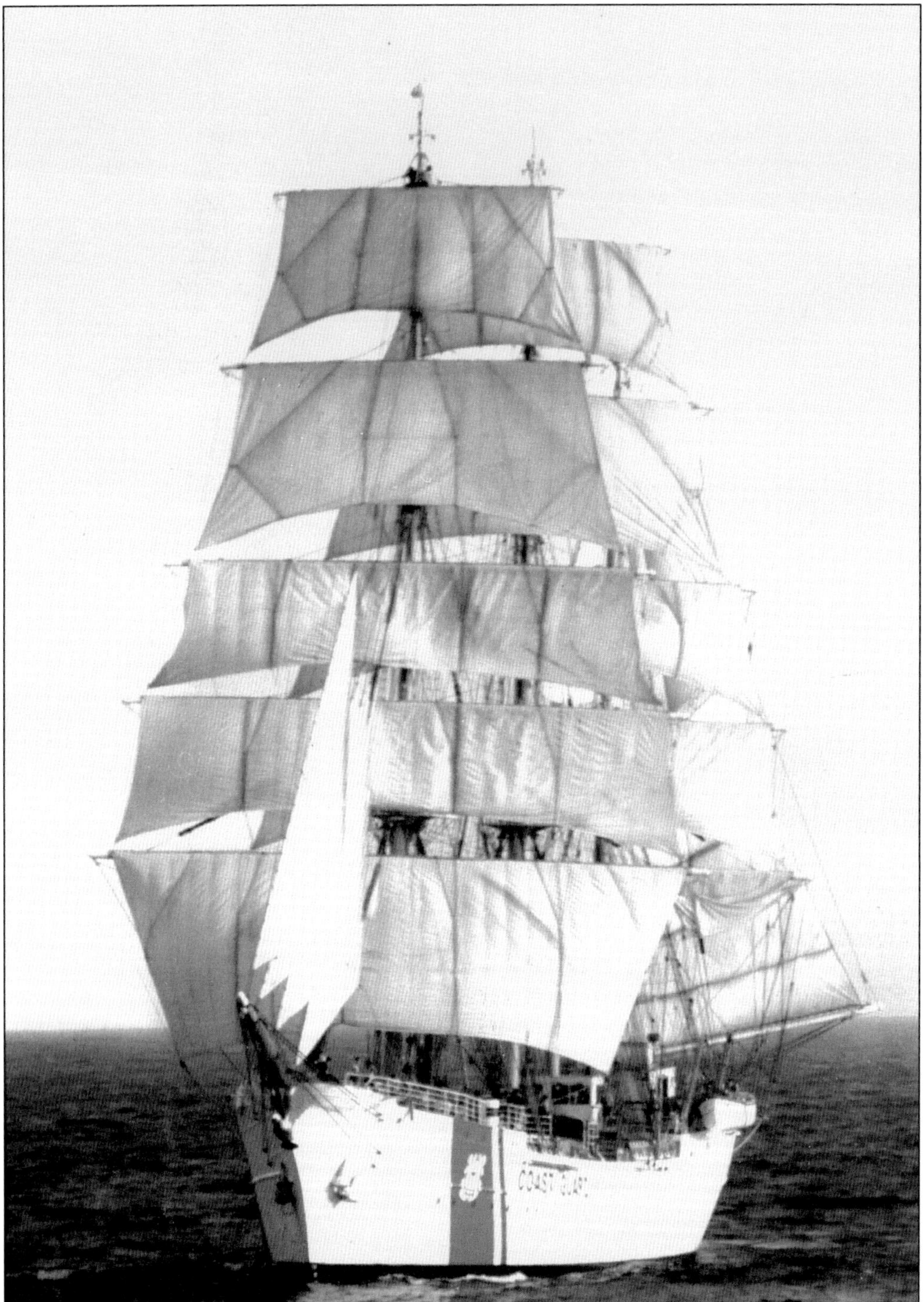

The *Eagle* is a three-masted sailing Barque with 21,350 square feet of sail. It is home ported at the U.S. Coast Guard Academy in New London, Connecticut. It is the only operational commissioned sailing vessel in the U.S. maritime services. The *Eagle* sails often in Narragansett Bay on training cruises and as part of tall ship regattas.

The Portuguese three-mast Barque sail training ship *Sagres* was built in 1937 in the shipyards of Blohm and Voss in Hamburg, Germany. It was the third of a series of four ships built by the German Navy comprising *Horst Vessel*, now *Eagle*, of the U.S. Coast Guard. This photograph is of the *Sagres*'s June 1964 tour of Narragansett Bay ports.

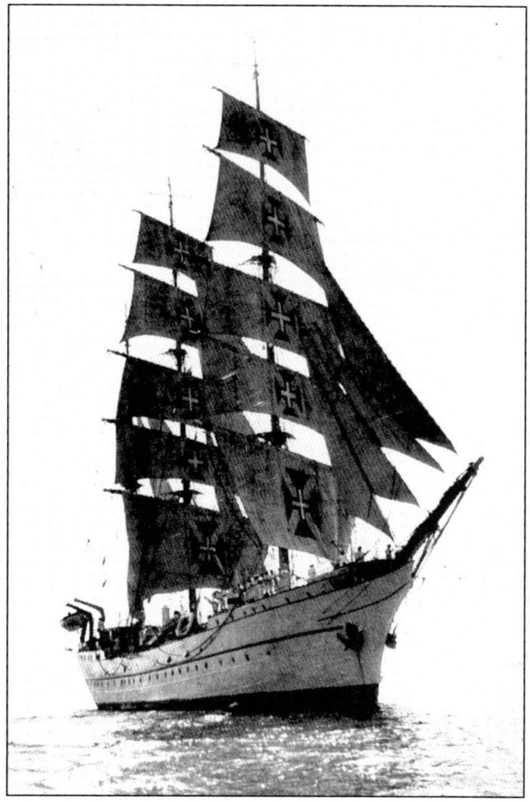

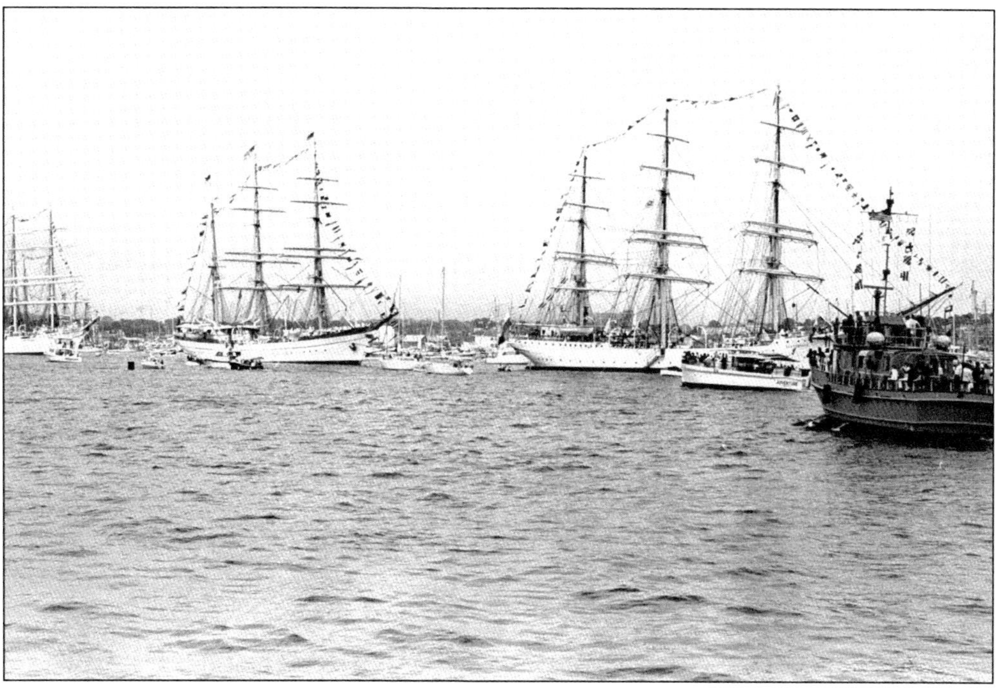

The tall ships are at deep water anchor in Newport Harbor during their 1982 tour. The large three-mast ship on the right is the ship from Poland, the *Dar Pomorza*.

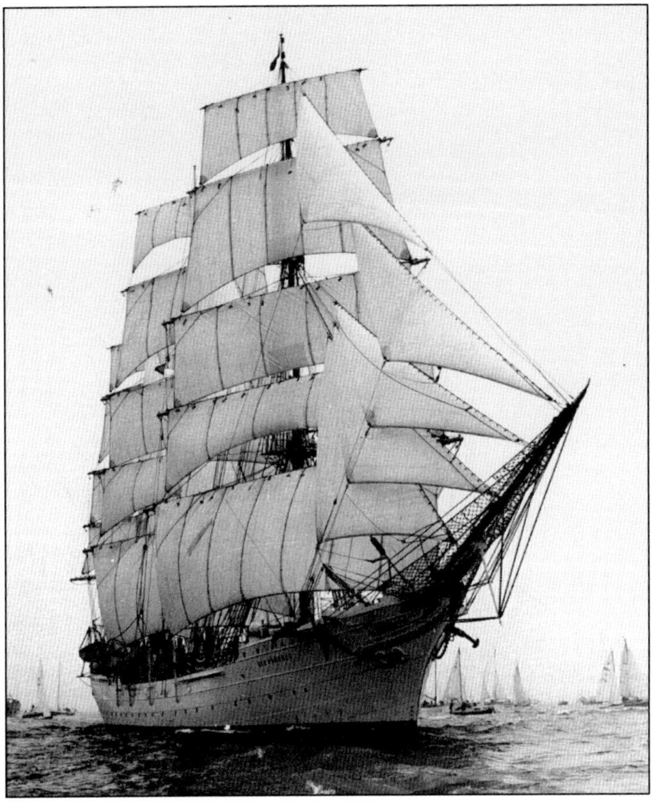

The *Dar Pomorza* was laid down on September 18, 1909, as the German training ship *Prinzess Eitel Friedrich*. In 1919, it was seized by the French. In 1929, still bearing the name *Prinzess Eitel Friedrich*, it was bought by the community of the Polish Pomerania as the new training ship for the Polish Naval Academy in Gdynia. It was given the name *Dar Pomorza*, which means "the gift of Pomerania."

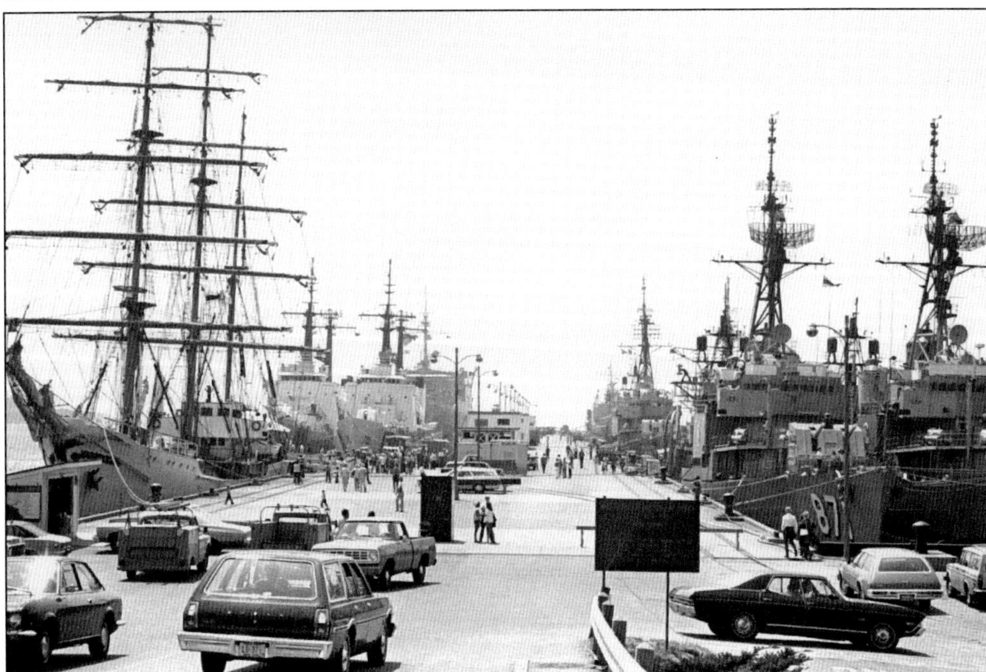

Antique and modern ships share dock space and services at pier 2 of the Newport Naval Base for the Tall Ships' Rendezvous in 1976.

The *Shenandoah* is the only vessel of its size and rig operating under the American flag. It has no engines, so sailing it means being at the whim of the wind and tide. Despite its size, it is remarkably agile, and the captain takes the vessel deep into small harbors with surprising ease and control.

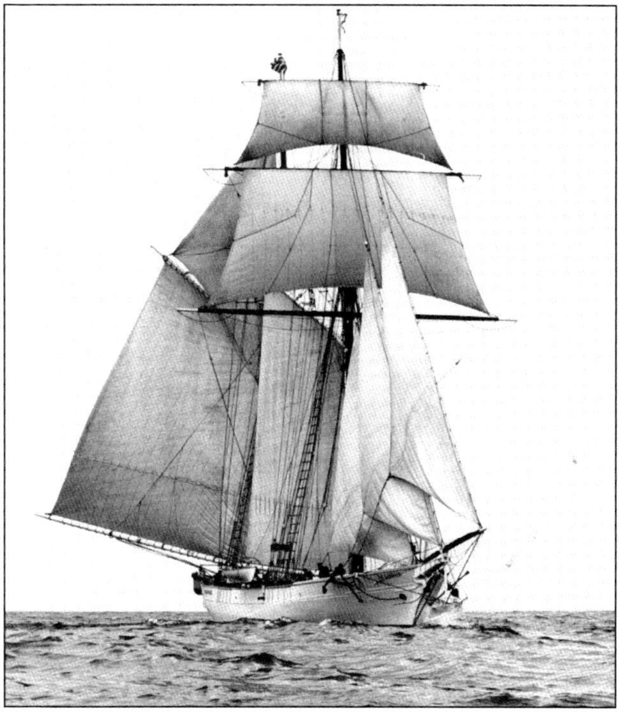

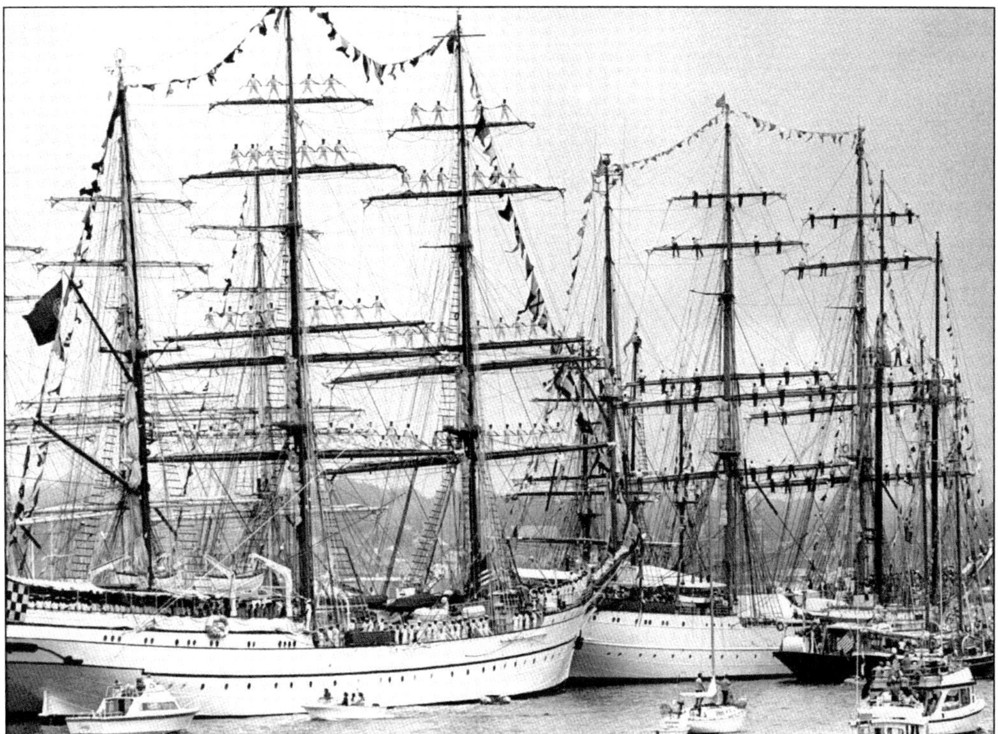

Two of the massive steel tall ships are birthed at Newport's Long Wharf during the 1976 regatta. Three additional tall ships are in the background (count the masts).

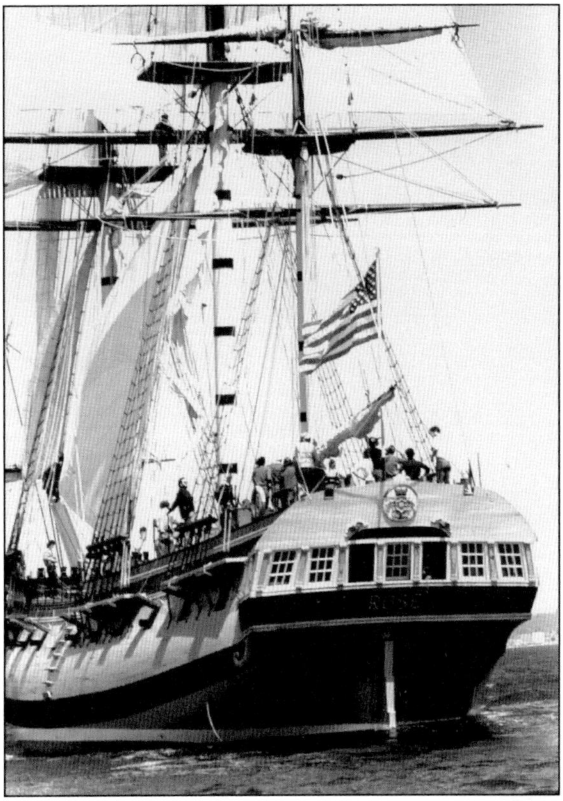

The replica HMS *Rose* was built in Lunenburg, Nova Scotia, in 1970 by Newport historian John Fitzhugh Millar, using original construction drawings from 1757 that were obtained from the National Maritime Museum in Greenwich, England. It spent the first 10 years of its life in Newport, Rhode Island.

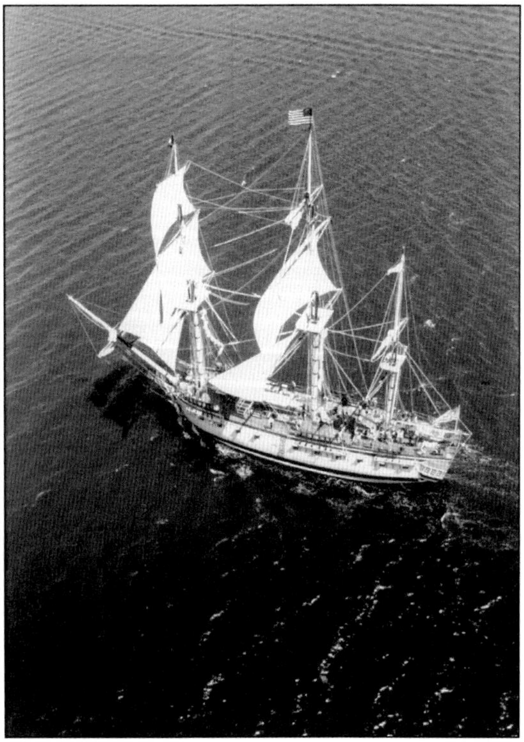

In 1990, the *Rose* toured the Great Lakes and in 1991 sailed the East Coast from Maine to Florida while displaying Rhode Island's original draft of the Bill of Rights. In September 1991, the *Rose* was certified as America's first Class-A size sailing school vessel by the U.S. Coast Guard, making it the largest sailing school vessel in the United States.

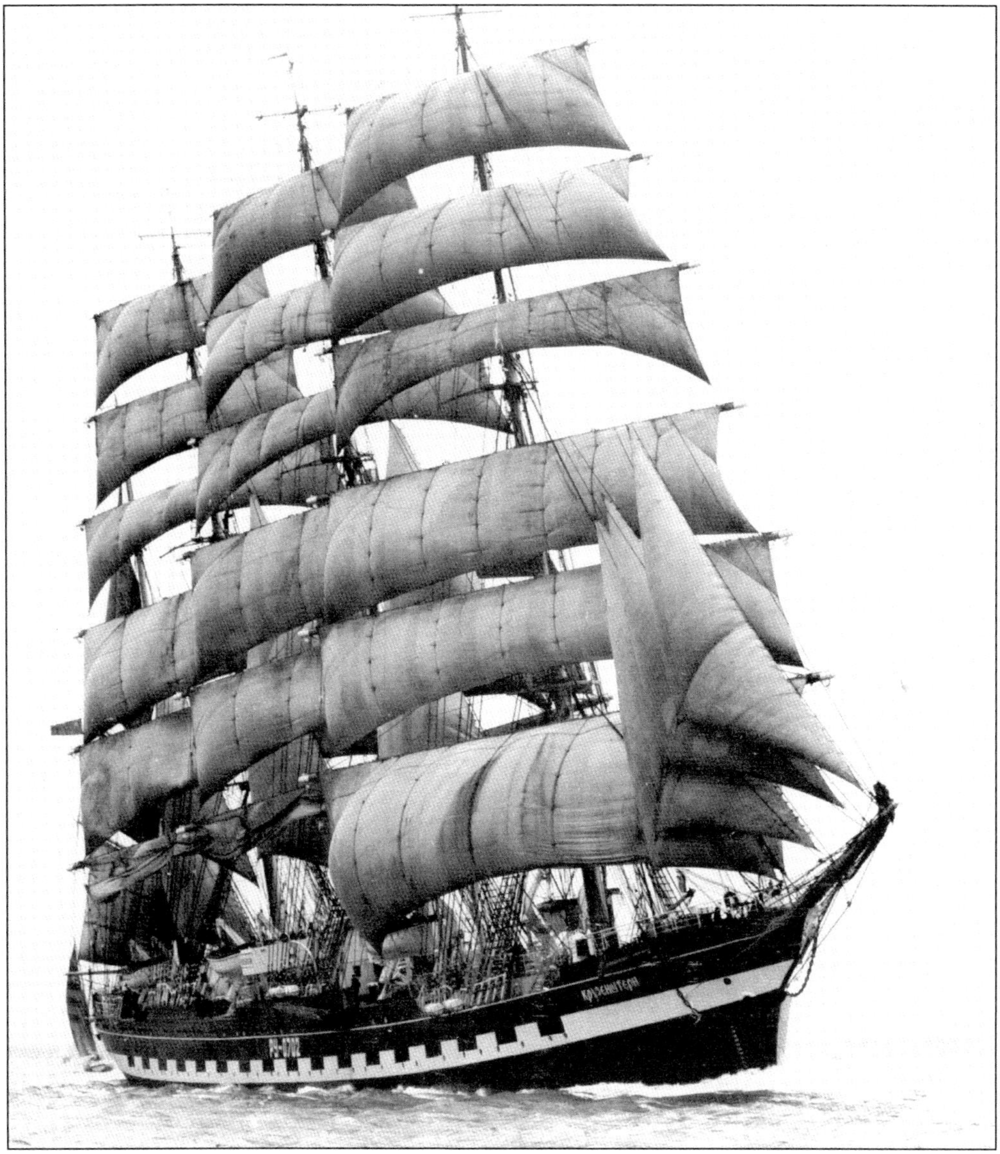

The *Kruzenshtern* is the second-largest sailing ship in the world, second only to another Russian ship, the *Sedov.* Originally called *Padua*, it was built in Germany in the 1920s as one of five clipper ships for the Flying P Line, which traded in the Atlantic, Indian, and Pacific Oceans. At the time it appeared in Narragansett Bay as part of the 1982 Tall Ships' Regatta, it was the property of the people of the USSR.

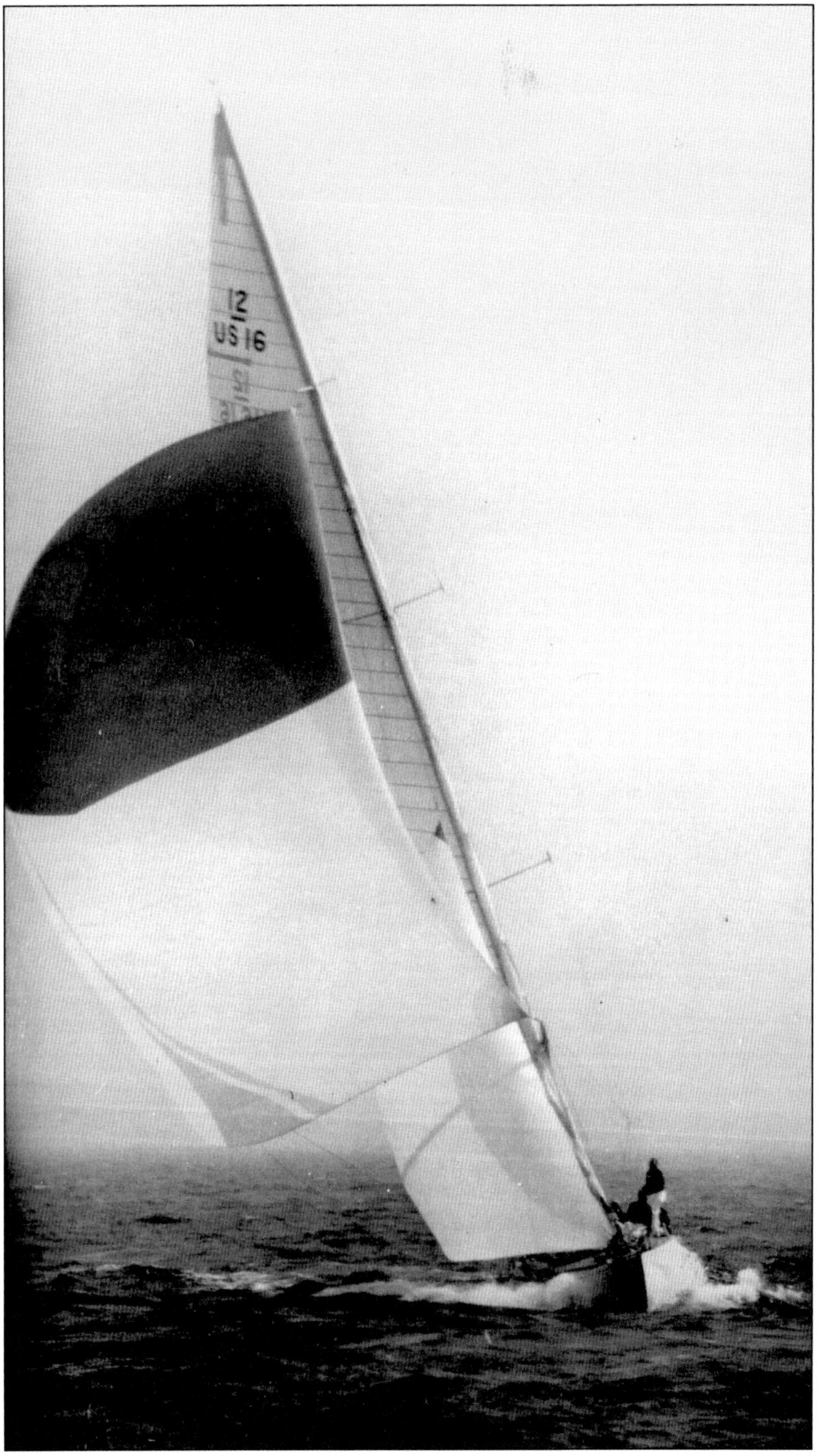

In September and October 1958, the America's Cup defender, the 12-meter yacht *Columbia,* decisively beat its British challenger *Scepter* in races held in the Rhode Island Sound.

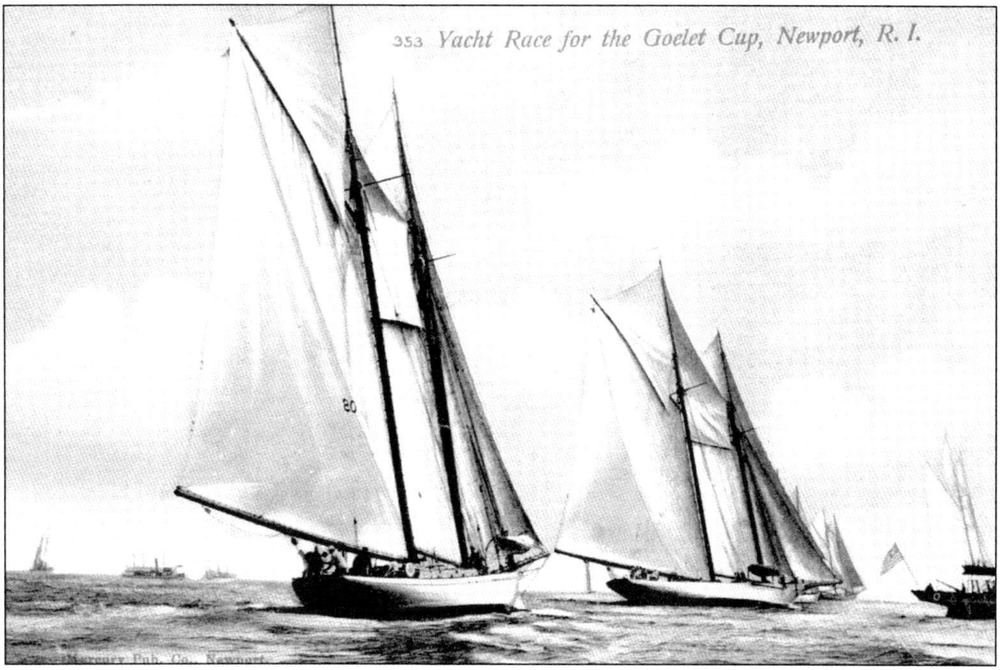

The Goelet Cup races were the trial races to determine the yacht privileged to defend the America's Cup. In 1930, the New York Yacht Club brought the America's Cup races to Narragansett Bay, home porting the yachts in Newport Harbor.

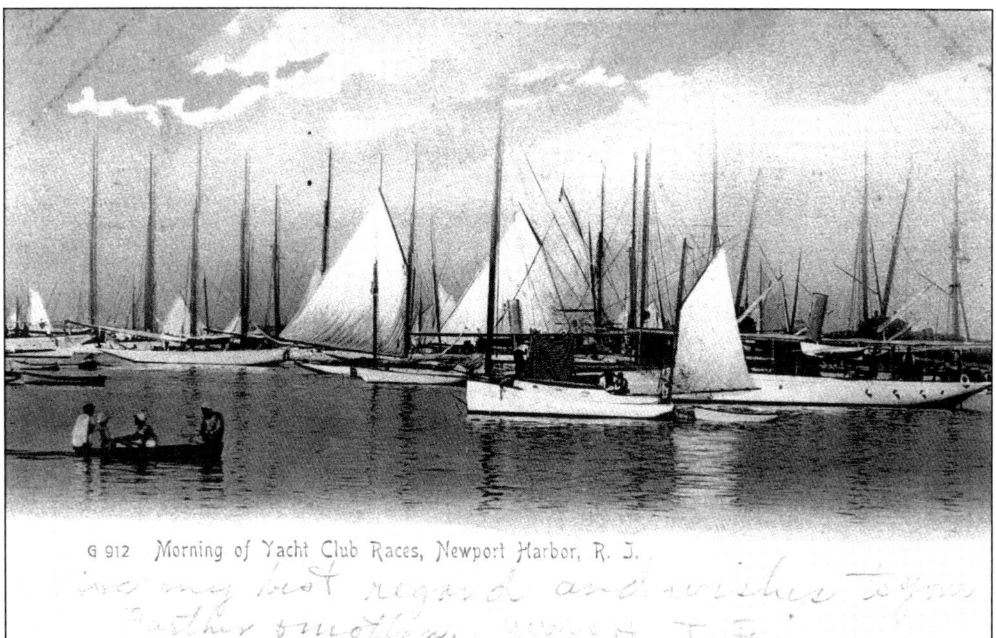

In this postcard postmarked August 1906, Newport Harbor is congested with sport sailboats of many shapes and sizes on, as it reads on the postcard, "[the] morning of yacht club races."

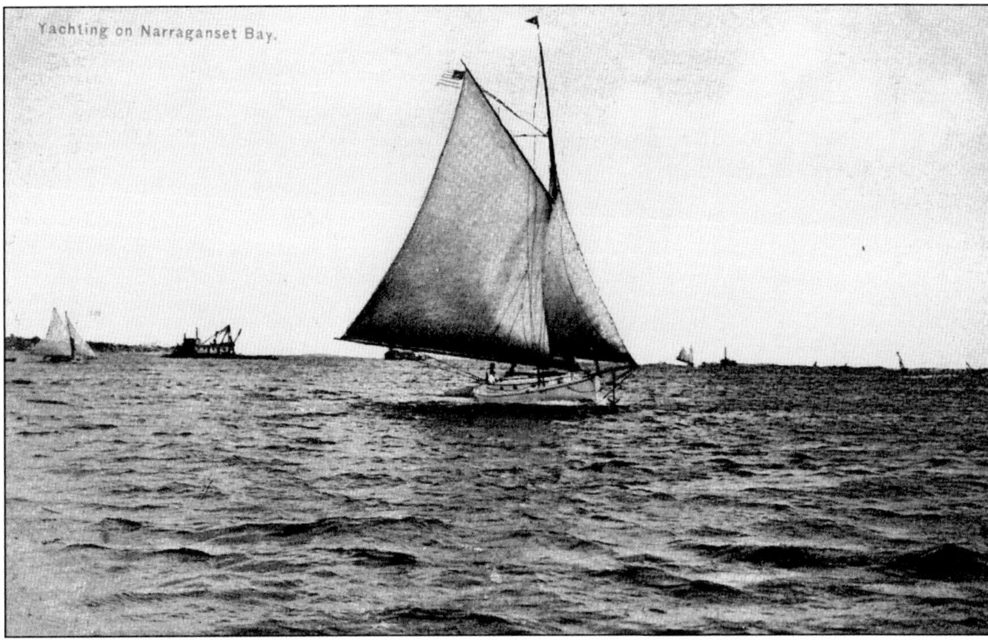

An unusually quiet day on the bay prompts a few to enjoy an afternoon of sailing.

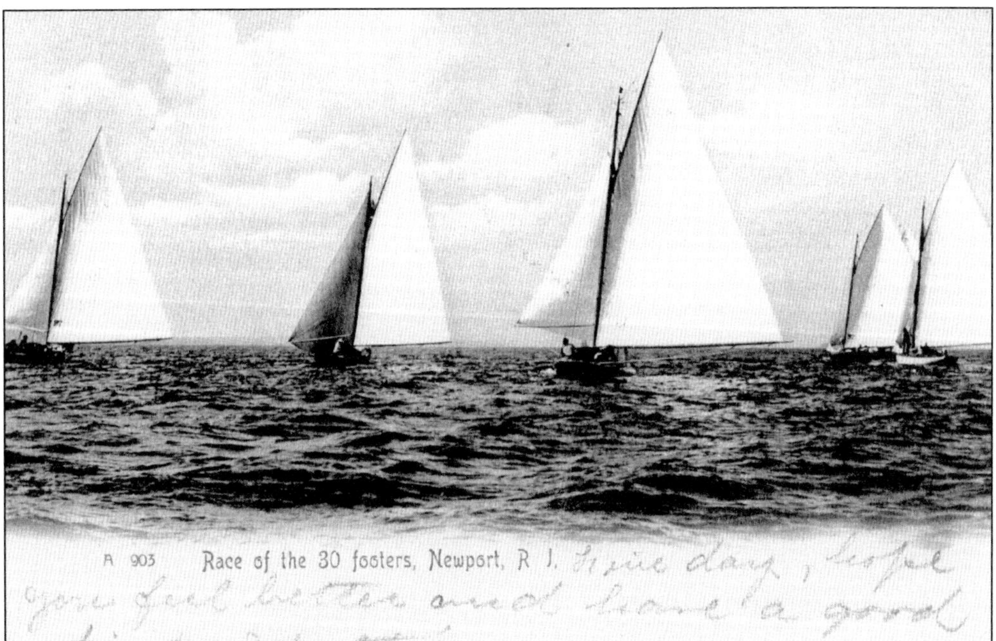

The Newport Yacht Club sent out a gaggle of their New York 30 footers to catch some fresh breezes.

This postcard photograph shows the struggle for the America's Cup between the Australian challenger *Gretel* and the successful American defender the *Weatherly* in the August 1962 races.

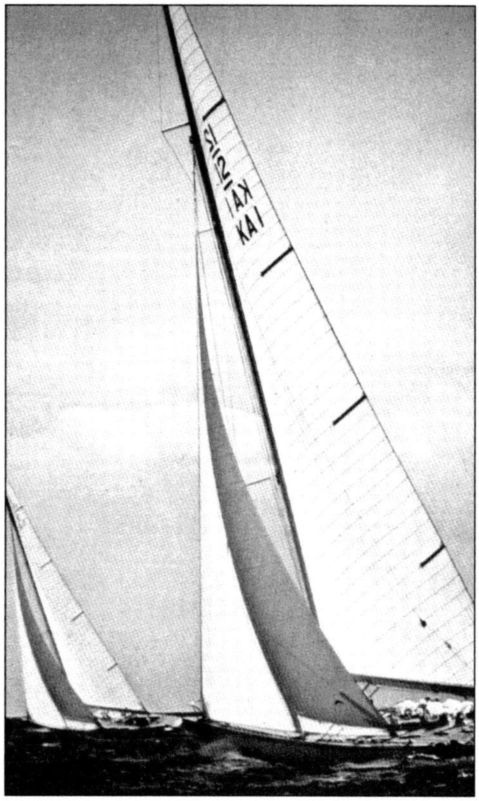

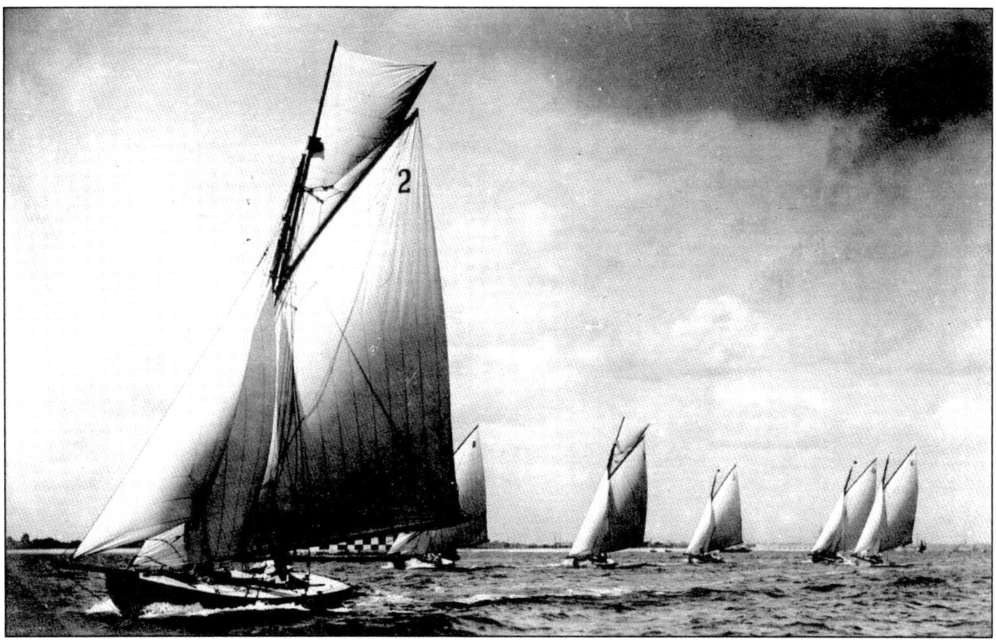

A squadron of 22-foot Sandbaggers is out on the bay for a stimulating day of sailing. Newport's Fort Adams can be seen in the distant right background.

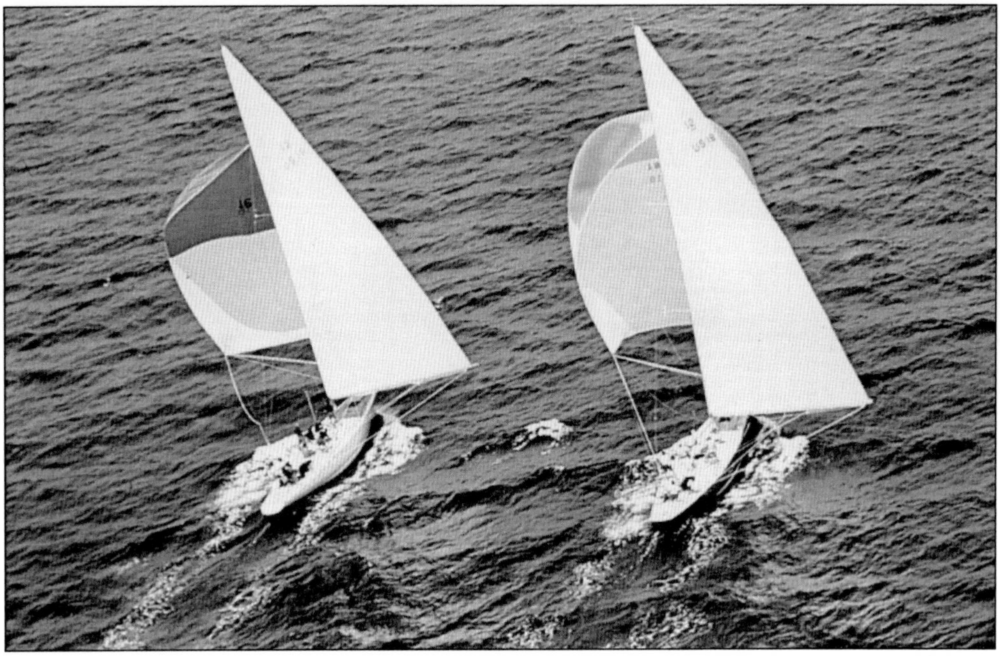

The 12-meter America's Cup yachts the *Columbia* (left) and the *Easterner* compete for the privilege of defending the America's Cup in the 1958 match races in Rhode Island Sound.

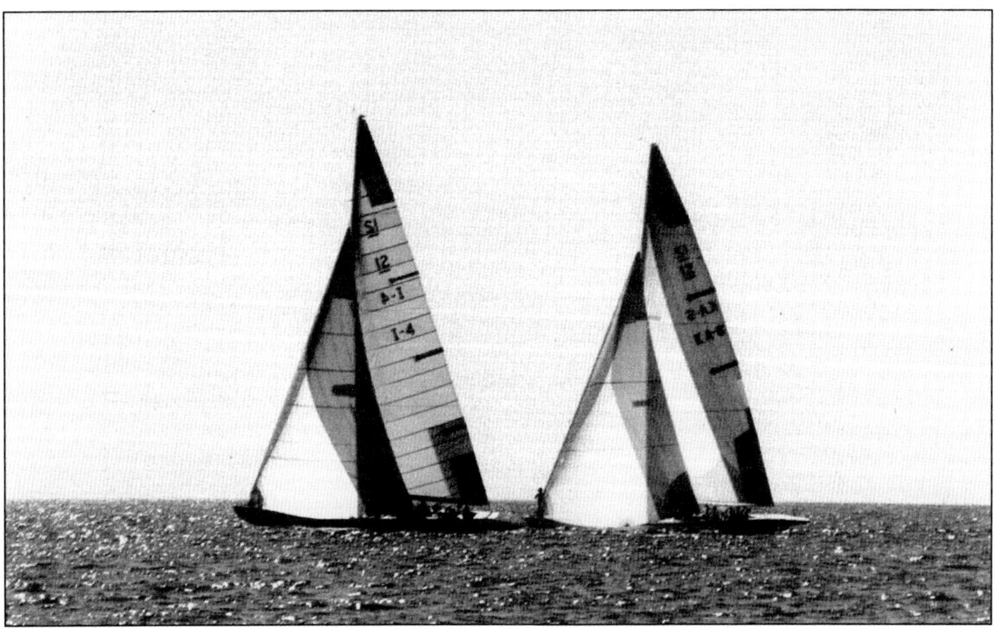

The end of America's Cup yacht racing in Rhode Island waters and the end of the New York Yacht Club's dominance in defending the America's Cup came in September 1983, when the Australian challenger the *Australia II* whipped the defender *Liberty*.

Three

Steamers and Ferries on Narragansett Bay

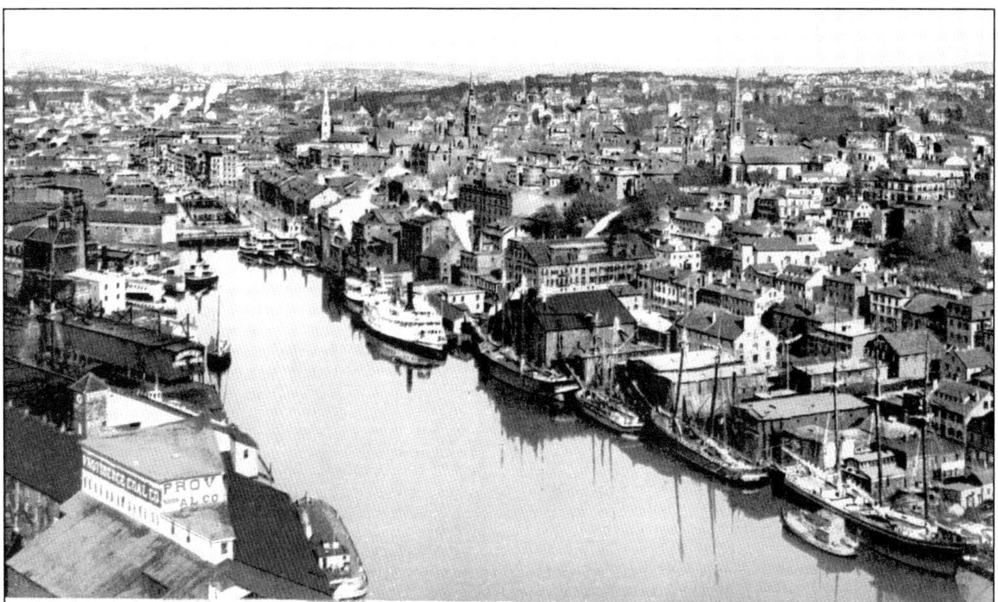

The Providence River, at the head of Narragansett Bay, was the terminus point for the major 19th-century passenger and cargo steamers. In this *c.* 1900 photograph, a few of the remaining packet sailors are seen in the right foreground.

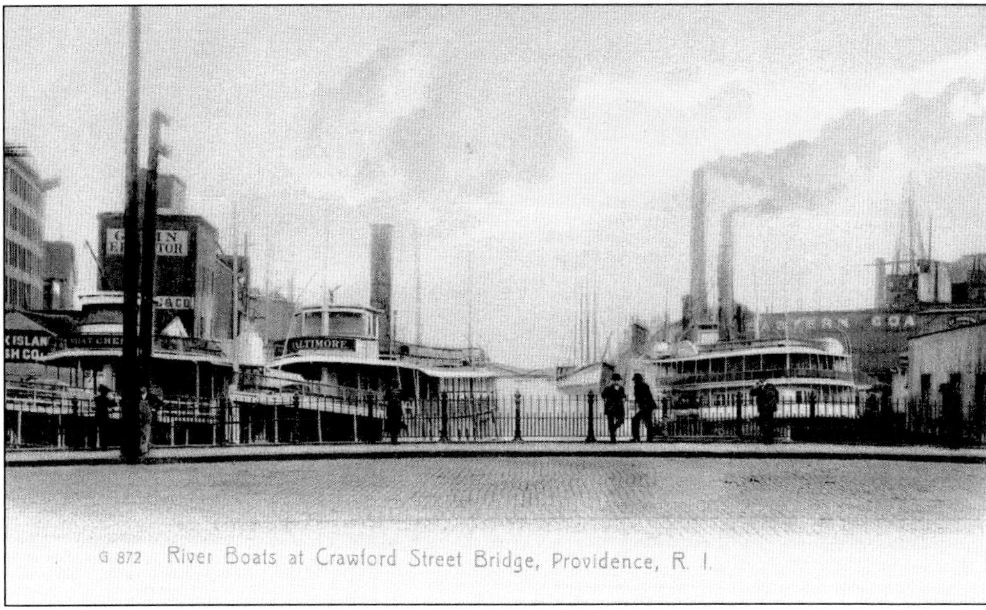

The steam passenger vessel the *Baltimore* is seen (left) in this view of the Providence River from the Crawford Street Bridge.

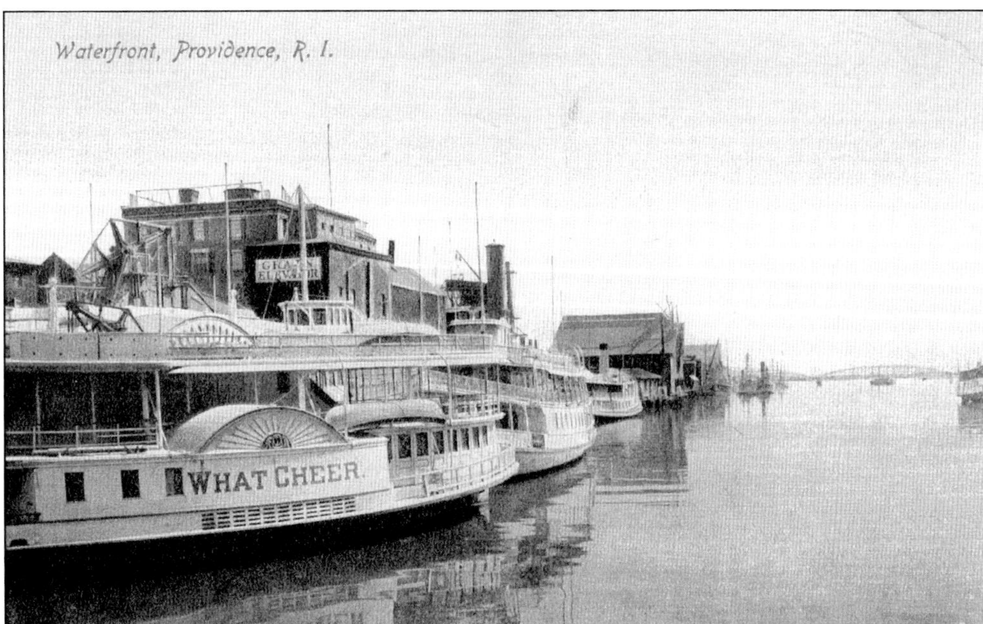

Here is a view of bay steamers awaiting passengers at their Providence River landings.

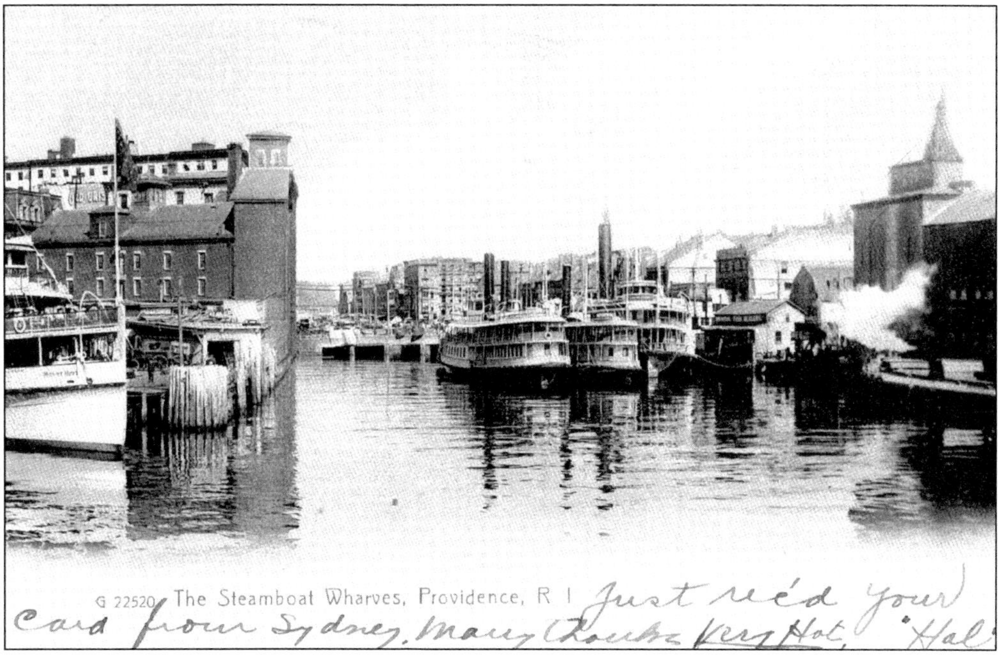

The paddle wheel steamer *Mount Hope*'s bow is seen (left) at its Providence pier. The Crawford Street Bridge is seen in the background around 1905.

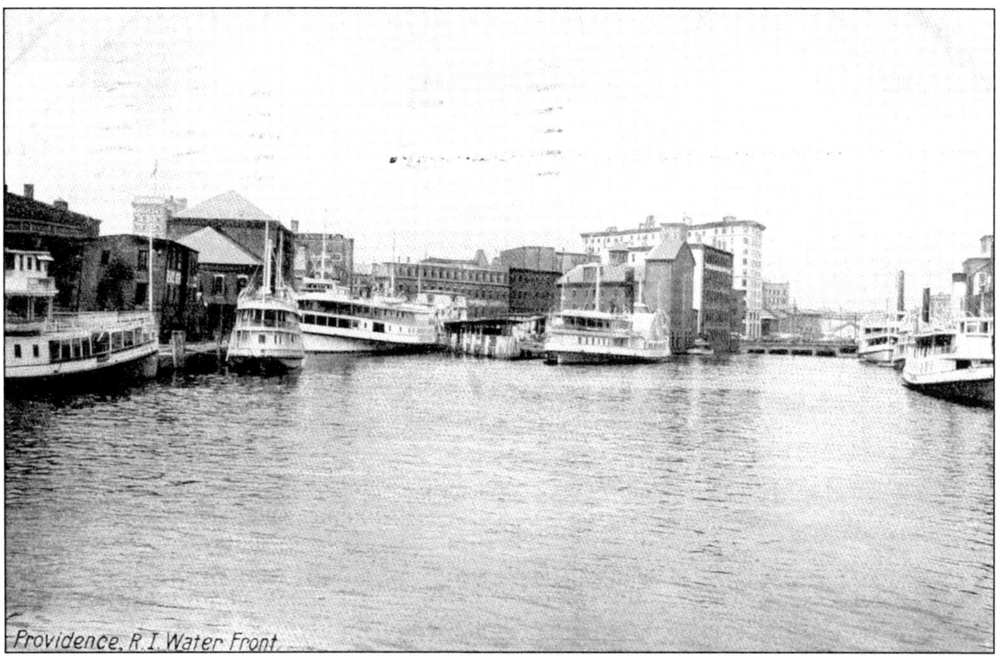

The Providence River's wharves were eventually choked by the massive steamers, which forced the sailing packets off the river and out of business around 1906.

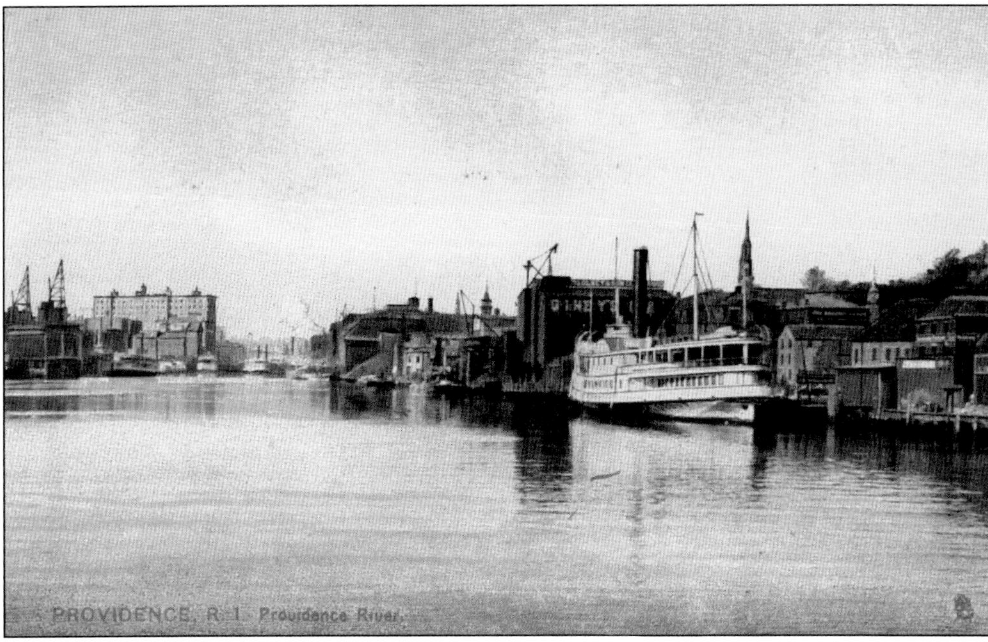

The *Mount Hope* is seen here in this *c.* 1916 photograph, taking on passengers at the South Water Street depot.

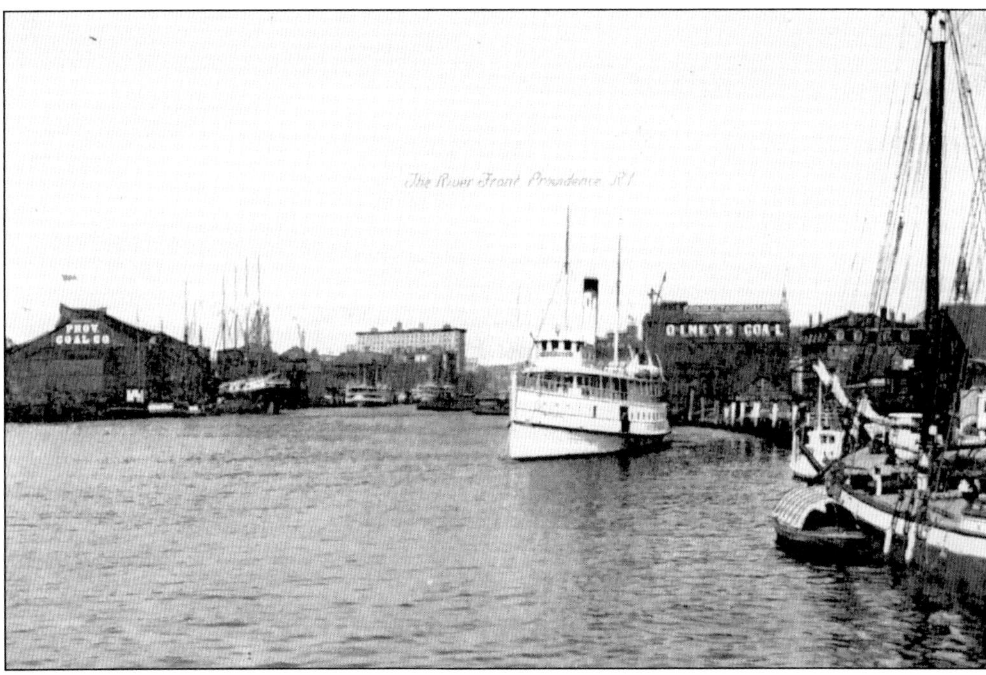

The *Mount Hope* departs Providence on its daily run to Block Island. In the left middle ground can be see the spars of several of the last sailing cargo vessels, and in the right foreground is a fishing boat with a covered launch alongside, around 1916.

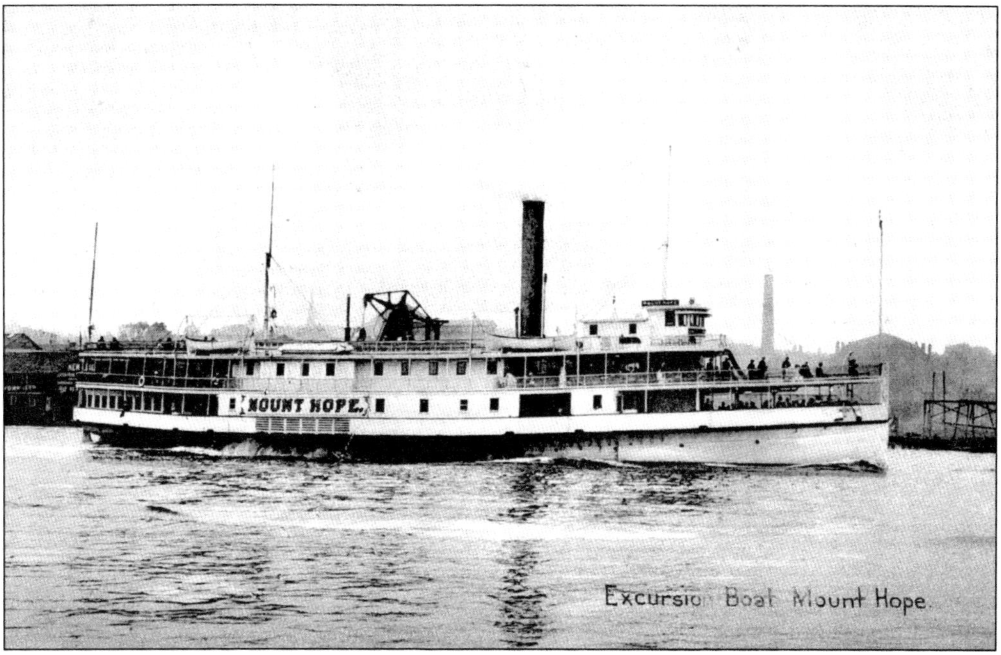

The "Queen of Narragansett Bay," the Providence to Block Island excursion steamer the *Mount Hope* makes its way down the Providence River to the open bay.

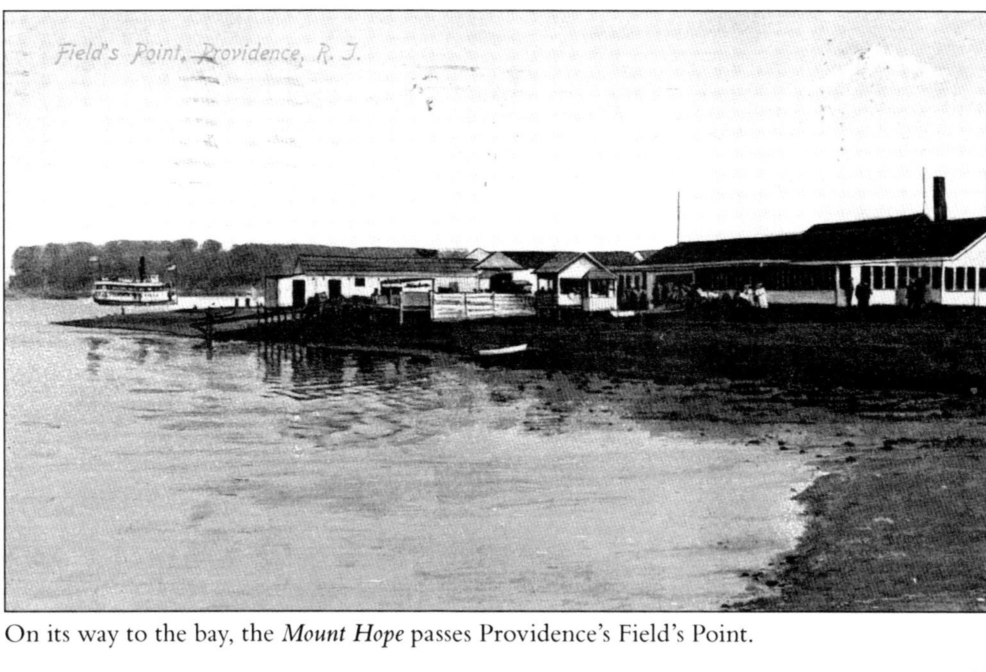

On its way to the bay, the *Mount Hope* passes Providence's Field's Point.

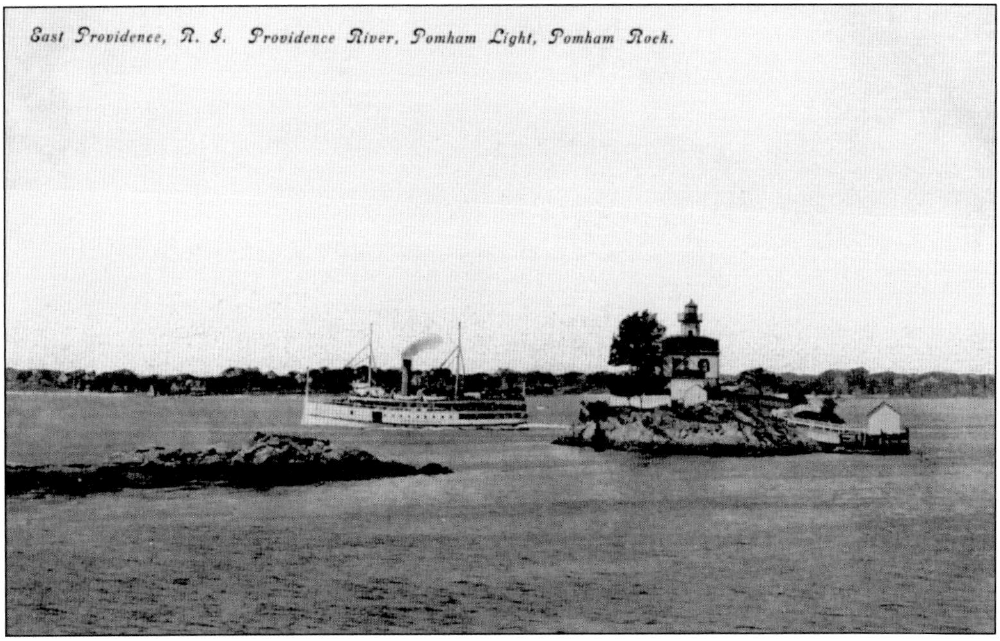

Entering the bay, the *Mount Hope* passes the Pomham Rock Light on Pomham Rock, East Providence (see page 125).

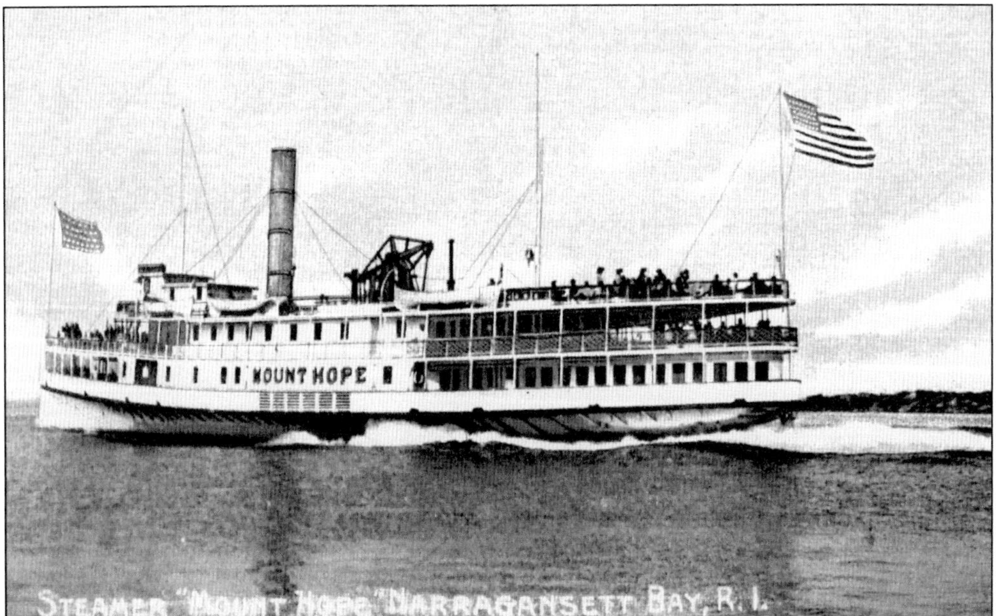

The *Mount Hope* was built in 1888 in Chelsea, Massachusetts; it was designed by George Pierce for the Montgomery and Howard Shipyard, and it was constructed by the W. and A. Fletcher Company.

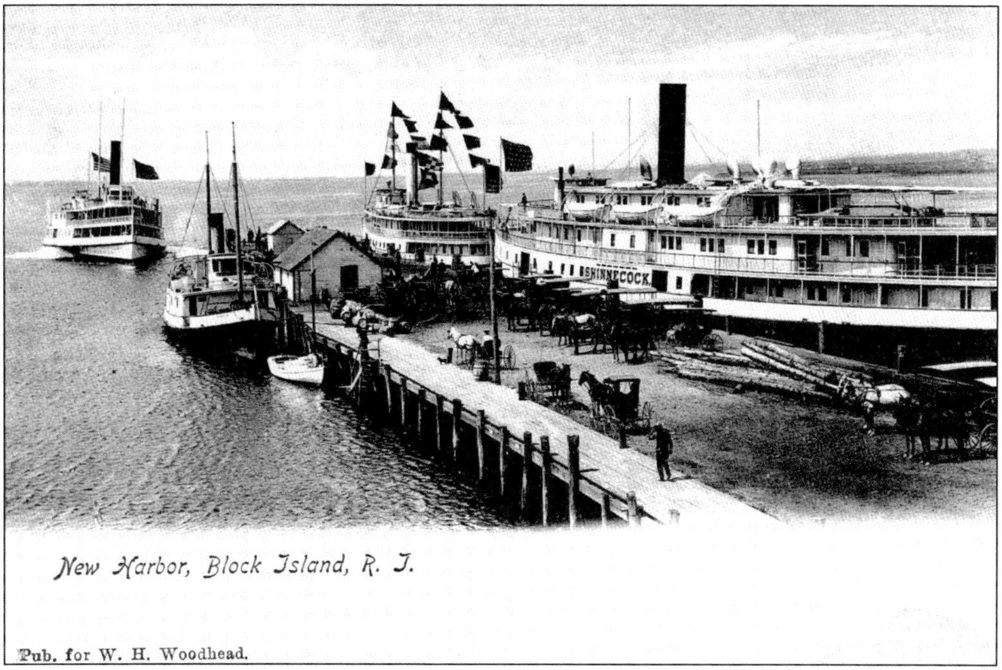

The *Mount Hope* approaches New Harbor, Block Island, as the sound steamer *Richard Borden* prepares to depart, and the *Shinnecock* stands by to receive passengers in this *c.* 1909 photograph. Notice the horse-drawn carriages and omnibuses on the pier.

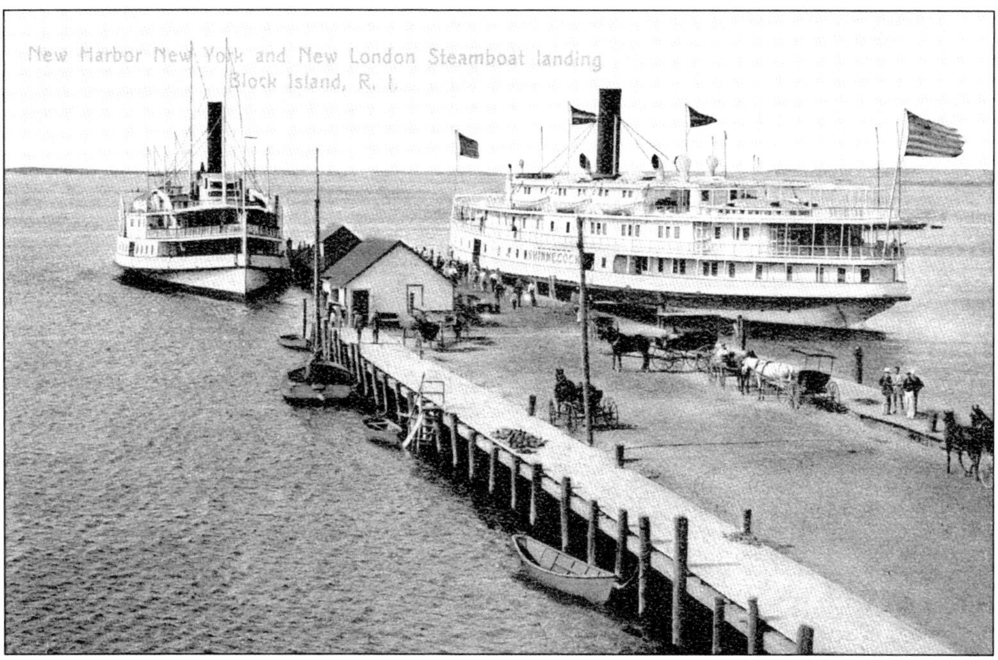

The *Mount Hope* draws close to its dockage at New Harbor, Block Island, as the *Shinnecock* departs around 1909.

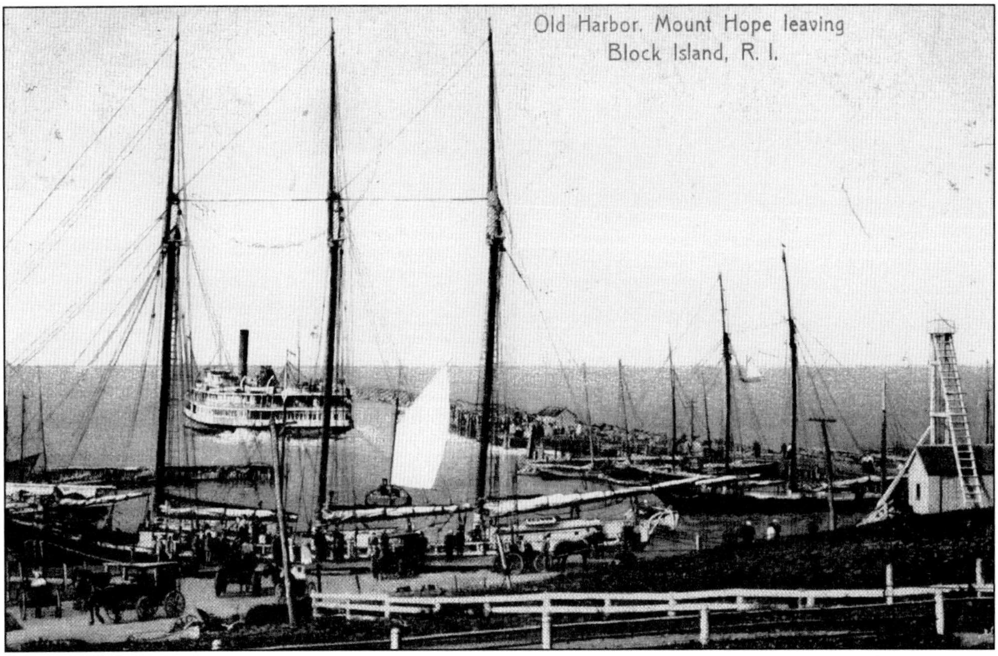

In this *c.* 1907 view, the *Mount Hope* departs from Old Harbor on Block Island. The *Mount Hope* was built for the Fall River and Providence Steamboat Company of Fall River, and began its career out of Fall River on May 24, 1888.

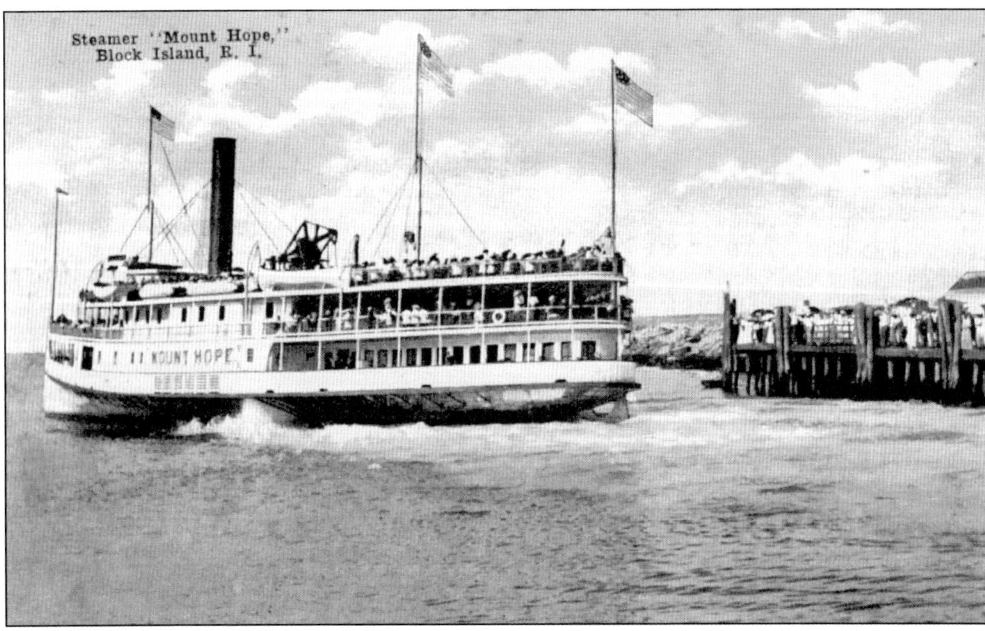

The *Mount Hope* was 193.1 feet long, with a beam of 58 feet, and it drew 11.5 feet. The engine was rated at 23 revolutions per minute, and it was certified to carry 1,650 passengers.

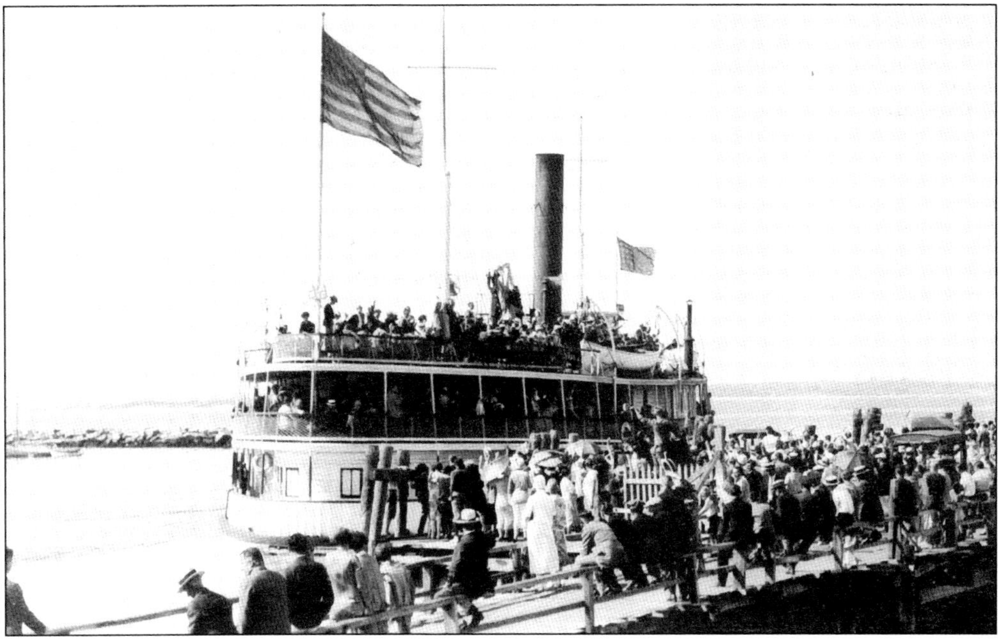

On Labor Day 1934, the *Mount Hope* is leaving Old Harbor, Block Island, on its last run. In 1896, the Fall River and Providence Steamboat Company was sold to the Providence, Fall River and Newport Steamboat Company of Providence. A valuable asset, the *Mount Hope* went with the sale.

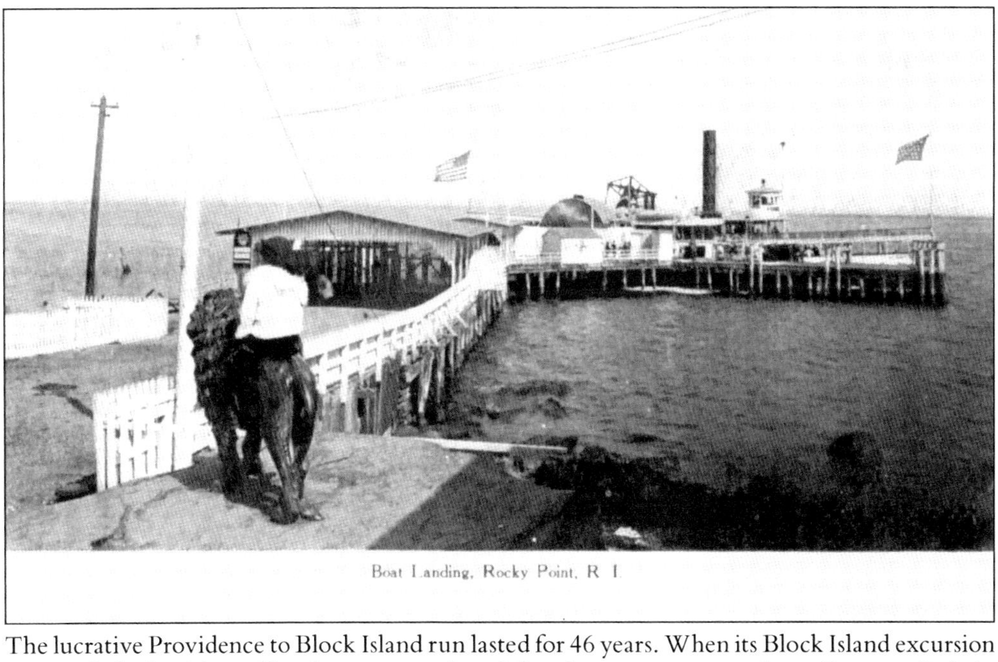

The lucrative Providence to Block Island run lasted for 46 years. When its Block Island excursion trips ended, the *Mount Hope* became employed ferrying summer crowds to Crescent Park in East Providence and Rocky Point Park in Warwick.

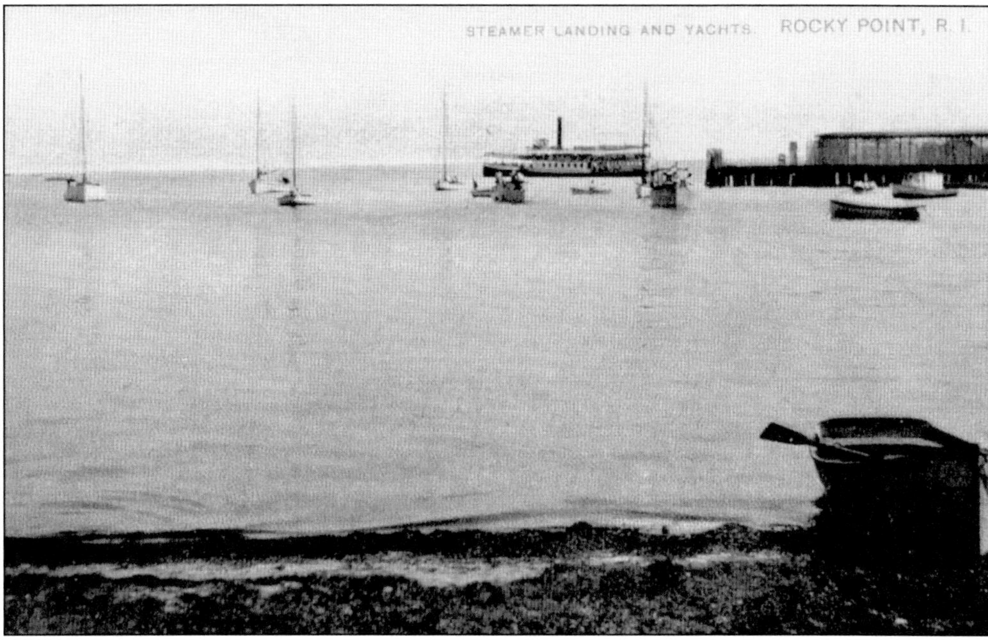

In the midst of a small fleet of anchored yachts, the *Mount Hope* leaves the Rocky Point Park landing.

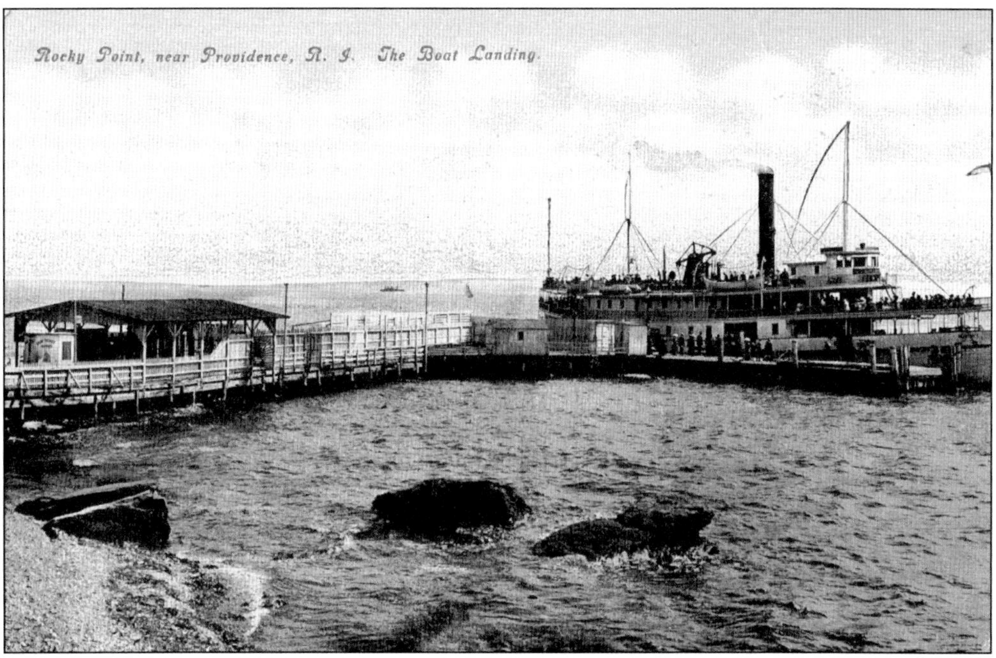

After a fun-filled day of amusements and shore dinners at Rocky Point Park, families board the *Mount Hope* for the leisurely cruise home to Newport, Bristol, Warren, and Providence.

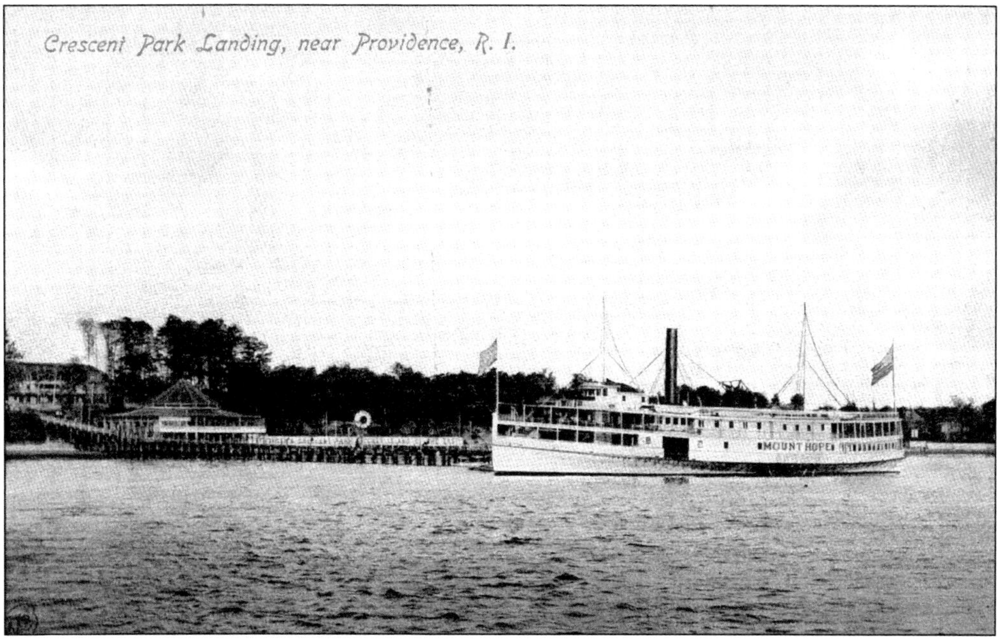

The *Mount Hope* waits to receive its passengers at the Crescent Park pier. The Crescent Park amusement park in the Riverside section of East Providence was famous for its roller coaster, shore dinners, and the moonlight dances at the Alhambra Ballroom.

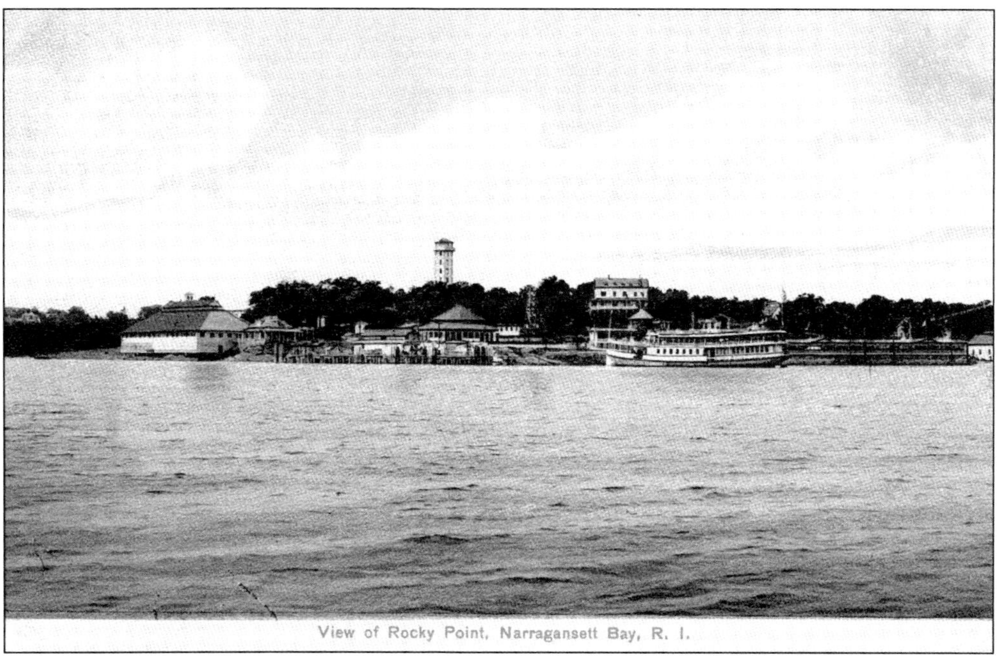

In this view of Rocky Point Park, one can clearly recognize the shore dinning hall (left), the carricle, and observation tower (center).

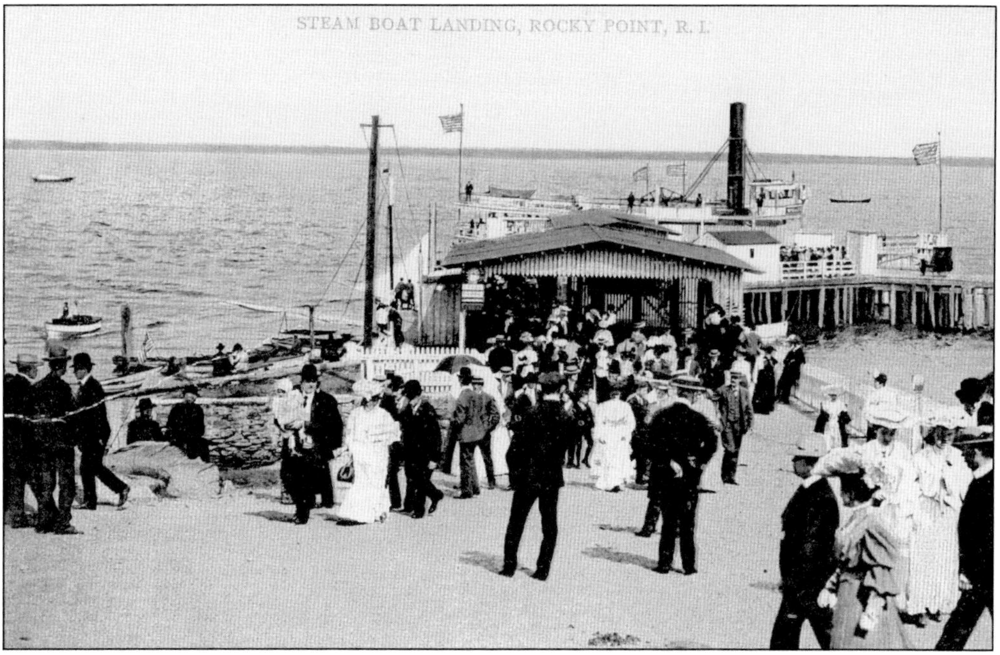

During those proper late-Victorian days of the early 20th century, gentlemen and ladies always attired themselves in presentable garments, albeit not particularly practicable for a hot, sticky summer afternoon at Rocky Point Park.

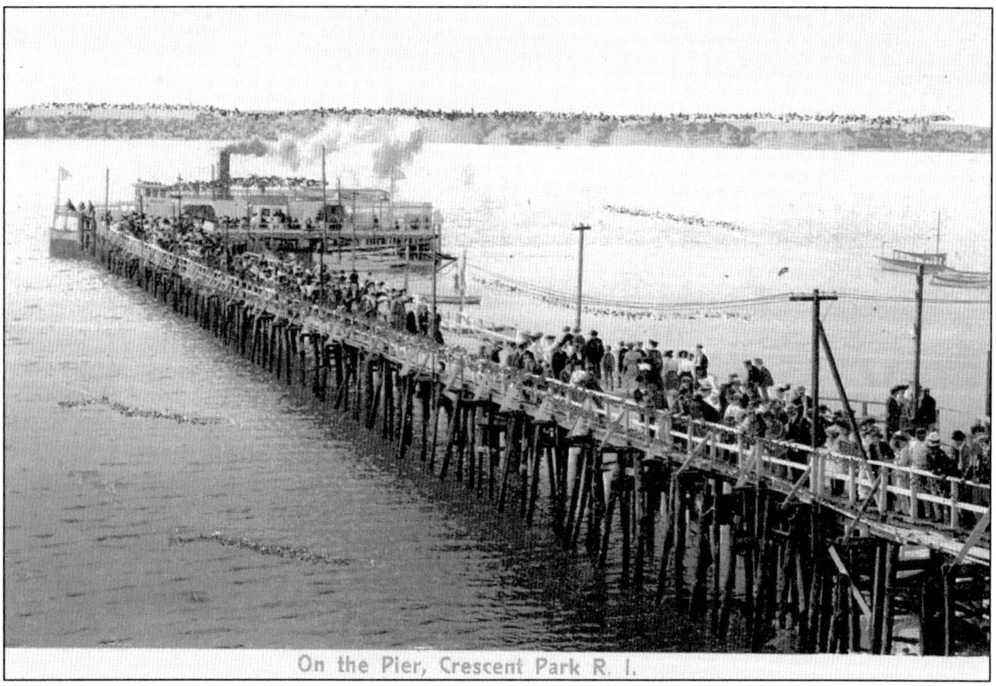

The Crescent Park pier appears rickety and unsound as commuters, coming and going, add their weight as they traverse its boards.

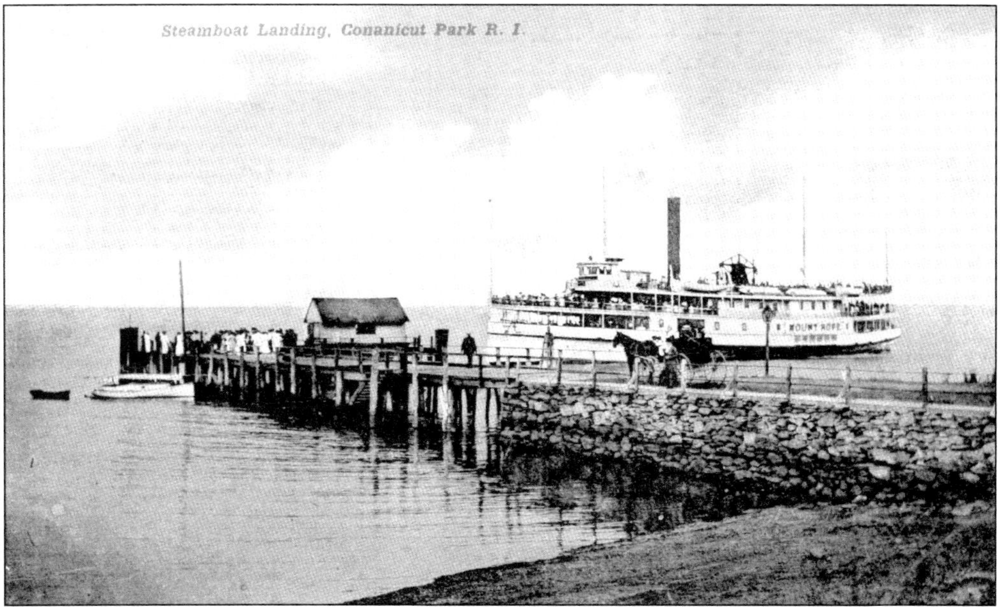

The *Mount Hope* approaches the Conanicut Park pier to pick up a small group of commuters. Conanicut Park was a residential community on the island of Jamestown in the middle of Narragansett Bay.

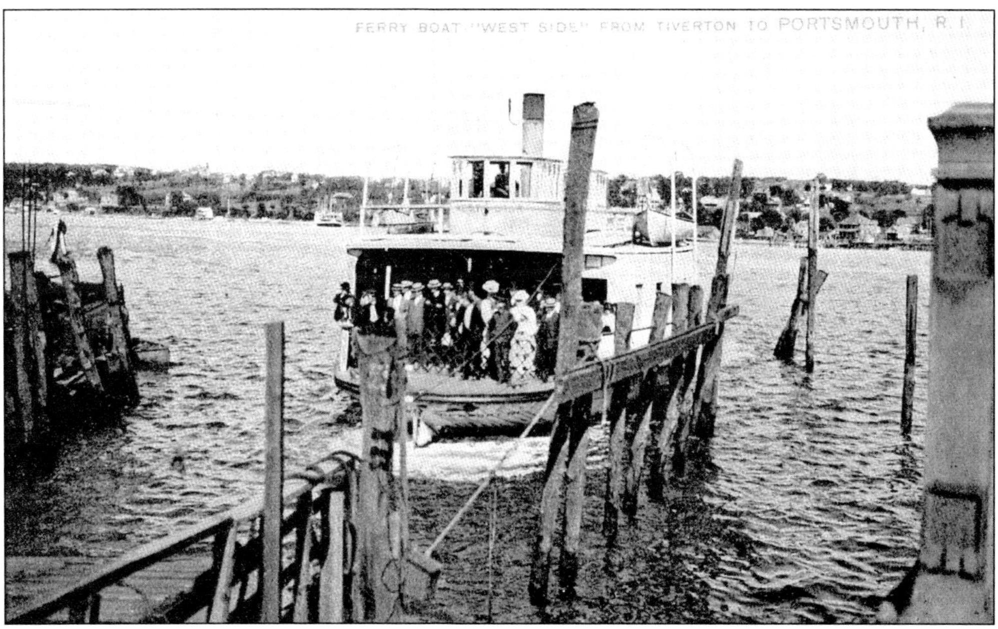

After the great hurricane of 1938 washed out Stone Bridge, the ferry boat *West Side* was pressed into service to carry passengers across the Sakonnet River from Portsmouth to Tiverton.

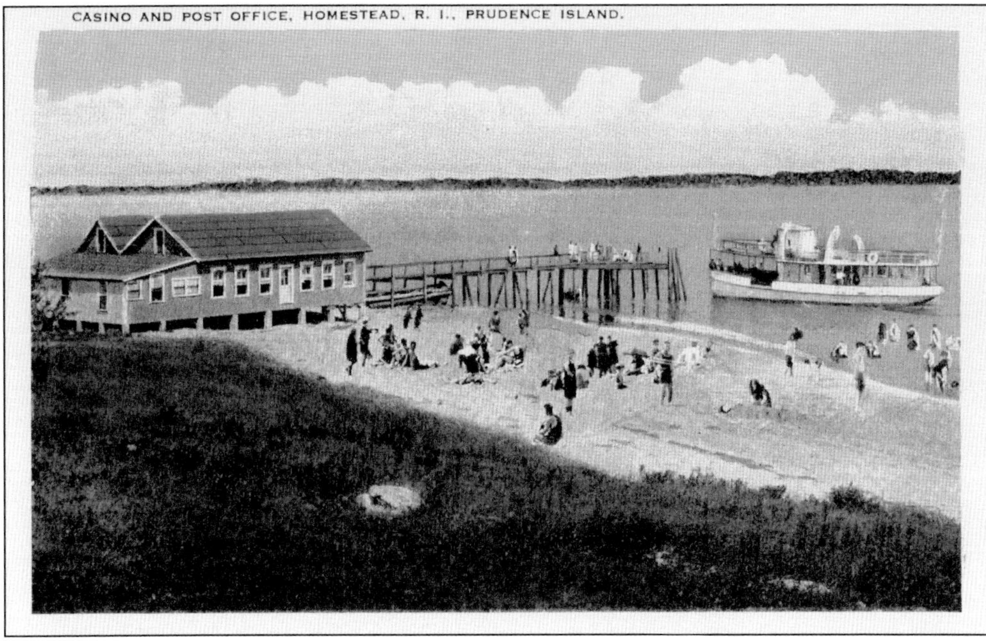

The MV *Harvest* approaches its dockage at Homestead on Prudence Island, Portsmouth, around 1918.

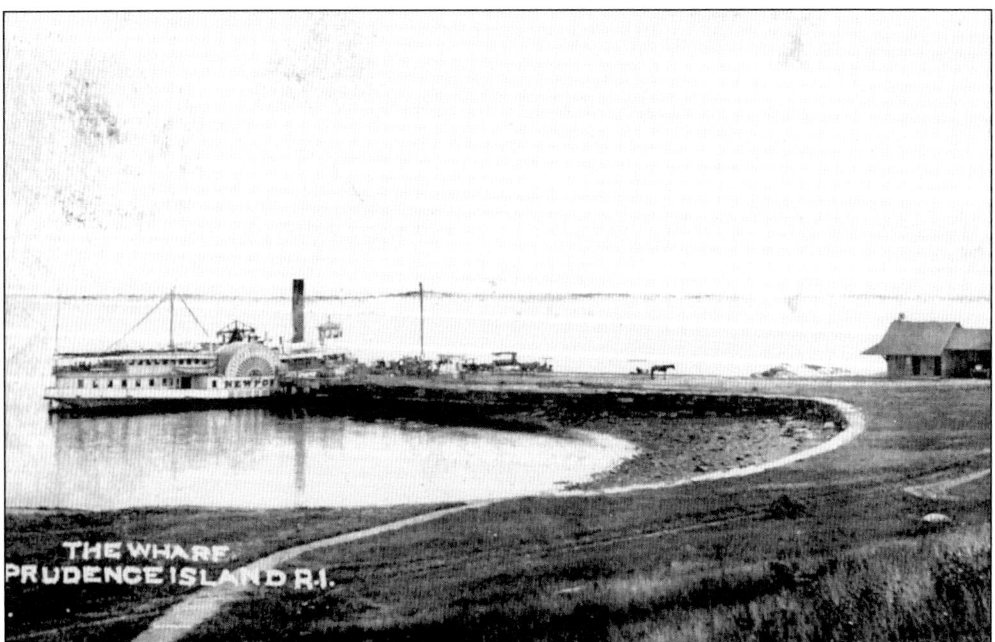

The Narragansett Bay excursion steamer the *City of Newport* dispatches summer residents at its Prudence Park landing on Prudence Island, Portsmouth.

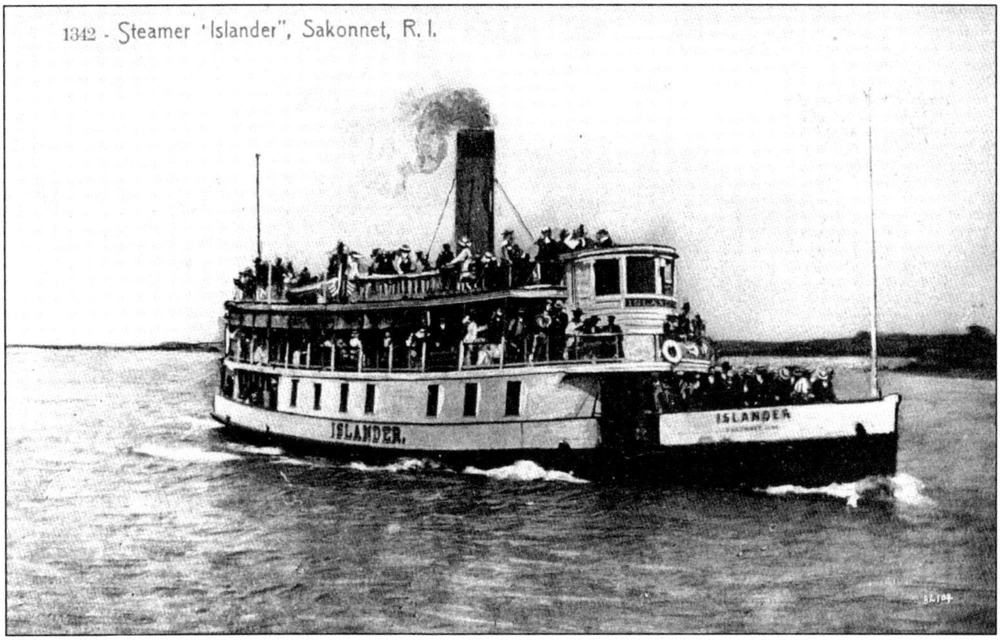

Beginning in 1886, the steamers *Awashonks*, *Queen City*, and *Islander* were operated by the Sakonnet Steamboat Company of Little Compton. The vessels operated between Providence and Sakonnet Point with stops at Bristol Ferry, Stone Bridge, and Fogland Point. The run continued each summer until 1919.

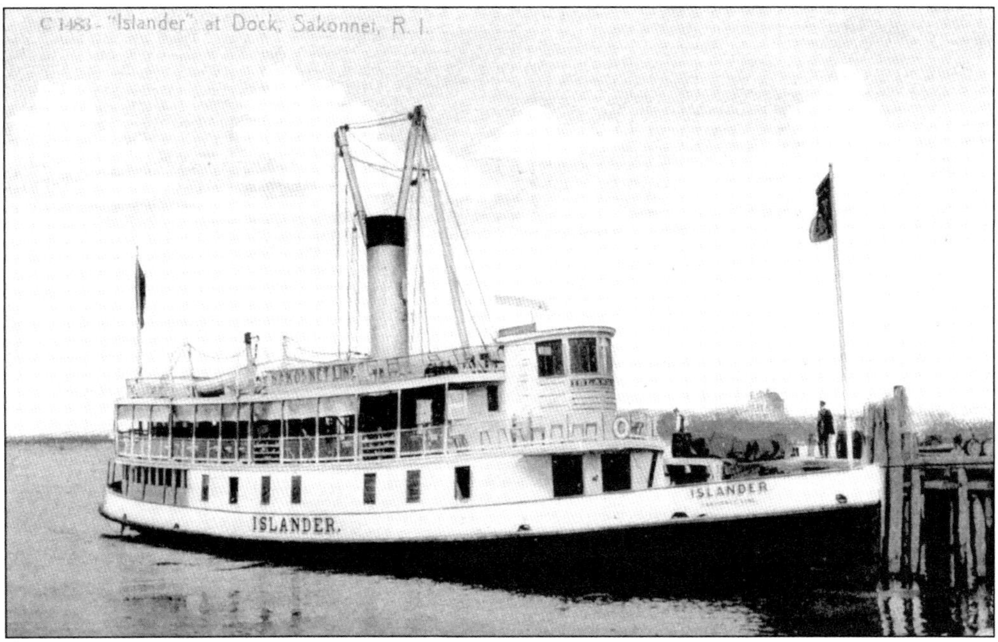

The 106-foot *Islander* replaced the *Awashonks*, which burned in 1901. This *c.* 1908 postcard image shows the *Islander* at its Sakonnet Point dock. Previous to the steam ferry service, a line of packet vessels served the summer colony in the Newport County towns of Tiverton and Little Compton.

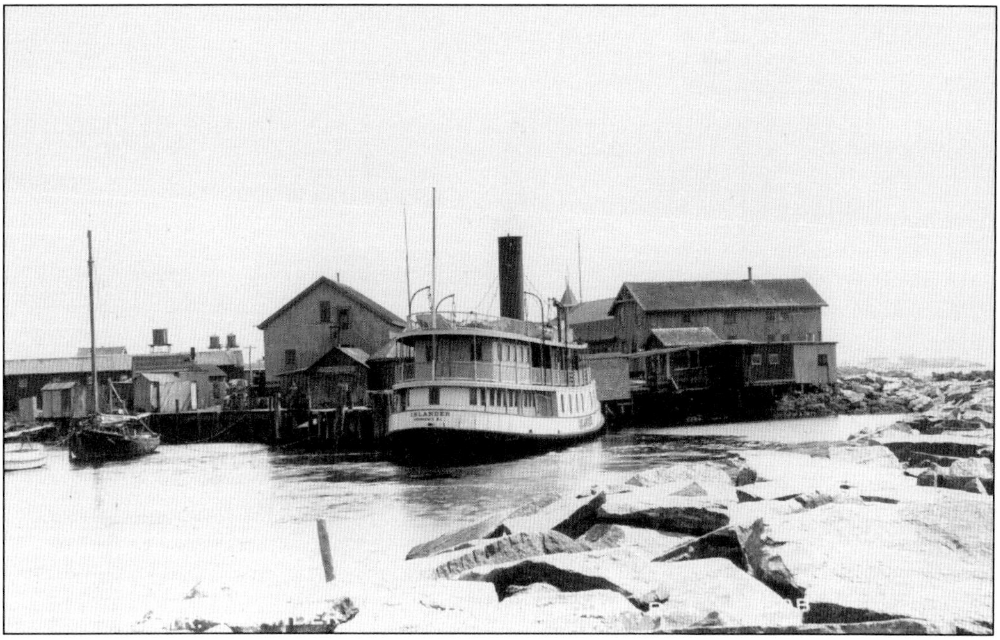

In this postcard image, taken around 1907, readers are graced by an aft view of the *Islander.* In 1886, Capt. Horatio N. Wilcox operated the ferry service between Providence and Sakonnet Point with the steamer ***Dolphin.*** Wilcox's steamer service opened the Providence market to farmers in the southeastern part of the state. In 1887, Capt. Julius A. Pettey and others organized the Sakonnet Steamboat Company.

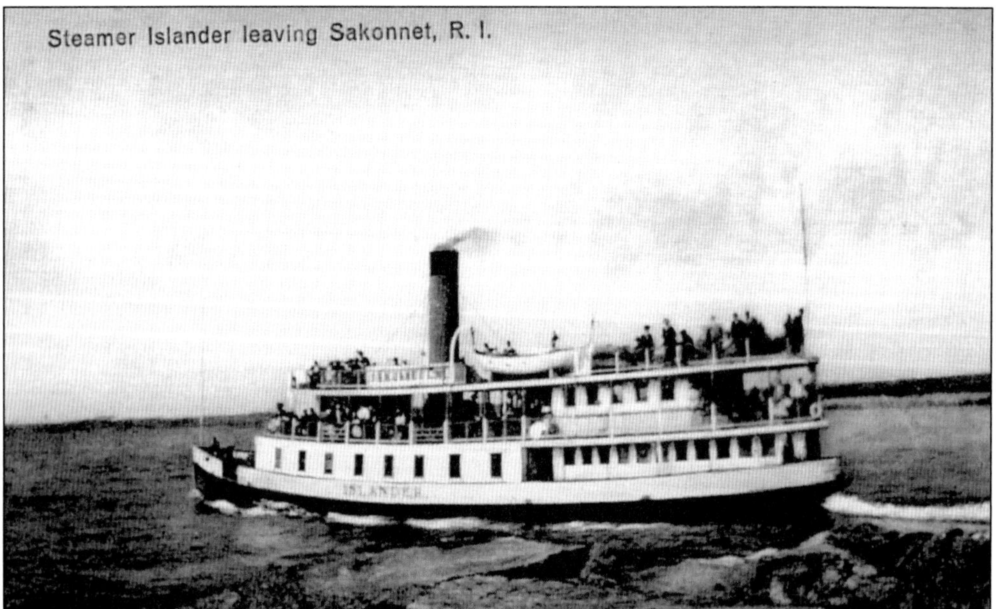

By 1915, only the *Islander,* owned by Philip W. Almy, made the Providence-to-Sakonnet run. Almy also owned the dining pavilion on the point; a round-trip ticket on the ferry entitled the bearer to a shore dinner.

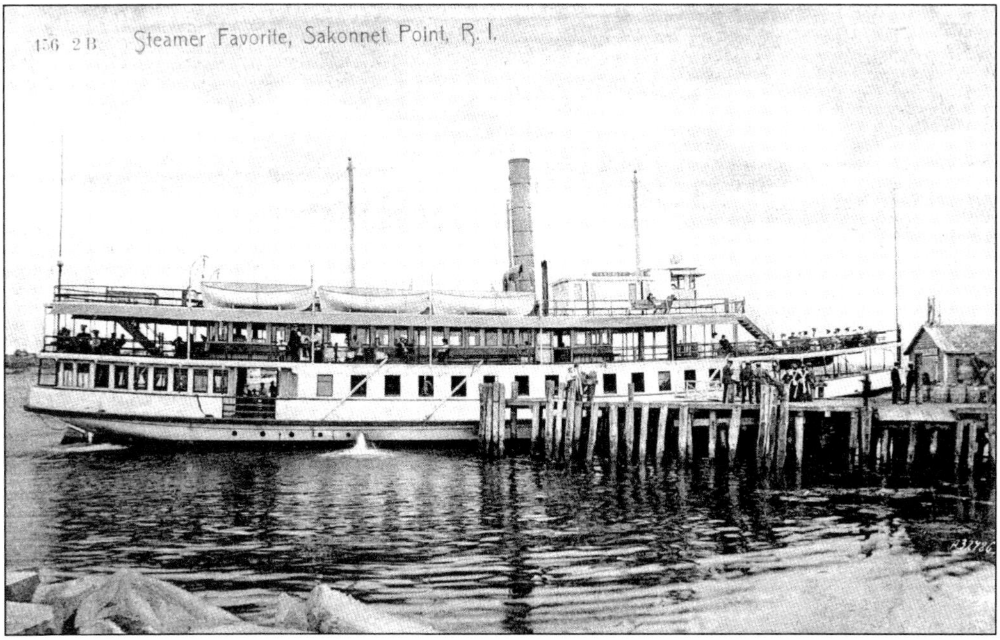

A *c.* 1910 view of the New York excursion steamer *Favorite* is seen here at the Sakonnet Point landing. Small excursion steamers and overnight sleepers such as the *Favorite* found it difficult to compete with old day-trippers like the *Islander,* which carried freight as well as passengers.

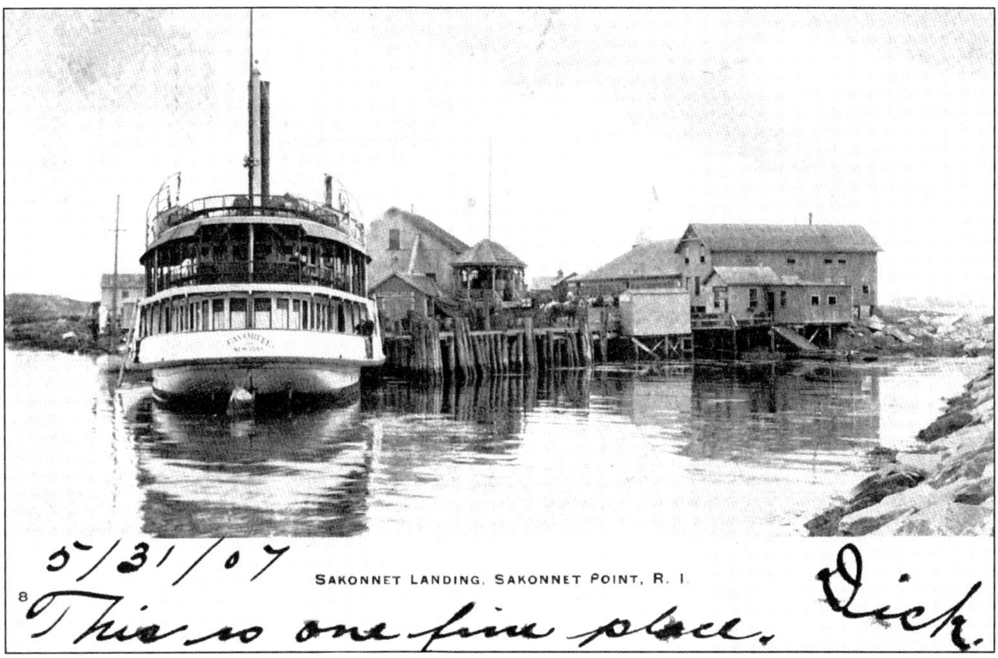

Here is another view of the *Favorite*, the Sakonnet Point steamer landing, and its fish processing buildings. The dining pavilion is the building in the background with the flag flying, taken around 1907.

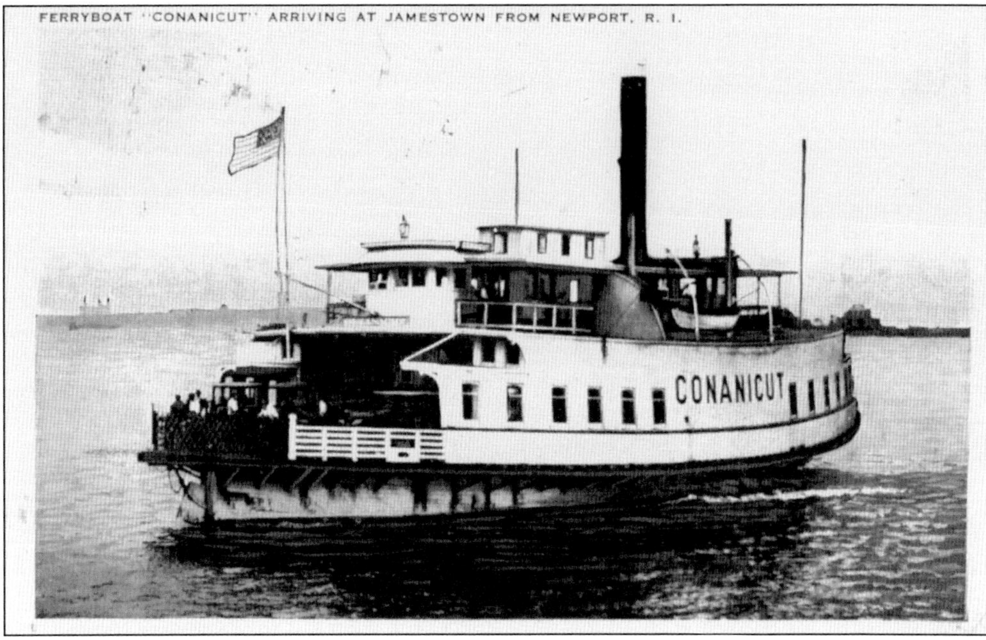

The *Conanicut* had a long career shuttling passengers between Jamestown and Newport, beginning in 1887, until it was replaced in 1927 by the *Governor Carr.*

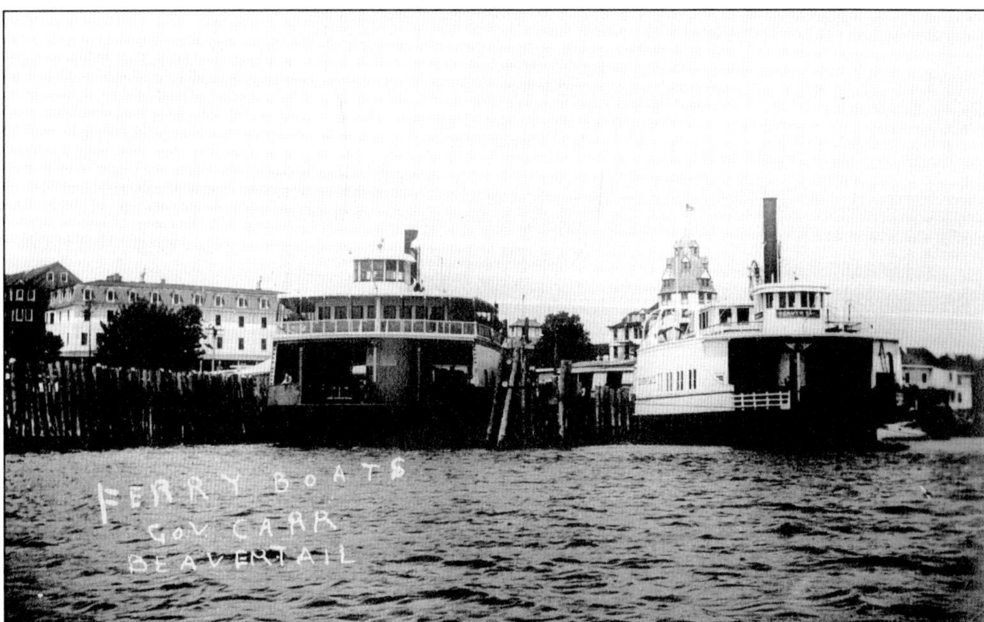

This is a view of Jamestown's East Ferry landing with the vehicle and passenger ferries the *Governor Carr* (left) and the *Beaver Tail.*

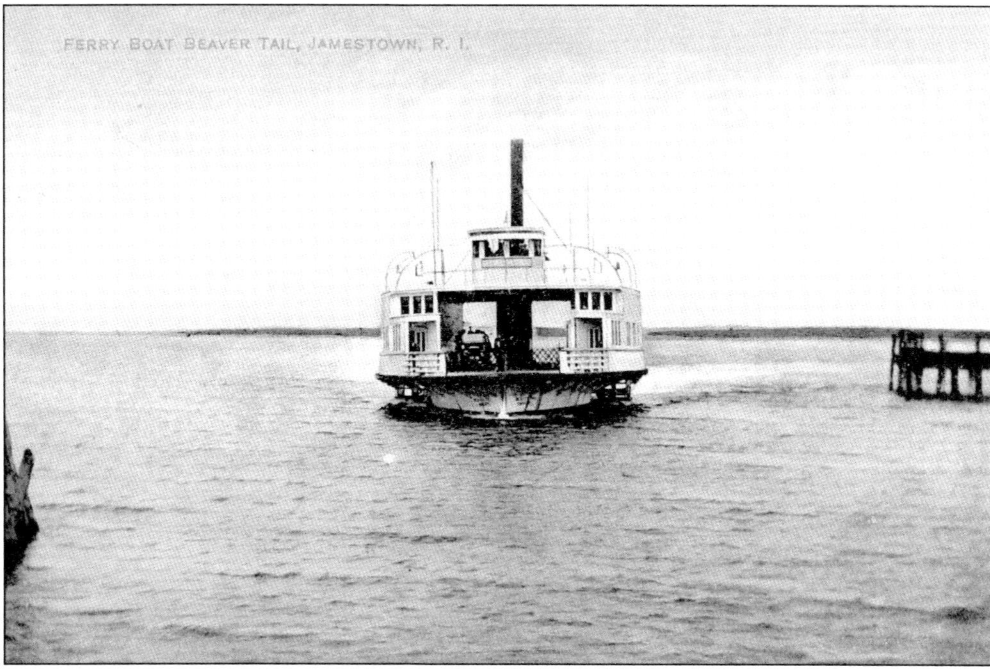

The *Beaver Tail* approaches its Jamestown slip around 1912.

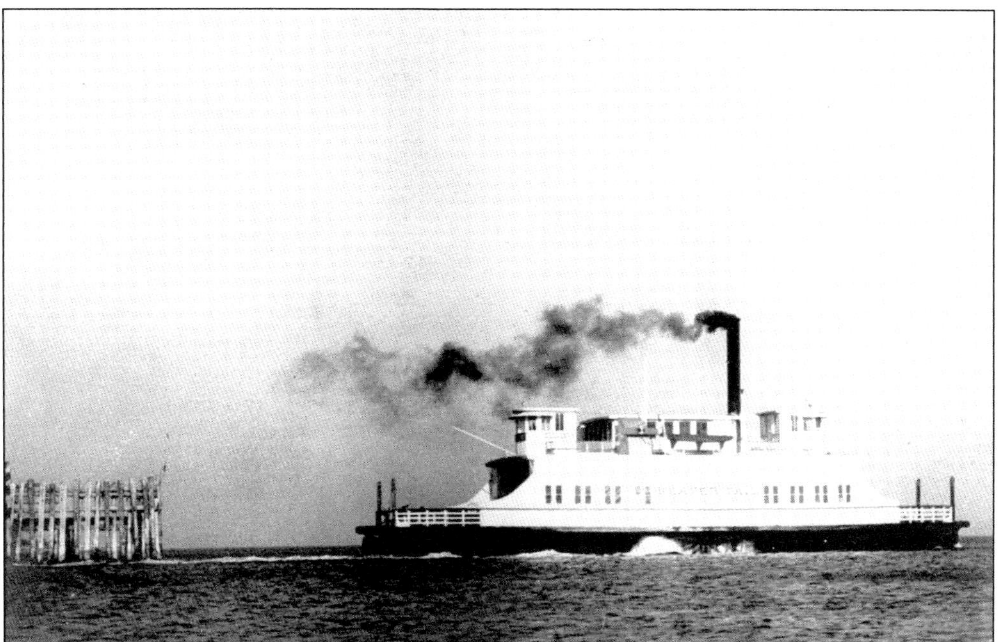

The *Beaver Tail* lays down a thick trail of black smoke, emanating from its coal-fired boiler, as it departs Jamestown for Newport around 1908.

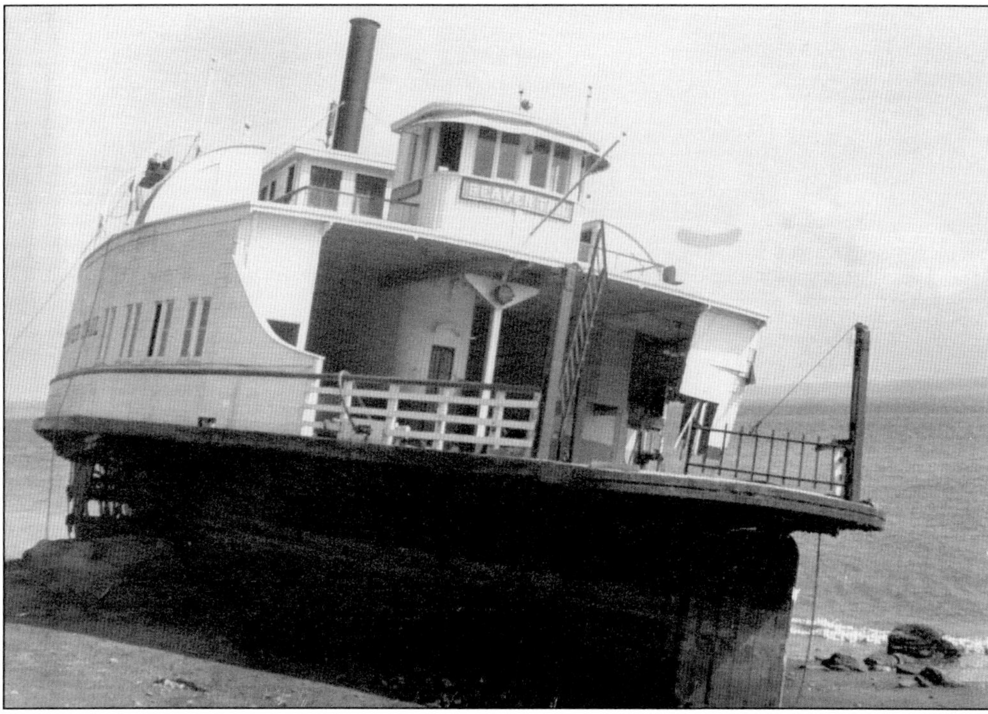

The *Beaver Tail* is seen high and dry on a Narragansett Bay beach.

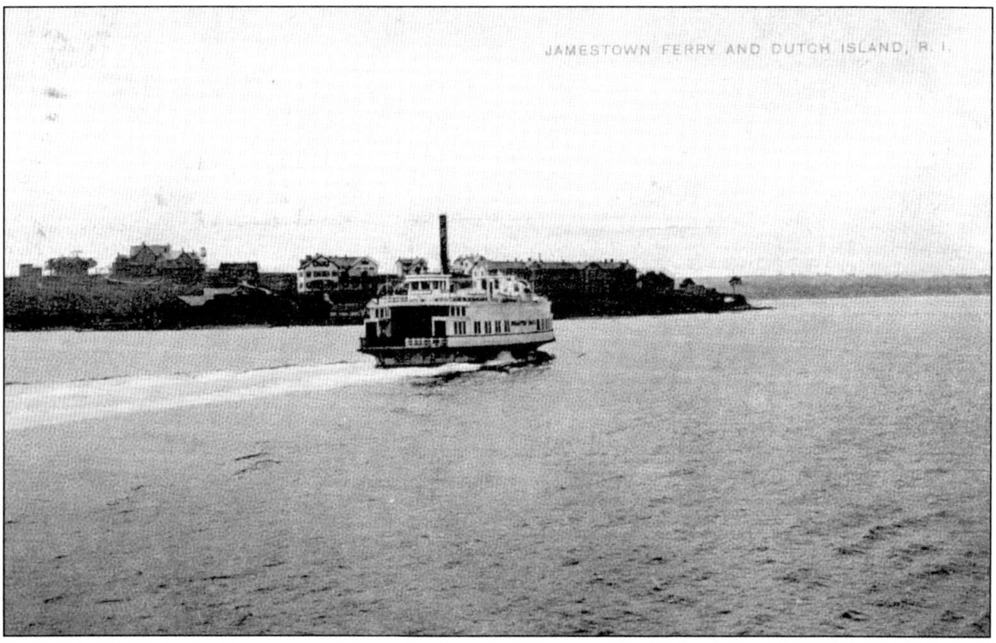

In this *c.* 1908 postcard, the *Beaver Tail* is seen steaming past Dutch Island. This is unusual because Dutch Island is on the west side of Jamestown; it is going in the opposite direction from its usual goal of Newport Harbor.

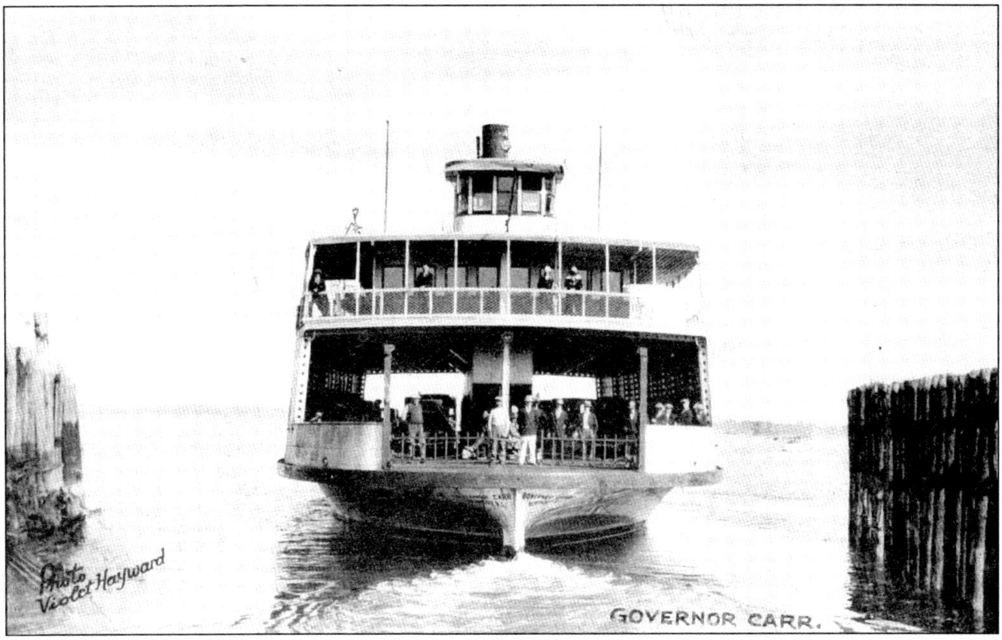

The new Jamestown-Newport ferry, the *Governor Carr*, was placed in service in 1927. Here it is seen leaving the Jamestown Ferry landing around 1944.

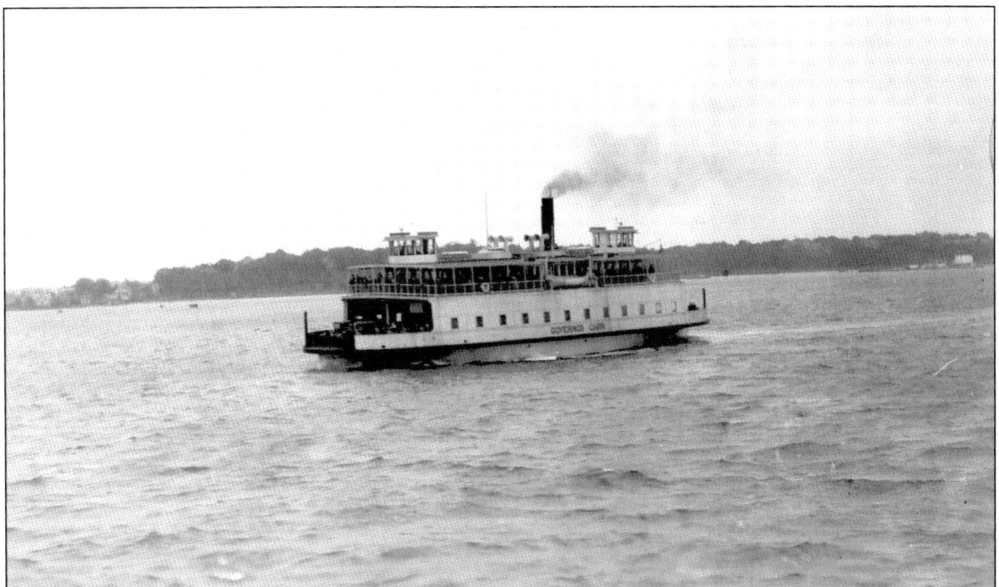
306 Governor Carr, Jamestown Ferry, Newport, R. I.

In this *c.* 1938 image, the fully loaded *Governor Carr* is in about the middle or the east passage of Narragansett Bay on its way to Newport Harbor.

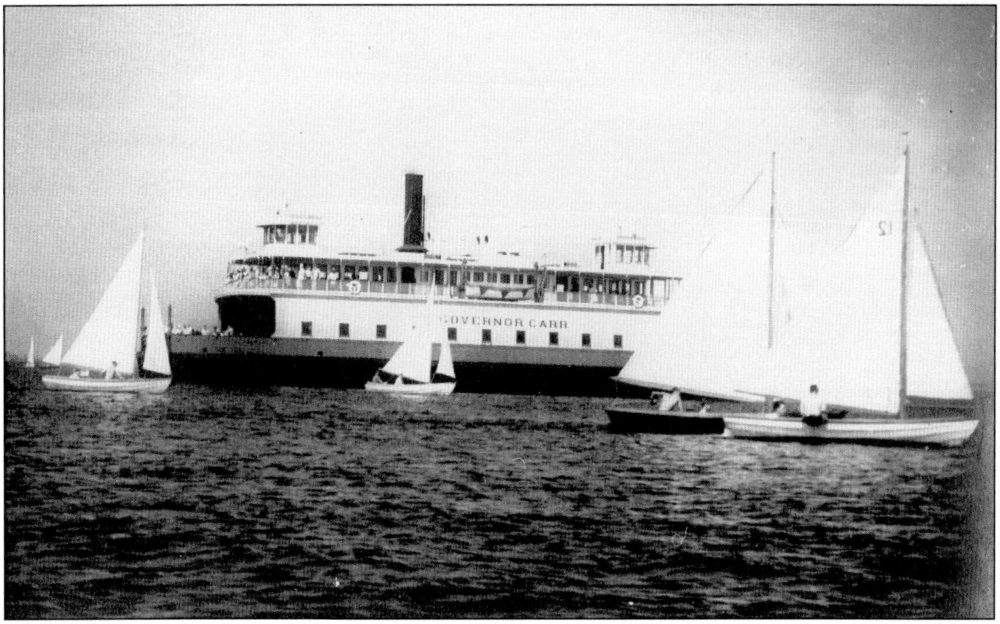

Small frolicking sailboats were always an entertaining sight for the *Governor Carr*'s passengers as they crossed the bay. This real-photo postcard is from around 1938.

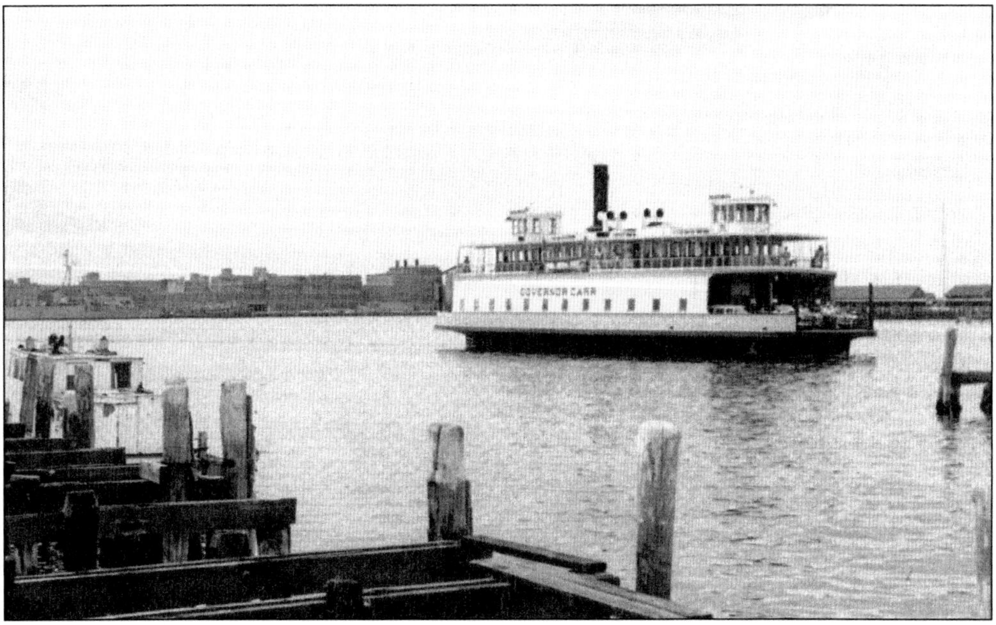

The *Governor Carr* approaches its Newport slip with Goat Island and the Naval Torpedo Station in the background.

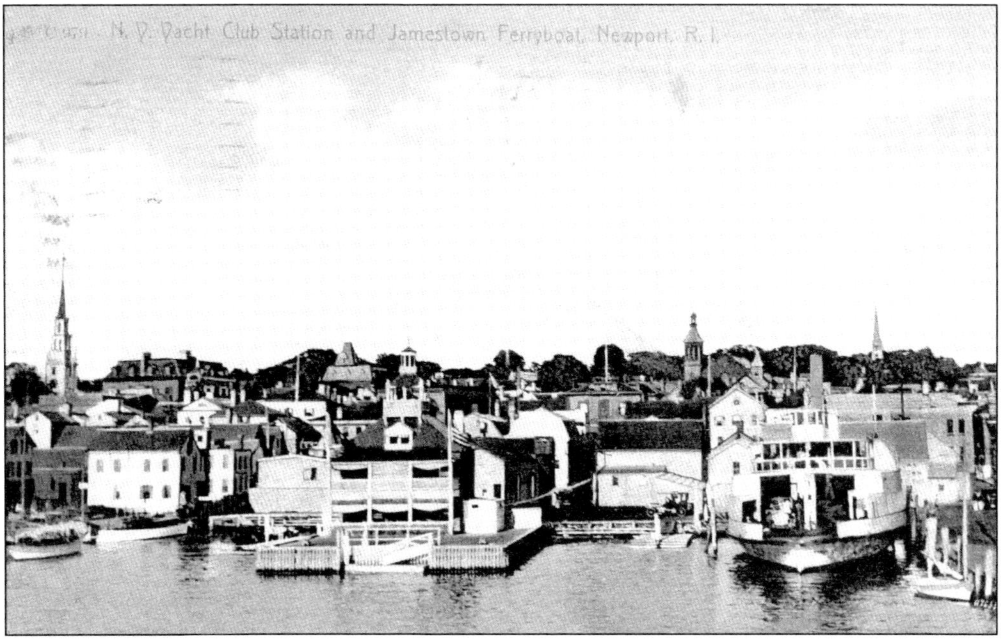

This is a *c.* 1909 view of the ferryboat *Narragansett* in the Newport ferry slip; to the left is the New York Yacht Club Station.

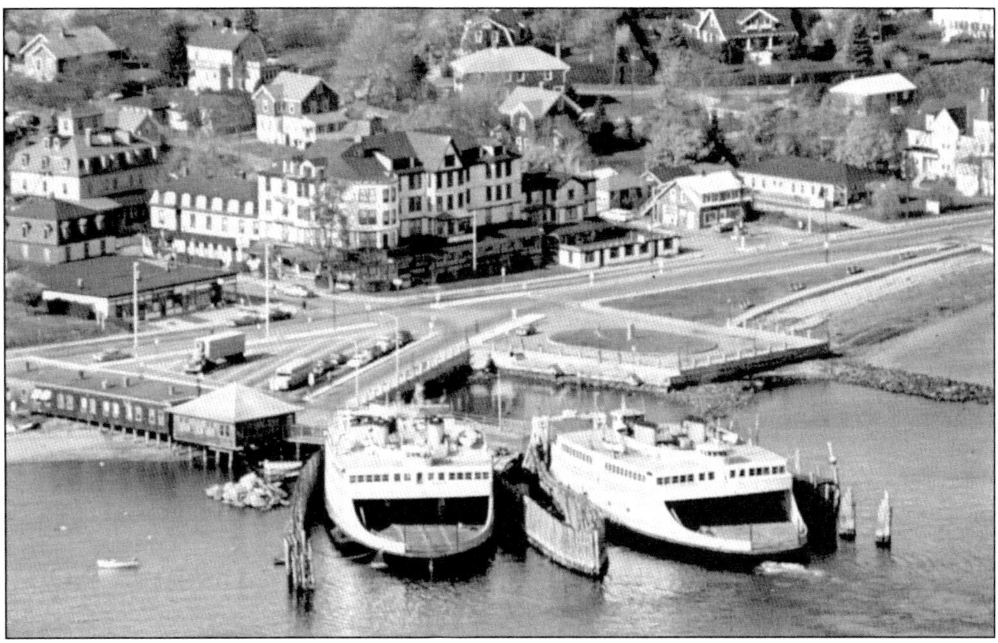

This is the Jamestown terminal of the state's Newport-Jamestown ferry system. In this aerial photograph is a view of the twin ferries, the *Jamestown* and the *Newport*. Also visible are the Bay View Hotel, East Shore Road, and part of Town Beach around 1960.

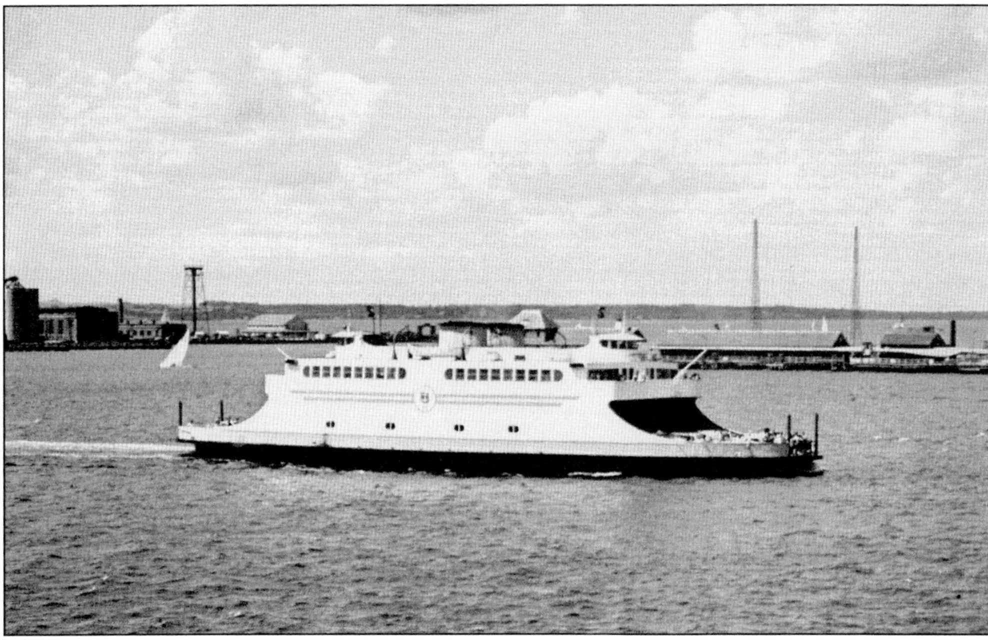

In this postcard photograph, the Newport-Jamestown ferry the *Jamestown* is seen entering Newport's inner harbor. When the Newport Bridge opened to vehicular traffic on June 28, 1969, operation of the ferry service ceased.

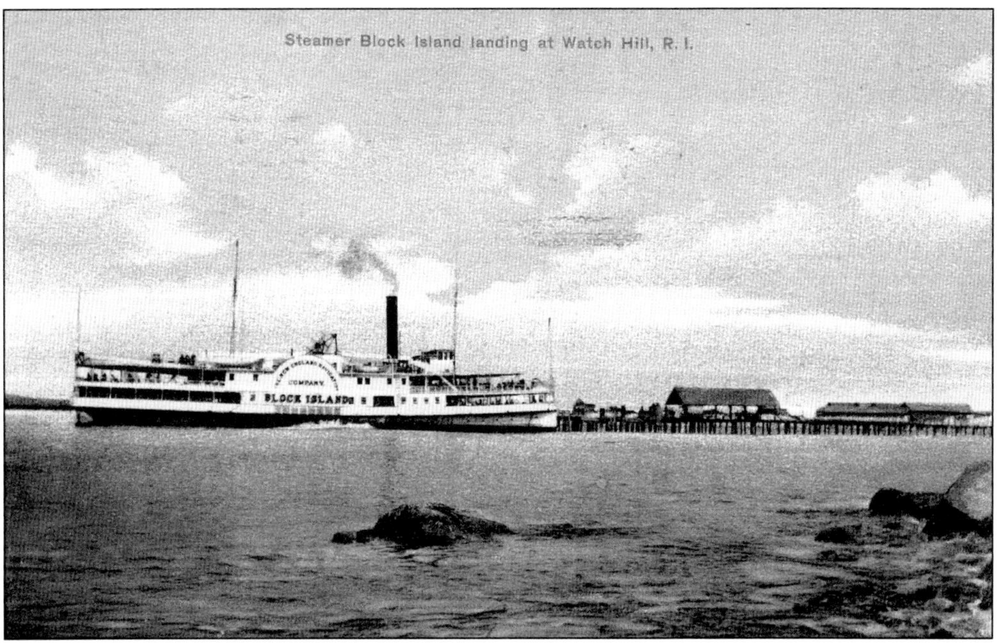

From around 1880 to present, there have been several different steamers on Narragansett Bay named *Block Island*. This steamer, *Block Island*, was owned and operated by the New England Navigation Company. Here it enters the Watch Hill landing around 1913. Worn-out, in 1930, it was towed to Dyer Island, off Melville, and burned.

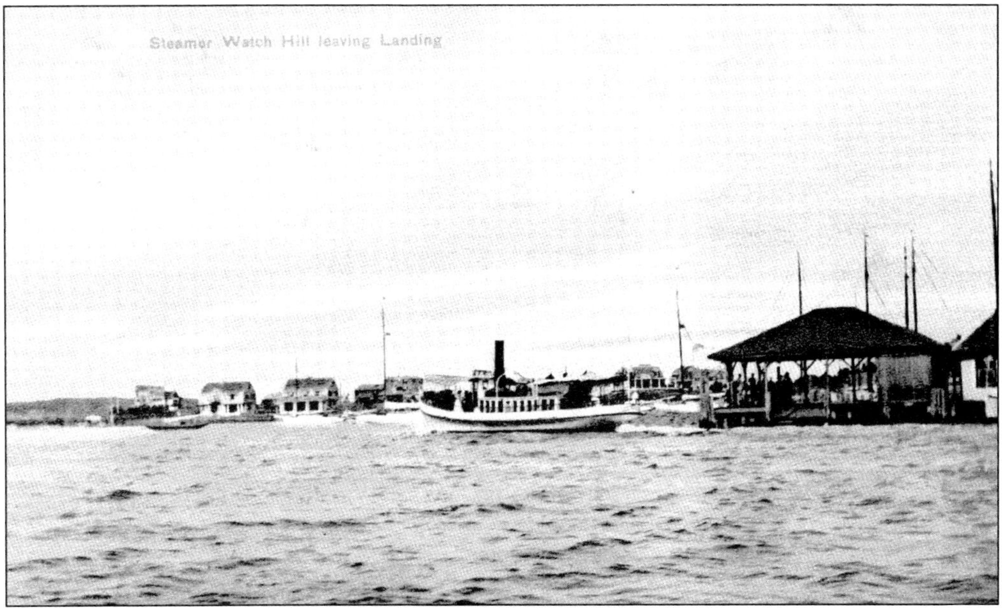

The intimate little steamer the *Watch Hill* chugs away from its Watch Hill landing around 1909.

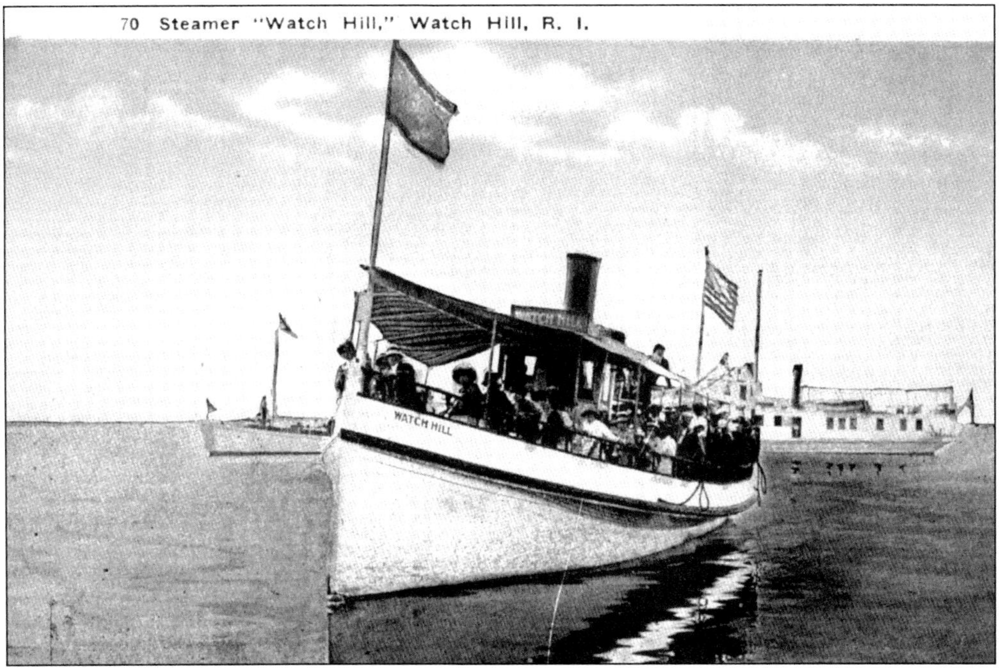

In this *c.* 1909 postcard image, the crowded ferry *Watch Hill* appears dangerously close to capsizing. These were the days before there was a U.S. Coast Guard to enforce safety regulations.

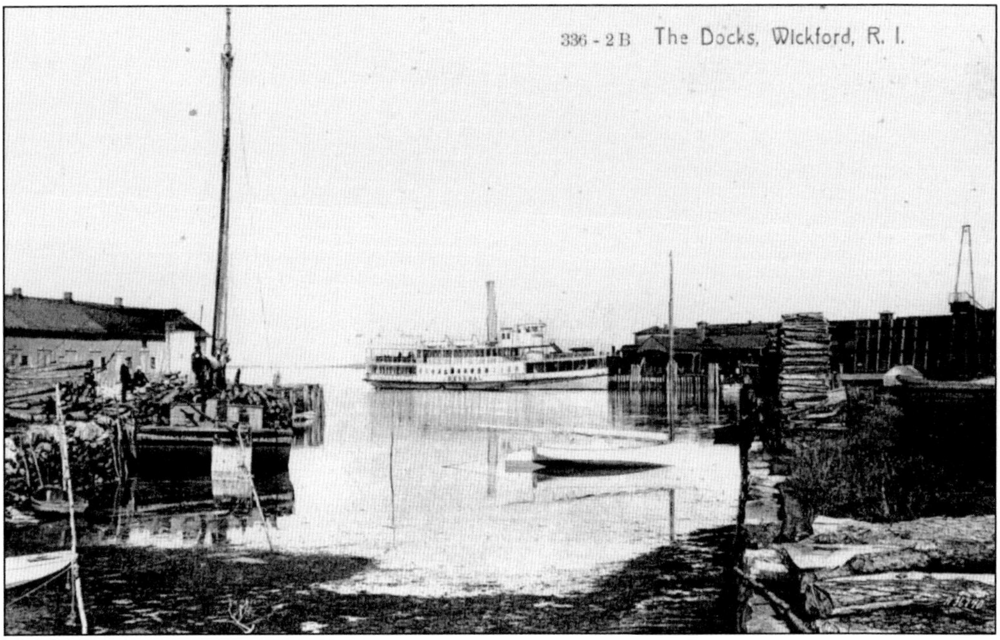

The *General*, built by the Continental Iron Works for the Hudson River Steamboat Company, was 332 tons. The Brooklyn-built steam ferry ran between Norfolk and Newport News, Virginia, until purchased in 1893 by the Newport and Wickford Railroad and Steamboat Company of Rhode Island.

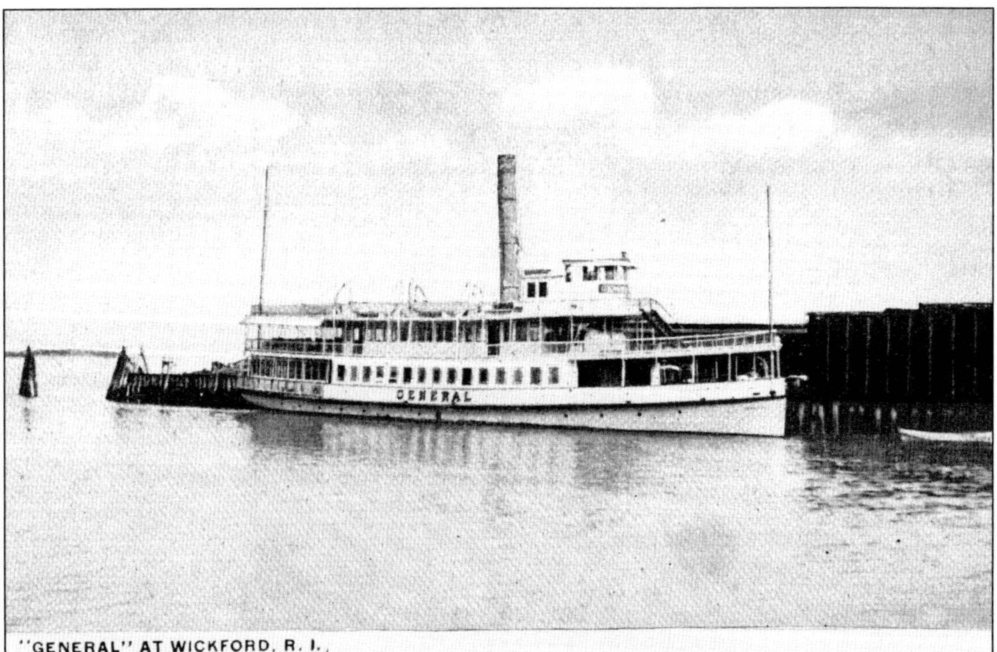

The *General* ran on the bay between Newport and Wickford until 1927. It was sold and used as an excursion boat for the city of New York until scrapped in the early 1930s.

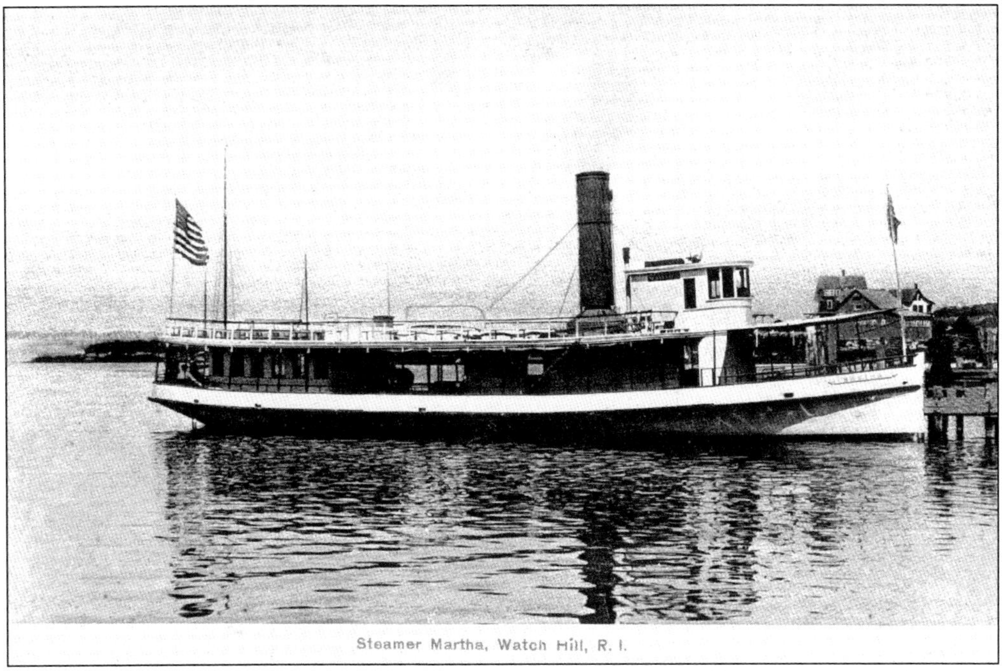

The passenger steam ferry *Martha* is seen dockside at its Watch Hill home port around 1910.

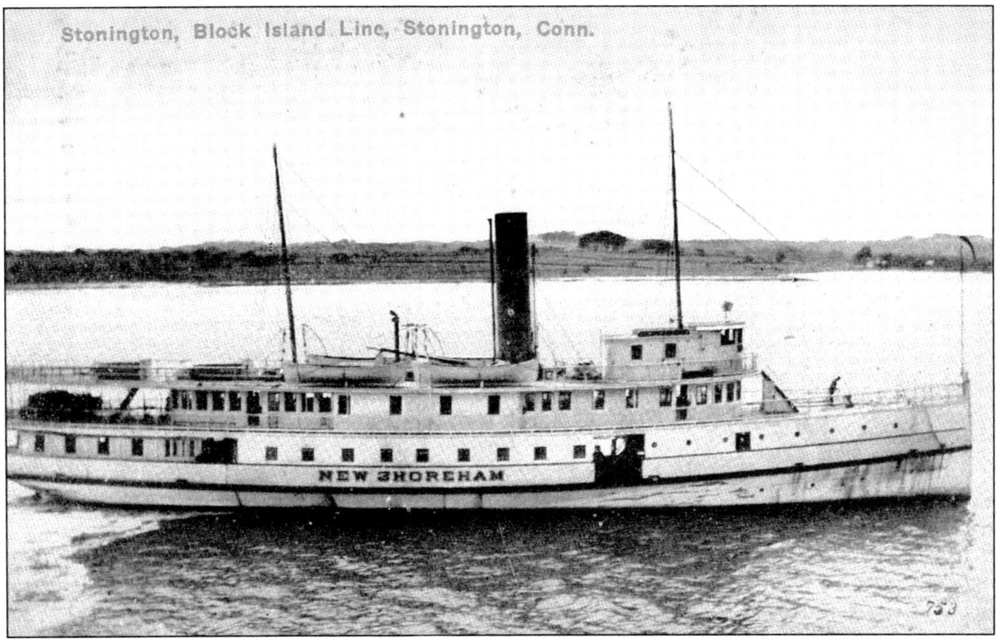

The *New Shoreham* of the Stonington, Block Island Line, is seen here around 1905. The *New Shoreham* was built in 1901 in East Boston for the town of New Shoreham for a year-round connection between Block Island, Newport, and Providence.

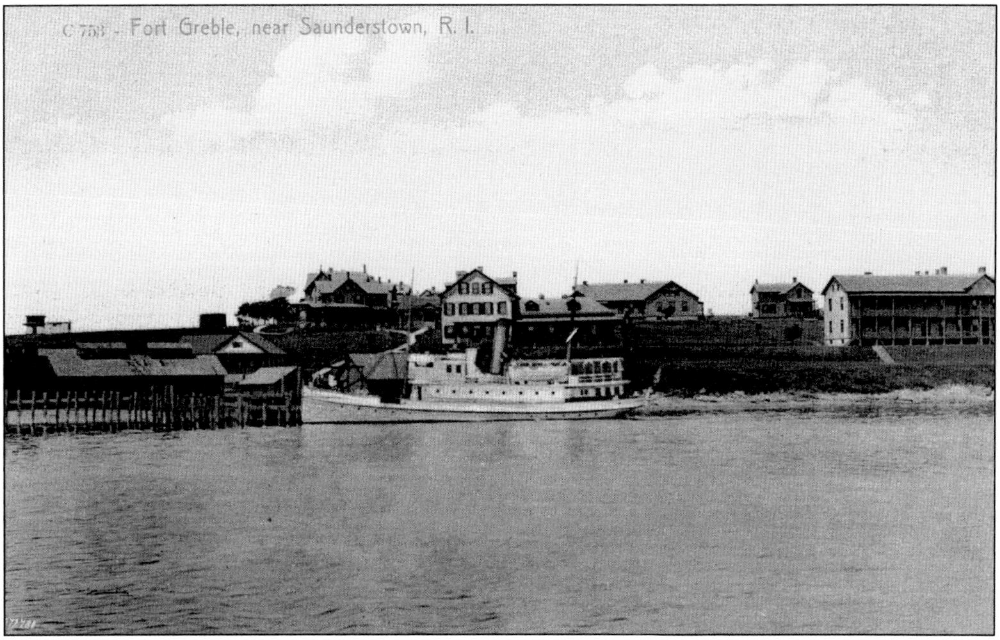

On this postcard, a small unidentifiable steamer is docked at the Fort Greble landing on Dutch Island at the southern end of the west passage of Narragansett Bay.

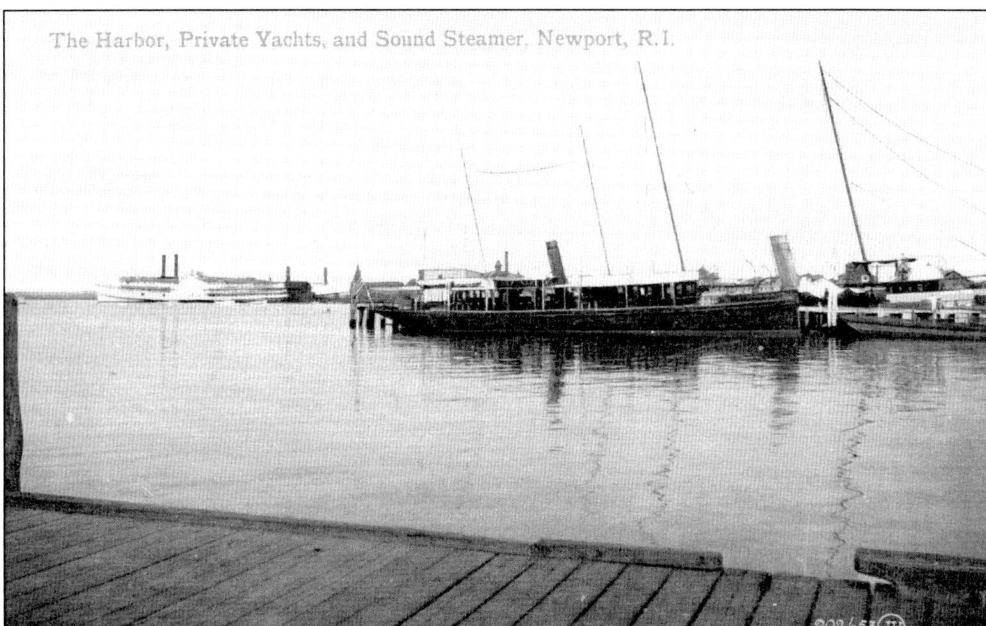

Private steam yachts are clustered in Newport Harbor as a sound steamer cruises past Goat Island around 1906.

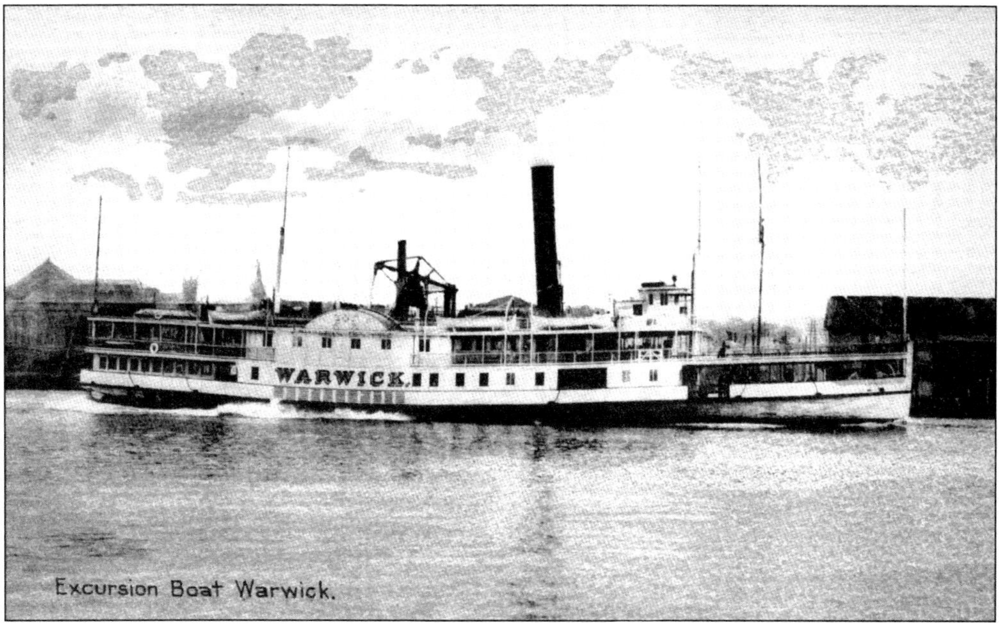

The steamer *Warwick*, formerly the *Day Star*, was built in 1873 by the Providence-based American Steamboat Company. On January 19, 1920, the *Warwick* sank off Commercial Wharf in Newport Harbor.

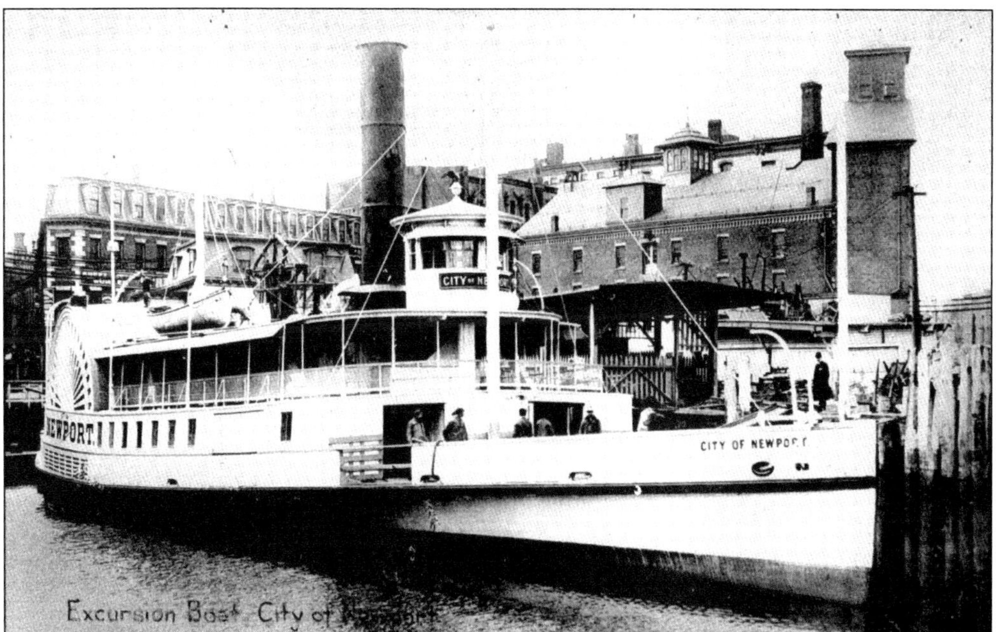

The American Steamboat Company was organized in 1864. The company's ferry *City of Newport* ran the lucrative Newport to Providence summer commute.

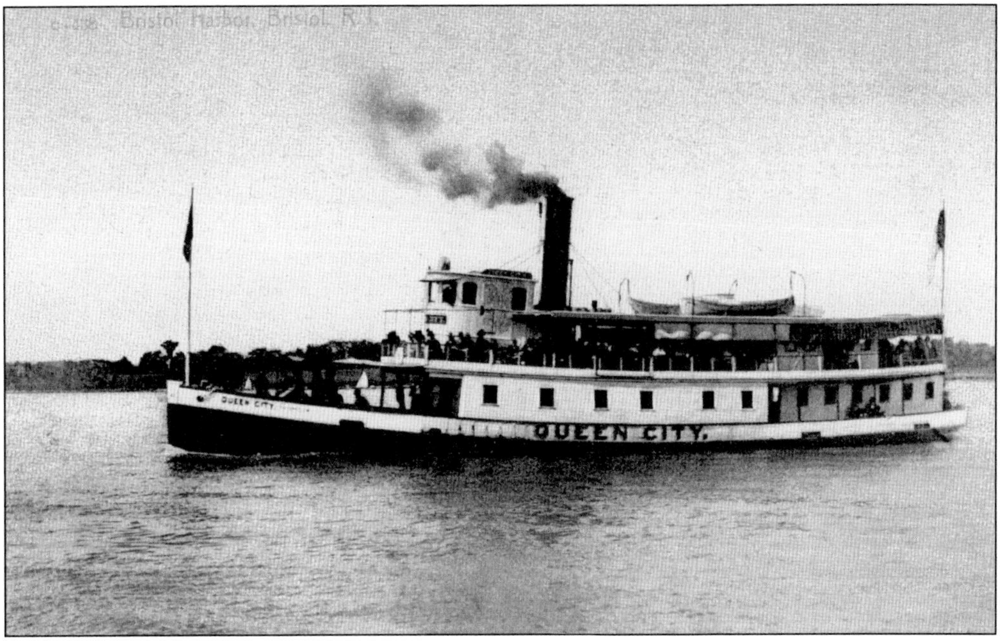

The Seaconnet Steamboat Company and partners put the 92-foot-long *Queen City* on the Providence to Sakonnet Point run. The company kept the run operating each summer from around 1887 until 1919.

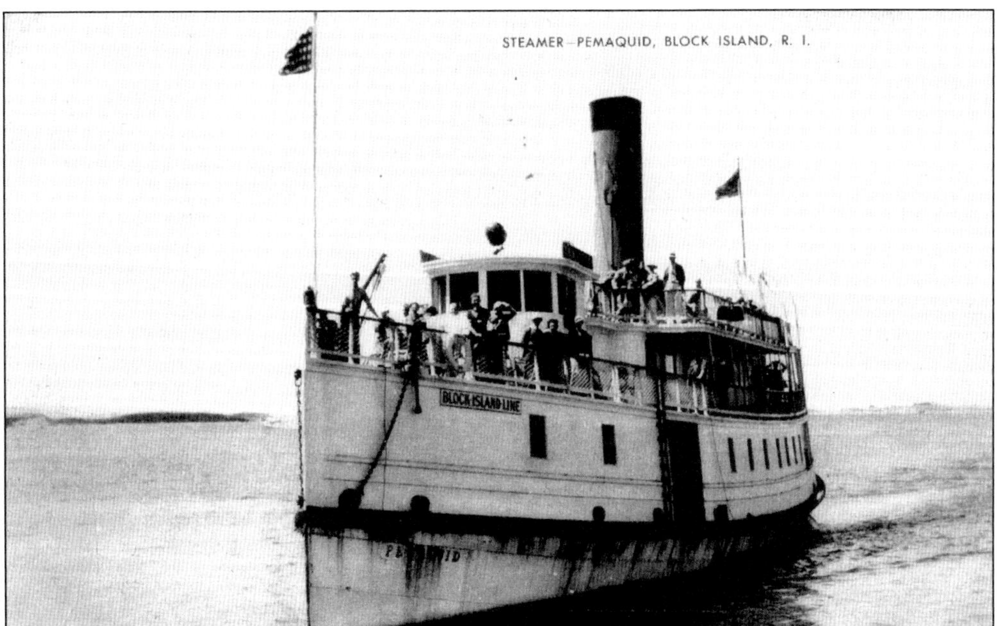

This is a *c.* 1910 image of the Block Island Line's day steamer *Pemaquid.*

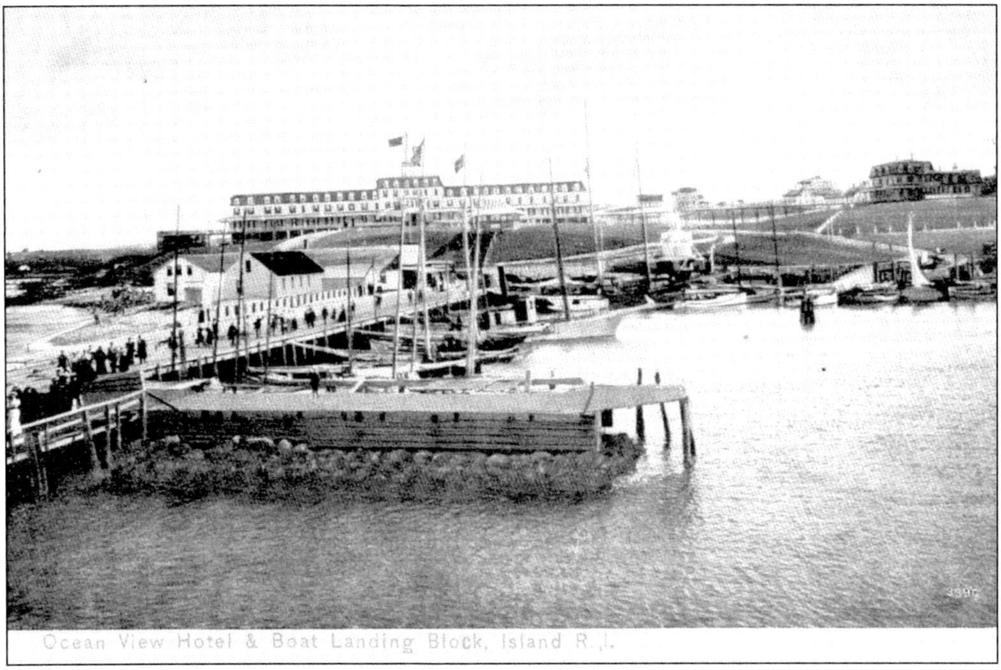

Block Island's Ocean View Hotel was the luxury resort hotel that many summer visitors to the island were heading; what an impressive first view they had as their steamer pulled into Old Harbor.

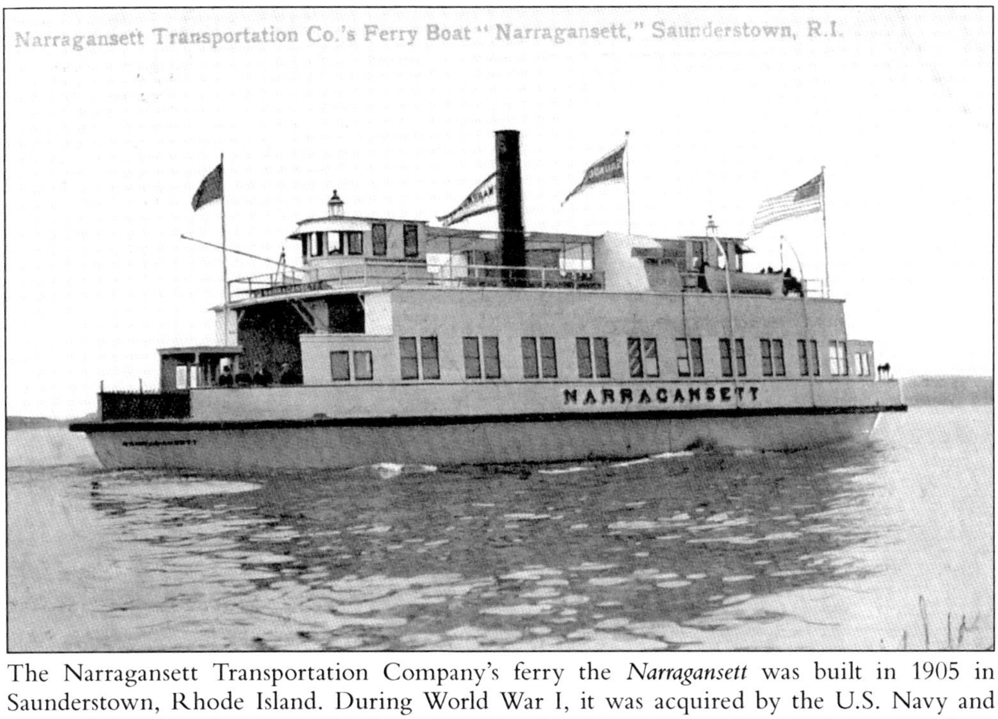

The Narragansett Transportation Company's ferry the *Narragansett* was built in 1905 in Saunderstown, Rhode Island. During World War I, it was acquired by the U.S. Navy and renamed the *Topsa*. It was used by the navy to shuttle military and civilian workers to and from the torpedo station on Goat Island.

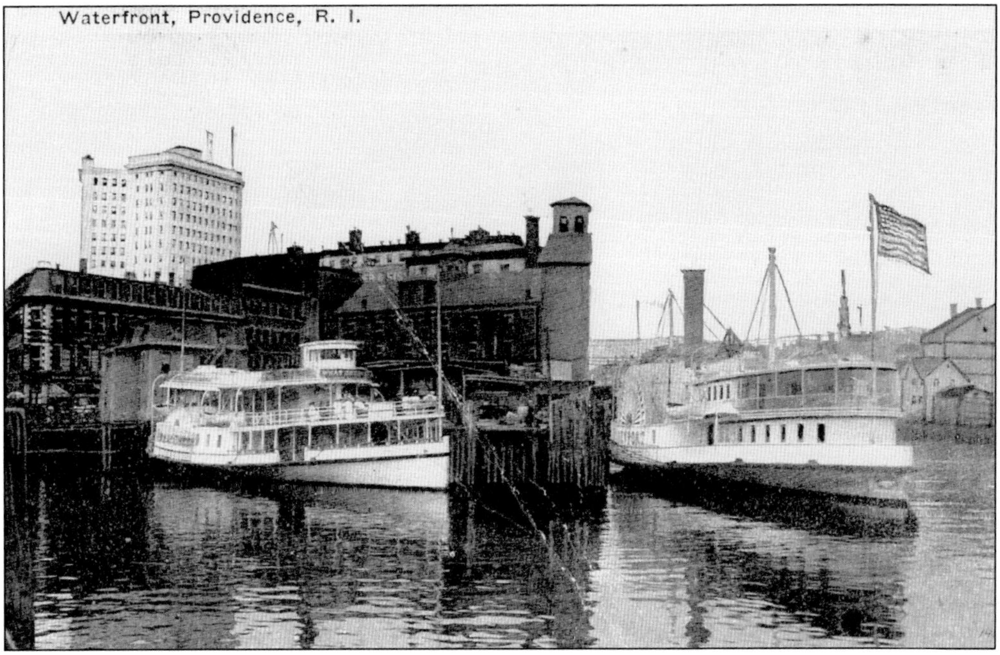

This image shows the bay steamers *What Cheer* and the *City of Newport* at their landing in the Providence River around 1909.

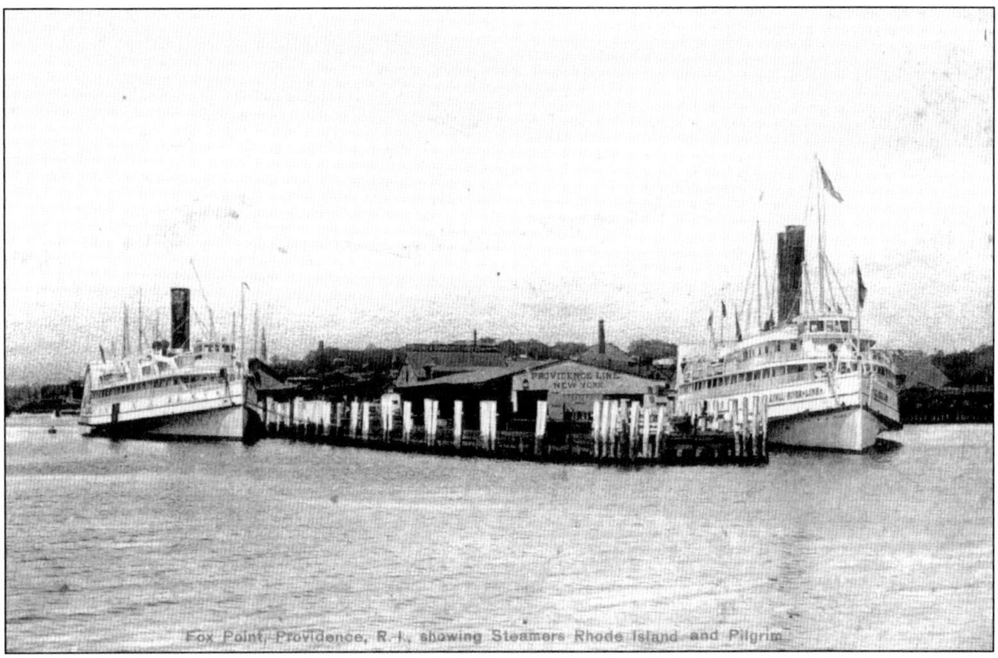

Here one can see the Providence to New York overnight excursion steamers the *Providence* (left) and the *Pilgrim* at their Fox Point landing around 1909. The *Pilgrim*, of iron construction, was rated at 3,483 tons and built in 1882. It was built for the Old Colony Steamboat Company; at the time, it was the largest inland steam passenger vessel built for the princely cost of $1 million. The steamer was broken up in New London, Connecticut, in 1920.

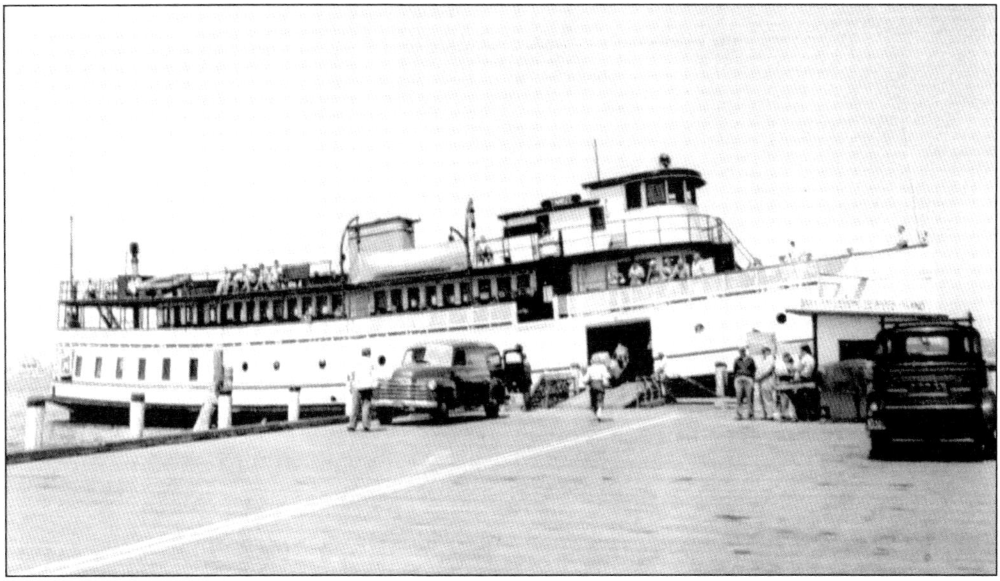

The *Yankee* is seen tied up at Point Judith getting ready for its daily run to Block Island. The *Yankee* was built as the *Machigonne* at Philadelphia in 1907. It made the summer run between Point Judith and Block Island until the *Quonset* took over in 1957.

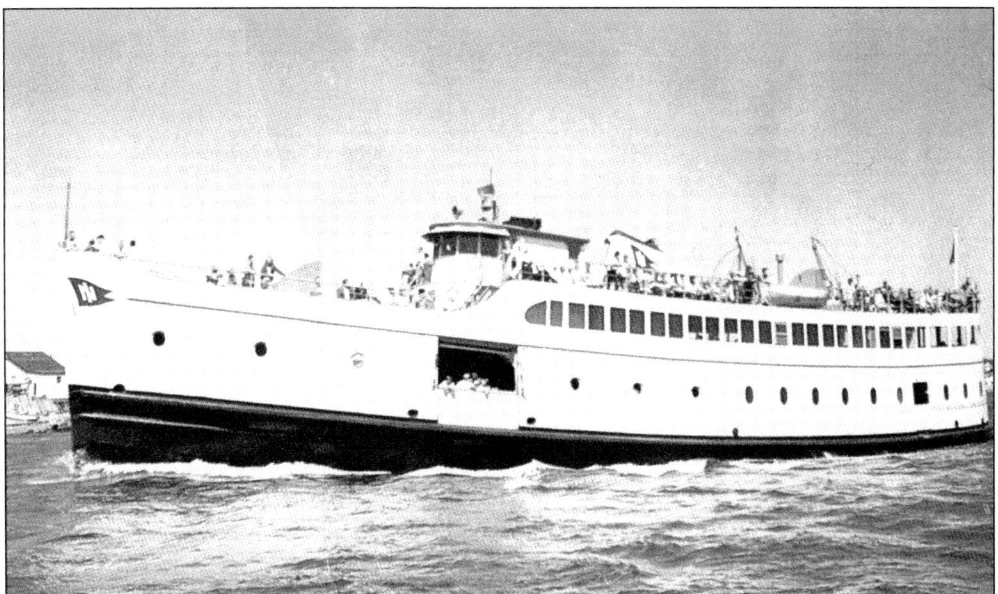

The motor vessel *Quonset* cruised the 14.5-mile run between Galilee to Block Island in 75 minutes.

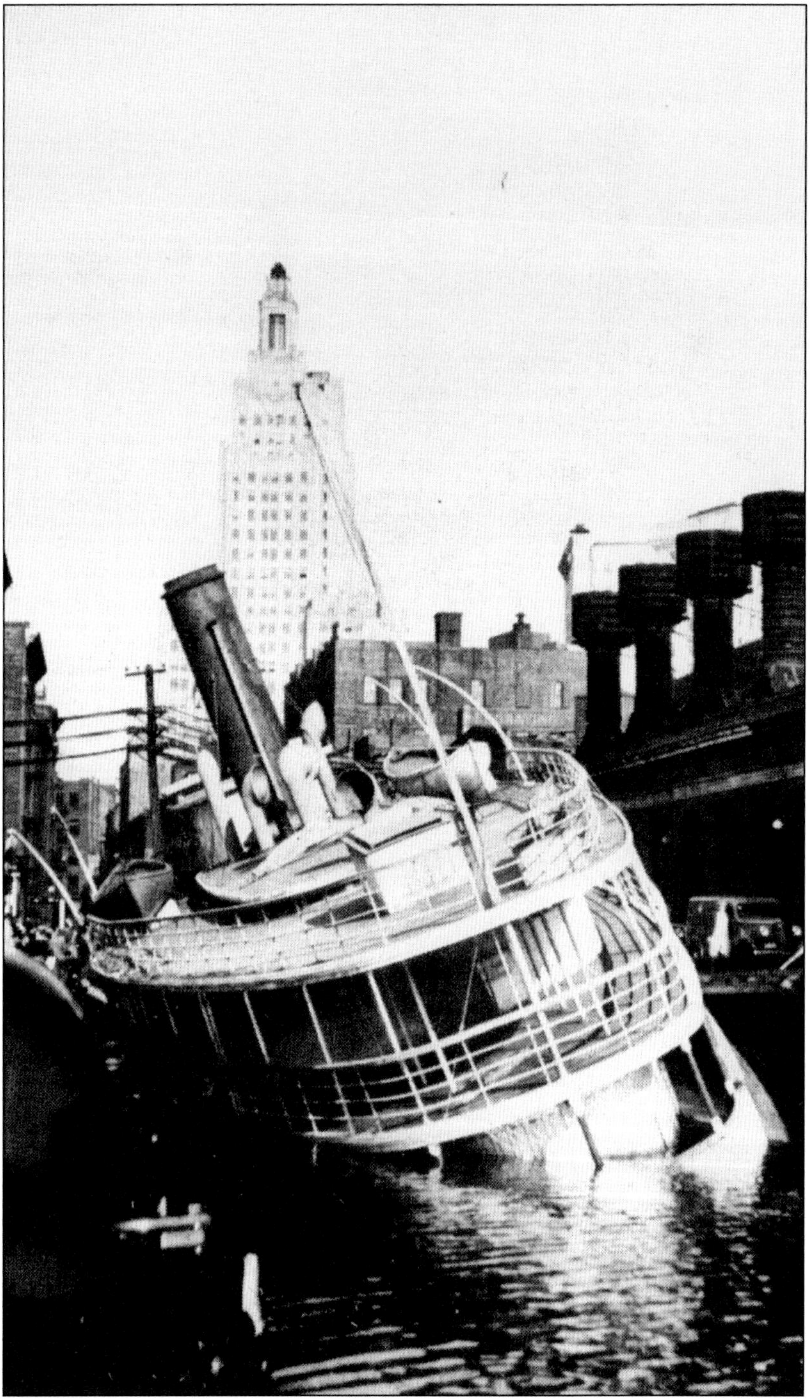

Its days of glory finished, the *Mount Hope* made short Providence to East Providence trips until abandoned in January 1935 in a section of the Providence River called "Rotten Row." In January 1935, it sunk at its pier in the Providence River. In February 1936, the *Mount Hope* was towed to East Providence where it was dismantled. The fleet and graceful "Queen of Narragansett Bay" is gone but never forgotten.

Four

SPANNING NARRAGANSETT BAY

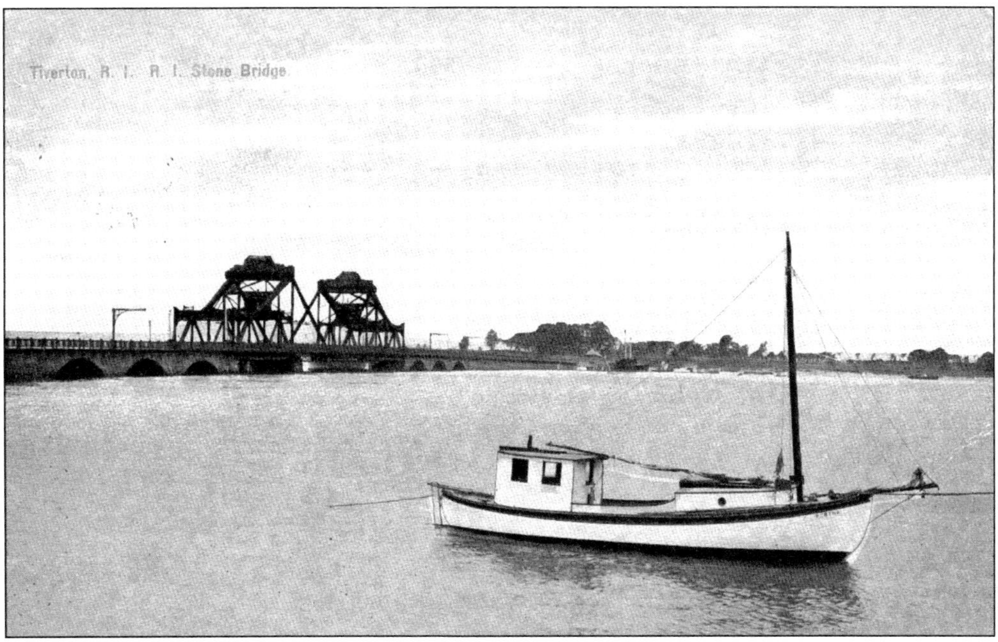

The Tiverton-Portsmouth Stone Bridge is seen here as it appeared in July 1907. The new drawbridge was constructed for the proposed Newport and Fall River Street Railway, requiring replacement of the old wooden draw with a more substantial iron and steel structure. The replacement draw was installed in 1898, and the first trolley traversed the span on June 18. The new bridge provided a 20-foot-wide roadway capable of supporting 20 tons.

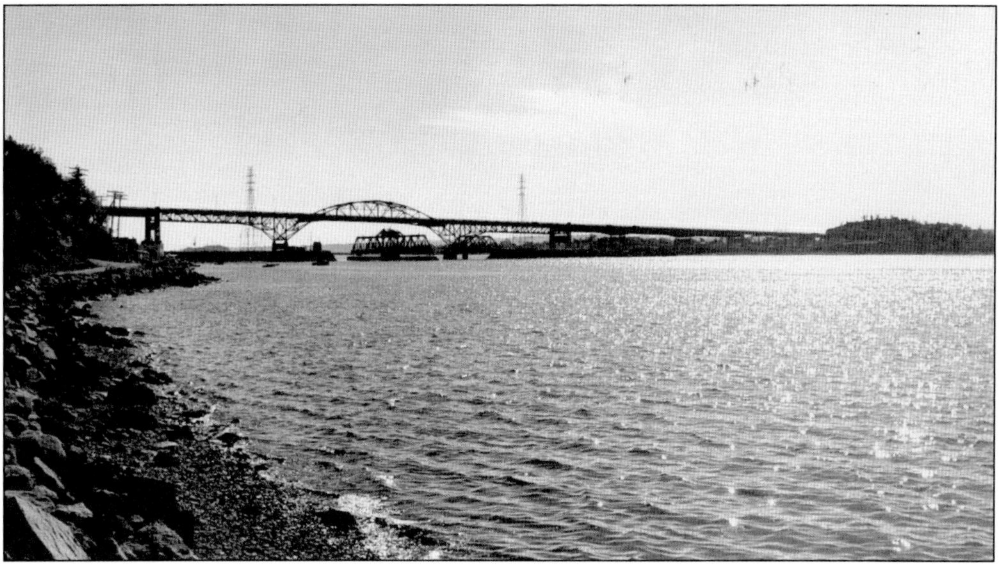

The Sakonnet River Bridge connecting Portsmouth (right) and Tiverton was completed in 1956. The railroad swing bridge is seen under the center arch of the span.

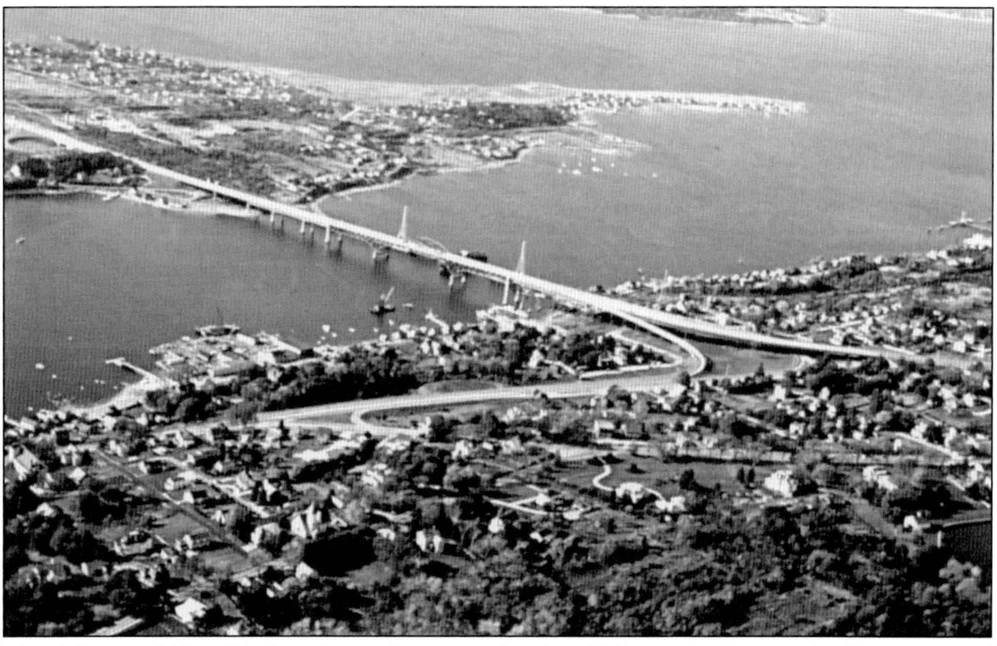

The Sakonnet River Bridge, the replacement for the old Stone Bridge, was built at a cost of $9 million; it opened with great fanfare on September 25, 1956. Because of poor maintenance over its 50-year life, the bridge is greatly deteriorated and plans are underway to replace it with a new span.

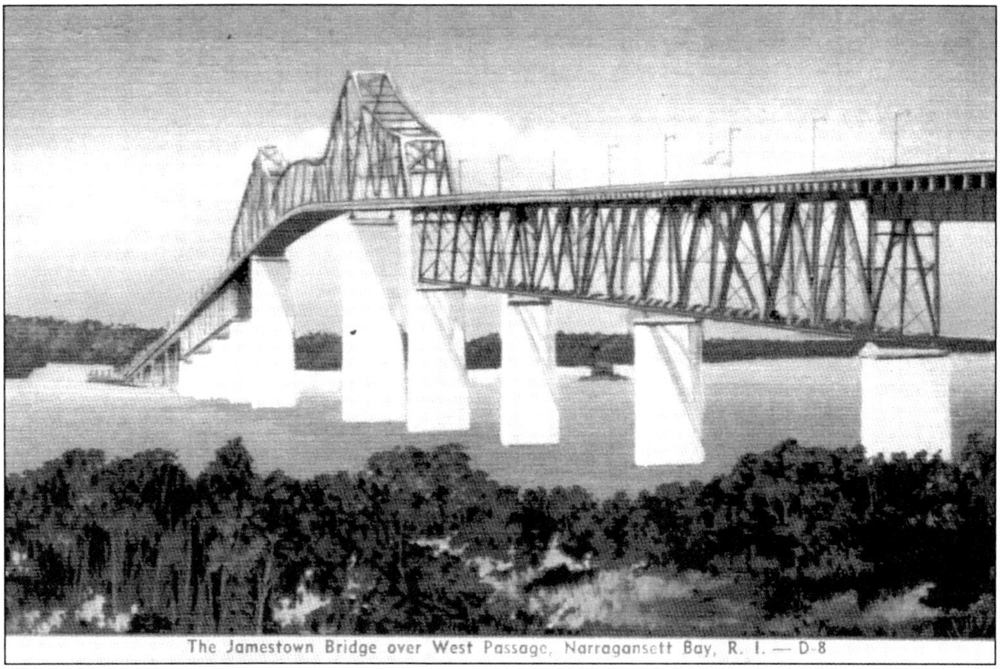

Construction of the Jamestown Bridge was financed by a federal grant of $1,404,000 by the Public Works Administration and the sale of state bonds for $1.7 million secured by bridge toll revenue. From the opening of the Jamestown Bridge in July 1940 until the end of the war, traffic from the Quonset Naval Air Station on the West Bay to the military installations on Aquidneck Island was significant.

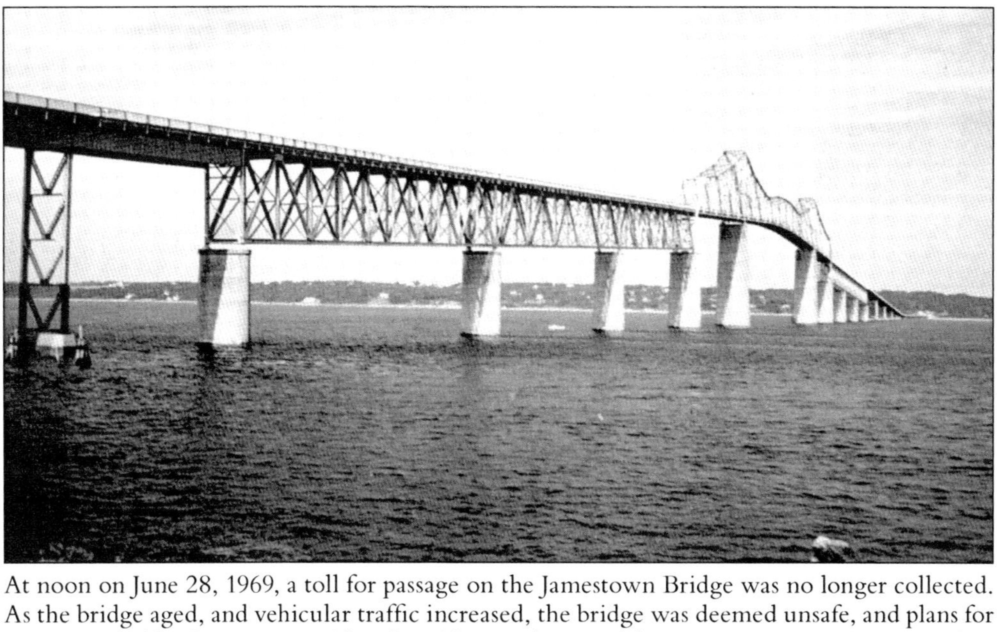

At noon on June 28, 1969, a toll for passage on the Jamestown Bridge was no longer collected. As the bridge aged, and vehicular traffic increased, the bridge was deemed unsafe, and plans for a new parallel bridge were considered. With completion of the Jamestown-Verrazzano Bridge, the old dilapidated Jamestown Bridge was closed. As of October 2005, cost of the planned dismantling of the bridge is $13.5 million.

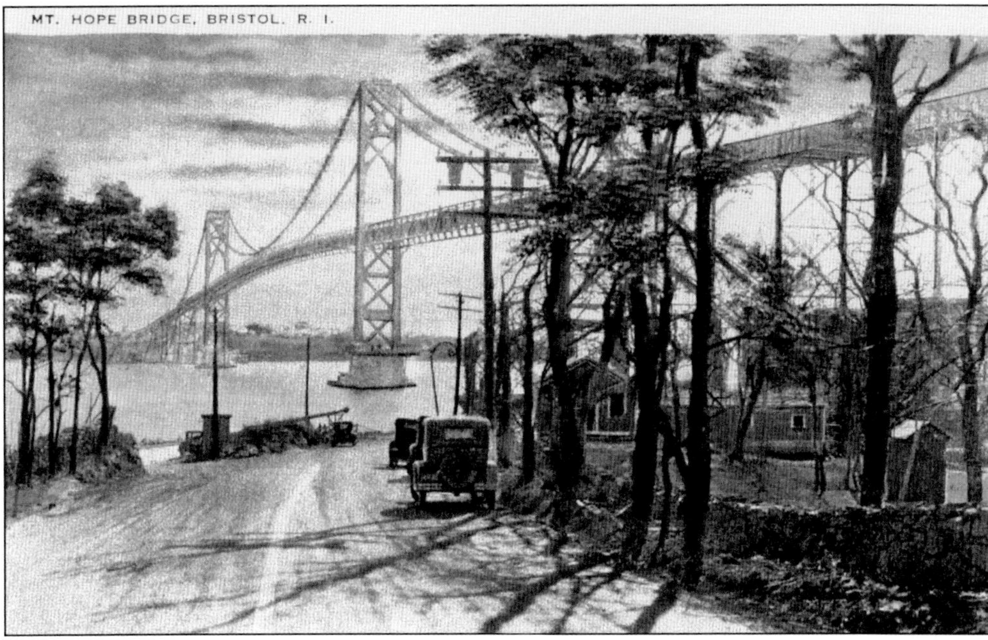

In 1926, the Mount Hope Bridge Commission was formed to study the feasibility of replacing the ferry service. The private Mount Hope Bridge Company was formed, and in 1927, the company awarded David B. Steinman of Robinson and Steinman of New York a contract to design a wire-cable suspension bridge at a projected cost of $3 million.

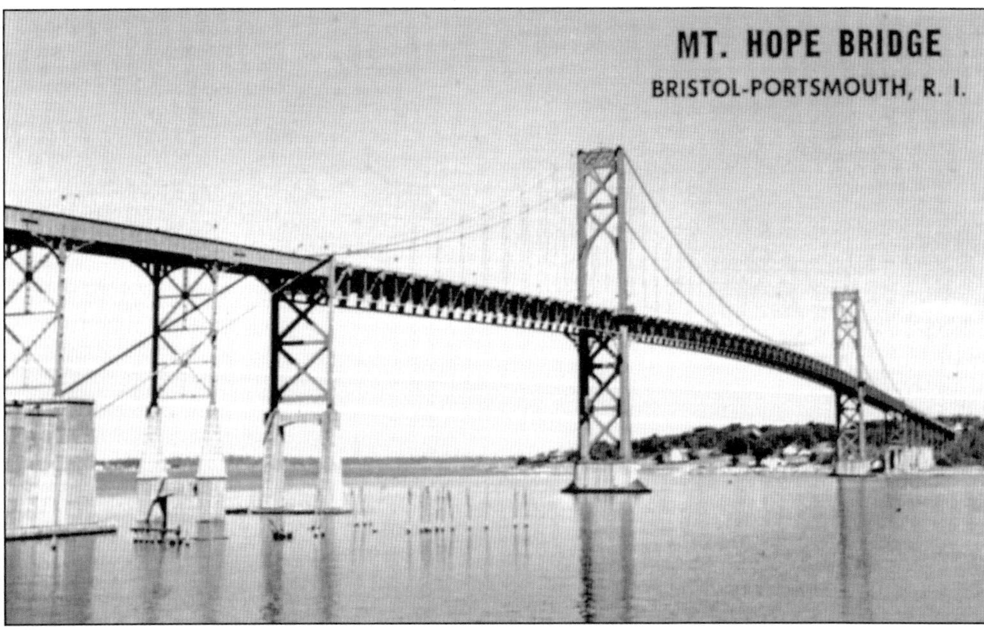

Opening and dedication of the Mount Hope Bridge occurred on October 24, 1929. The ensuing Depression and low toll revenues led to the privately held bridge company's default in 1931. At a public auction in 1932, a new company, the Mount Hope Bridge Corporation, led by Rudolf H. Haffenreffer, purchased the bridge. Beginning on April 2, 1998, toll-free crossing of the bridge became a reality.

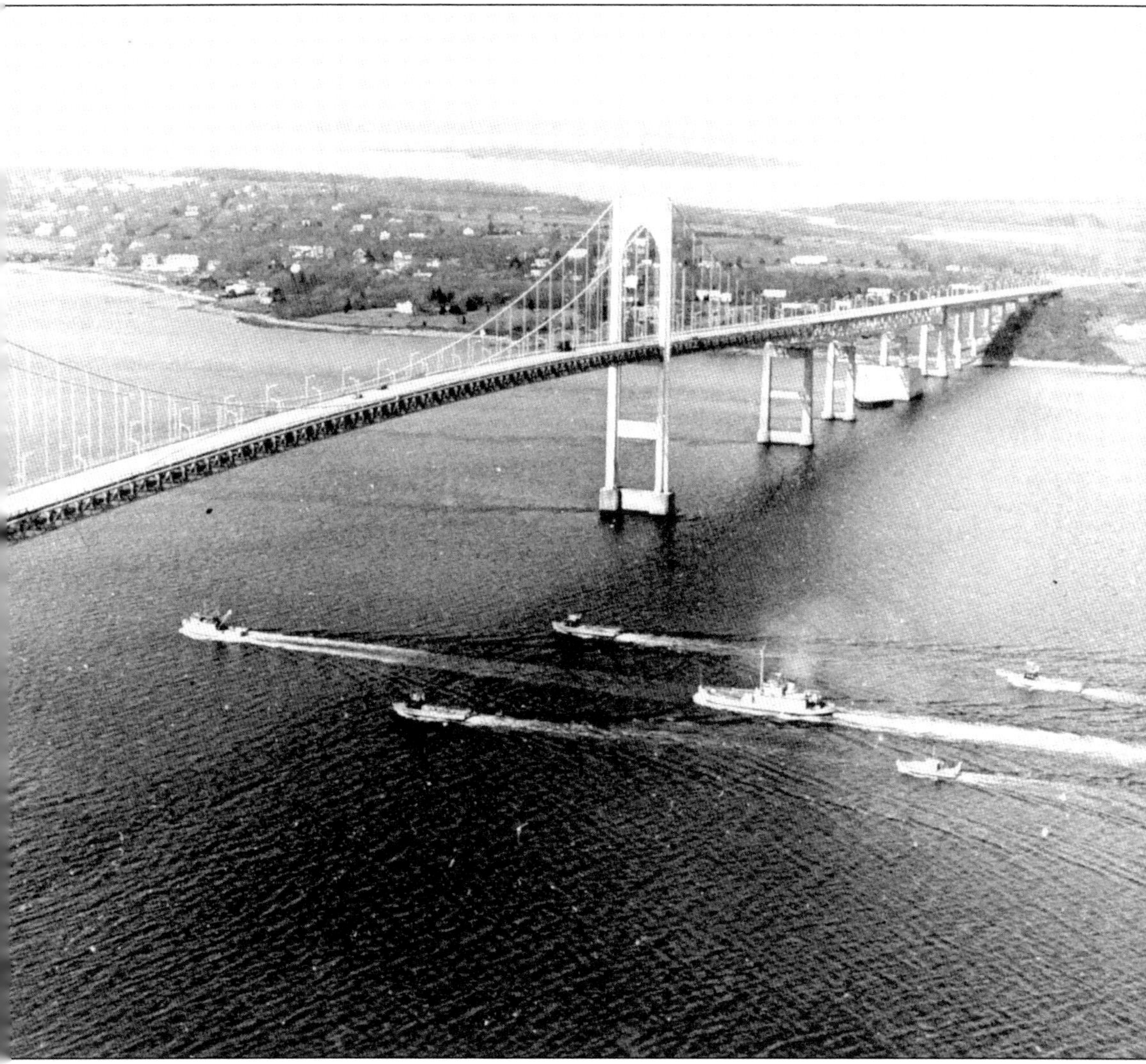

A 1960 referendum to build the Newport-Pell Bridge was not approved by voters, but in 1964, the bonding measure was finally ratified and later reapproved in 1965. The Newport-Pell Bridge faced many challenges in its construction, but the benefits of its existence have far outweighed the cost of its creation. The bridge has grown with Newport and the surrounding areas, encouraging trade, travel, and tourism for over 30 years.

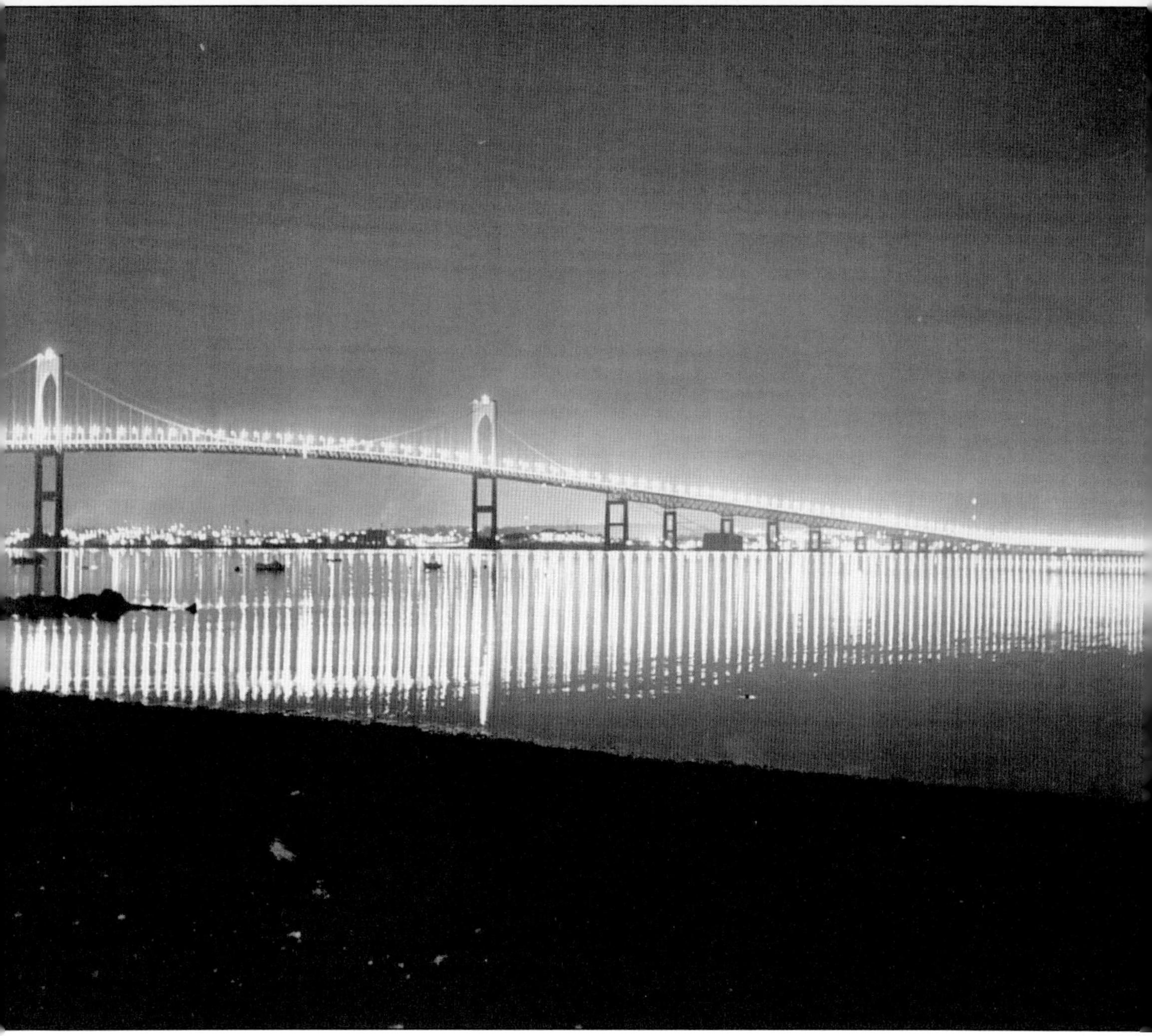

The Rhode Island Turnpike and Bridge Authority was responsible for the construction of the Claiborne Pell Bridge (formerly the Newport Bridge), which was opened for traffic on June 28, 1969, and has been responsible for the operation and maintenance of the Mount Hope Bridge between Bristol and Portsmouth, Rhode Island, and the Claiborne Pell Bridge between Newport and Jamestown, Rhode Island, since 1964 and 1969, respectively.

Five

Rhode Island Yacht Clubs

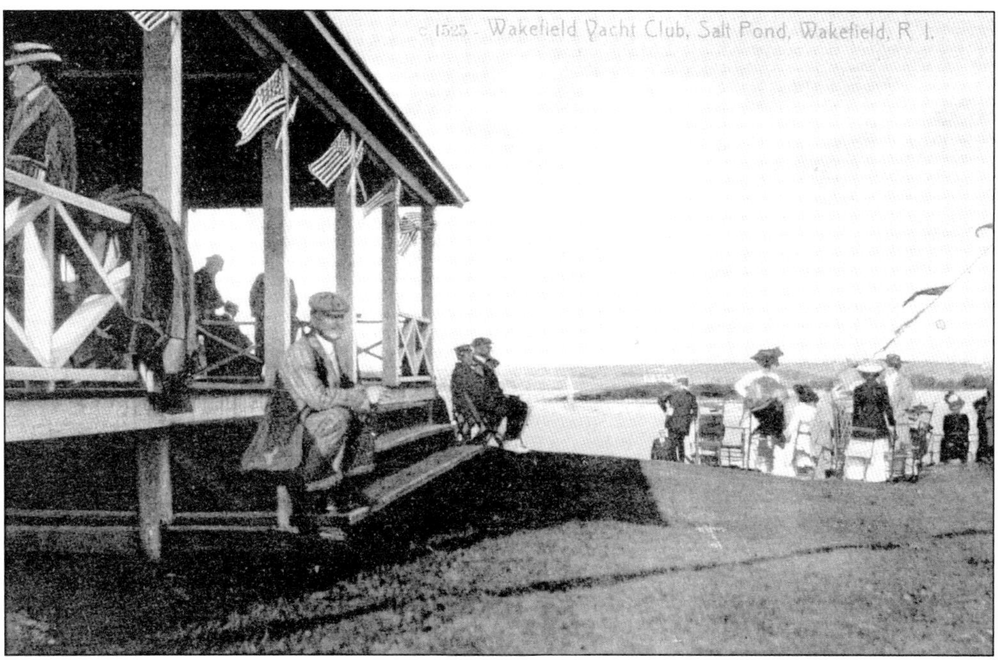

Members of the Wakefield Yacht Club enjoy a summer afternoon lolling on the clubhouse lawn that borders Upper Pond. Here are located handy boatyards and two yacht clubs: the Point Judith Yacht Club and the University of Rhode Island Yacht Club.

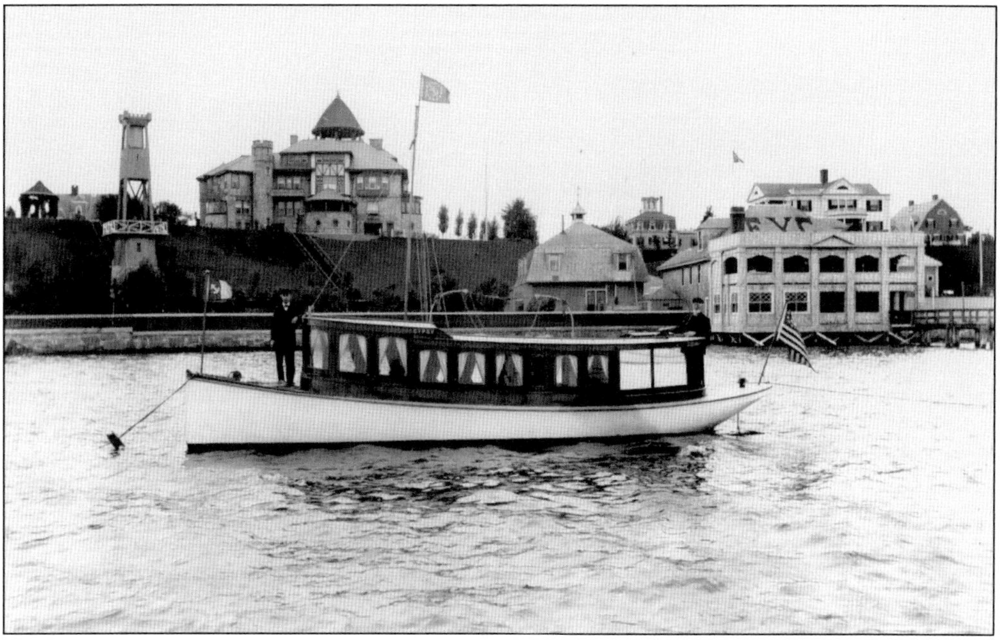

The Edgewood Yacht Club was organized June 1, 1889, as the Edgewood Boat Club. In 1908, the clubhouse was destroyed by fire; the new clubhouse was built along the lines of the original. This pre-1908 photograph is courtesy of the Edgewood Yacht Club archives.

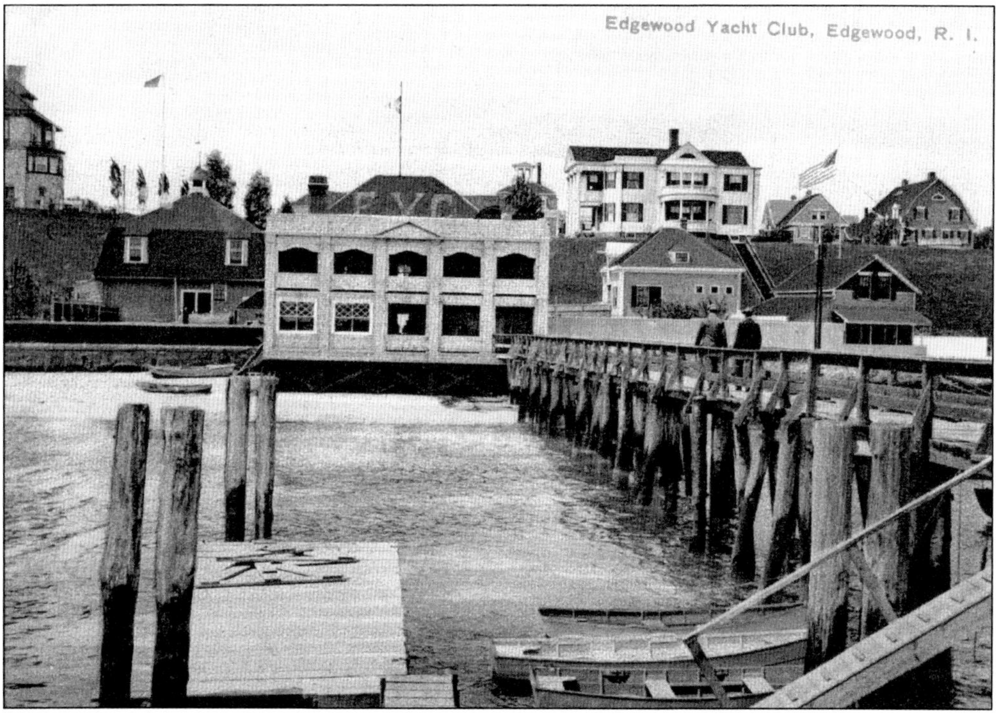

The original clubhouse provided covered porches where members could enjoy panoramic views of the bay, chat with fellow members, or promenade in the shade. When Hurricane Carol struck on August 31, 1954, the water rose nearly to the ceiling of the first floor.

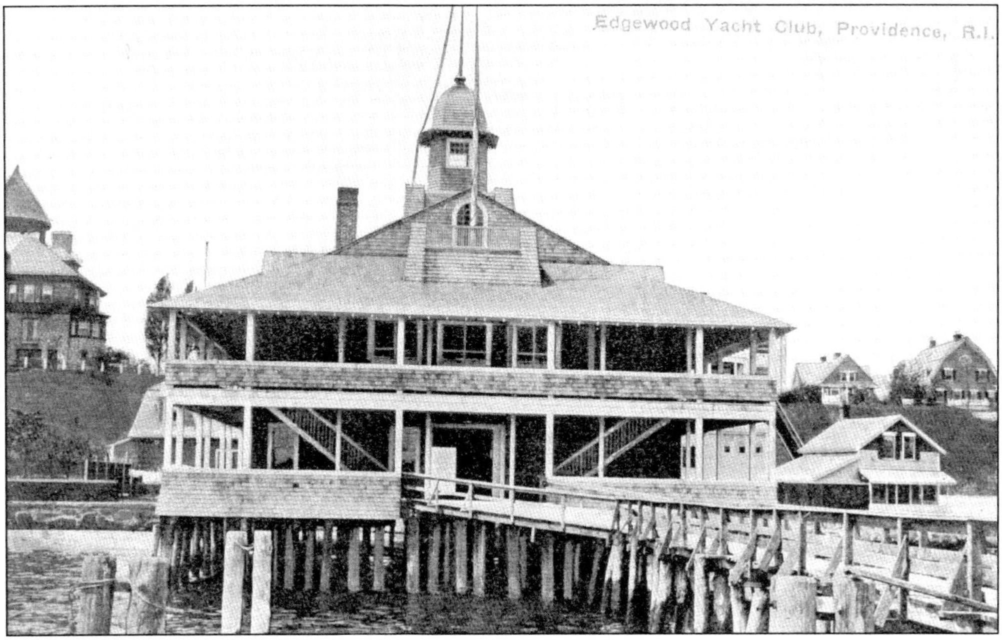

The Edgewood Yacht Club combines a nice blend of yachting and sociability, pleasure for the adults, and instruction for the youngsters. Functions originate from this historic and unique clubhouse; it is an extraordinary setting for relaxation, socializing, and making new friends.

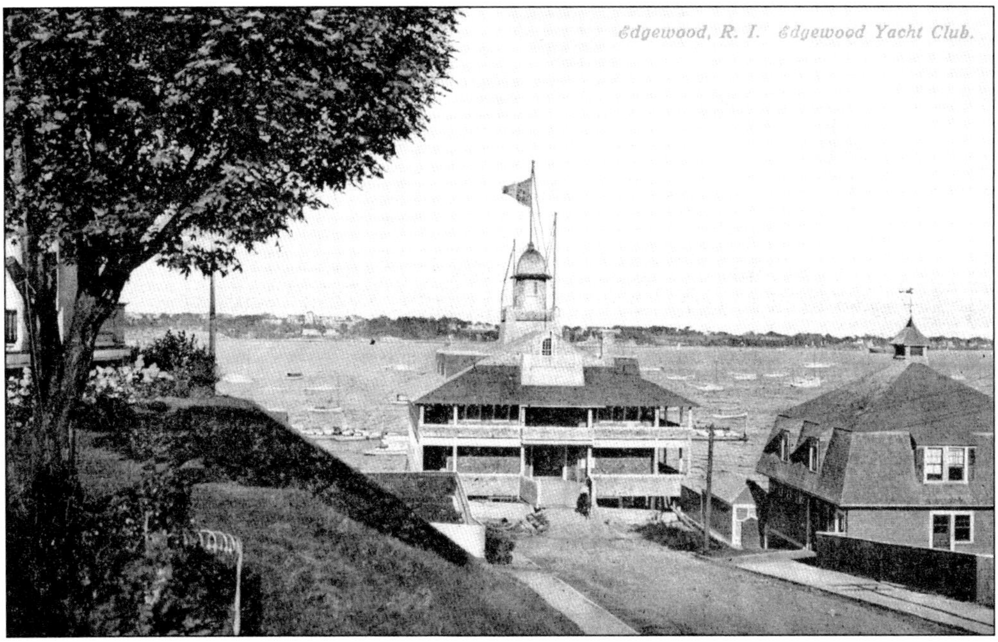

The Edgewood Yacht Club is located at the bottom of Shaw Avenue in the Edgewood section of Cranston.

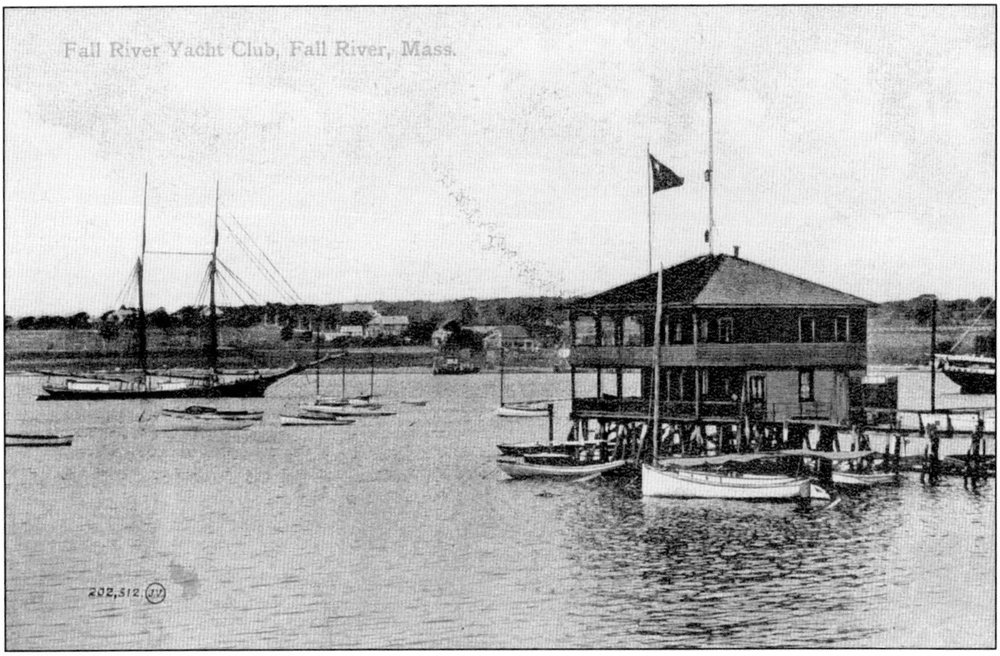

The Tiverton Yacht Club was organized, in the most part, by members of the former Fall River Yacht Club, which was washed away by the hurricane of 1936. In this *c.* 1908 postcard one can see how vulnerable the clubhouse was to the tidal surge.

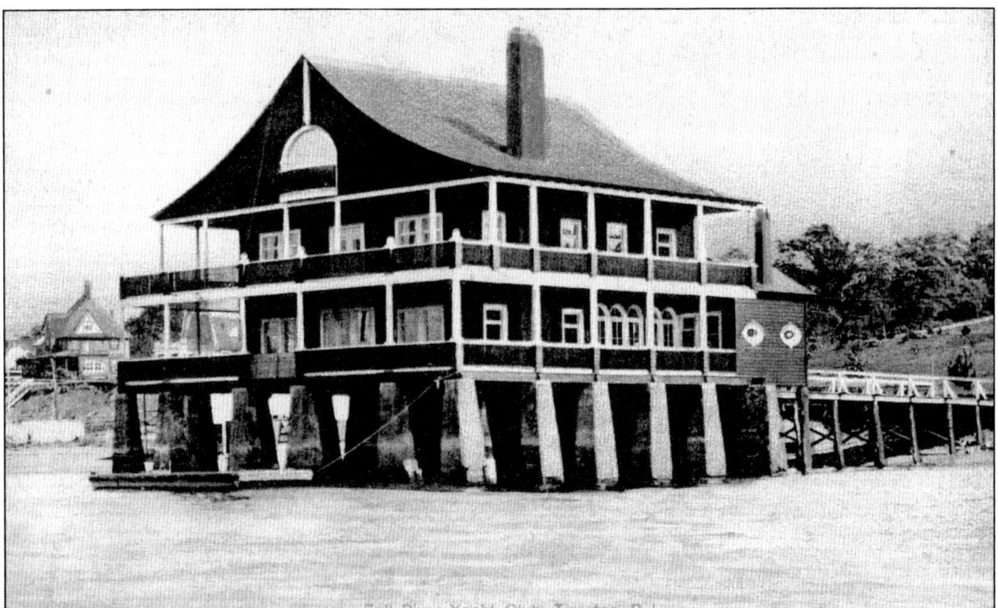

As membership grew, yachting and social activities developed side by side. In 1946, the Tiverton Yacht Club elected Stewart Grinnell as its first commodore. When the club moved its operations to Tiverton, it leased the second floor of a building on a dock on the Sakonnet River. For more on the Tiverton Yacht Club, see *Tiverton and Little Compton, Volume II*, Arcadia Publishing, 1998.

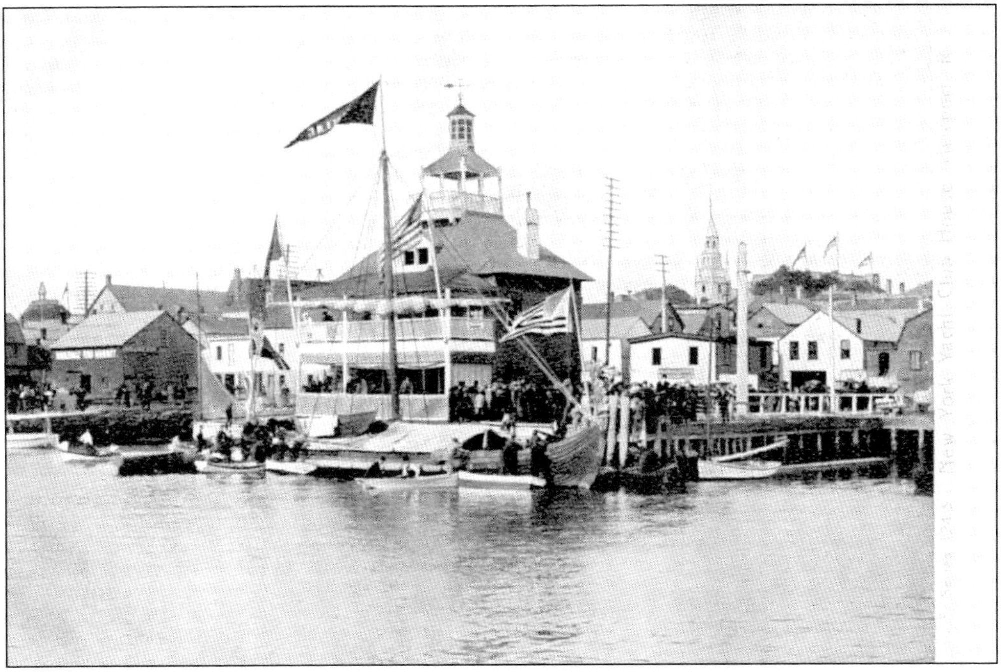

The New York Yacht Club, organized in 1844, for cruising and racing on Long Island Sound and Rhode Island Sound deserves to be included in the roster of yacht clubs on Narragansett Bay. Shortly after a cruise to Newport in 1844, the New York Yacht Club established a station on Newport's waterfront.

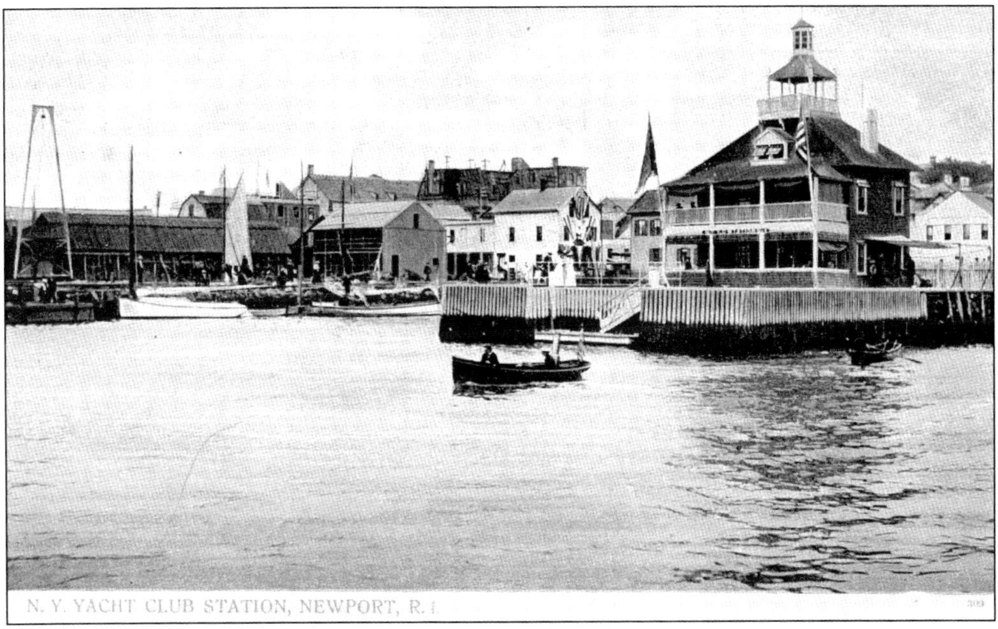

For many years, the New York Yacht Club fleet has made Newport its principal rendezvous. These two *c.* 1903 postcard images show the number of warehouses, chandleries, and fish processing businesses clustered close to the waterfront. For more on the New York Yacht Club, see *The America's Cup Yachts: The Rhode Island Connection*, Arcadia Publishing, 1999.

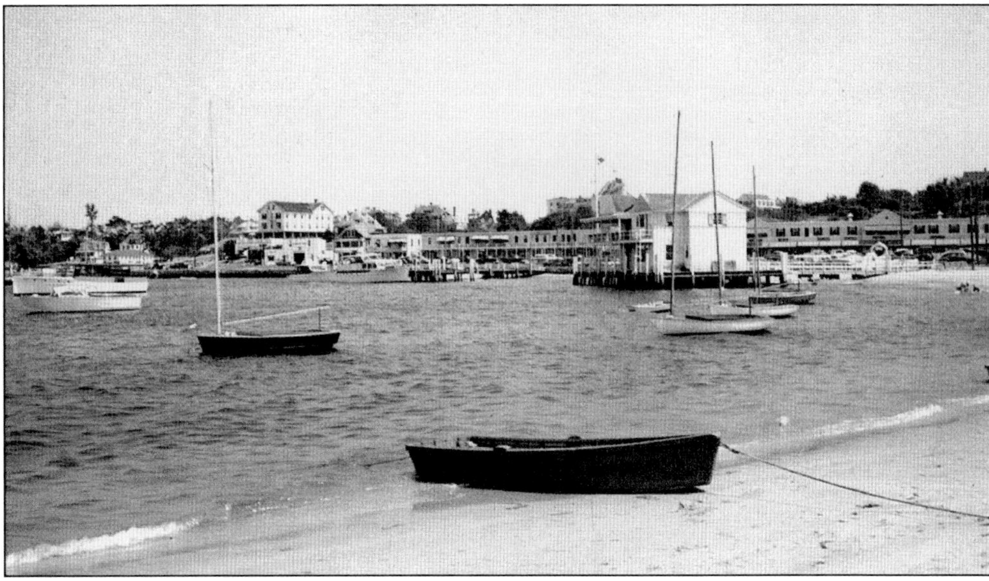

For the purpose of conducting small sailboat races and having a meeting place for kindred souls, a Watch Hill Yacht Club became desirable. In July 1912, Commodore John Watts received permission from the Watch Hill Fire District to remove from the Watch Hill dock the building formerly used as a ticket and express office for the steamer *Watch Hill.* On July 19, 1913, a constitution and bylaws were adopted (see page 63).

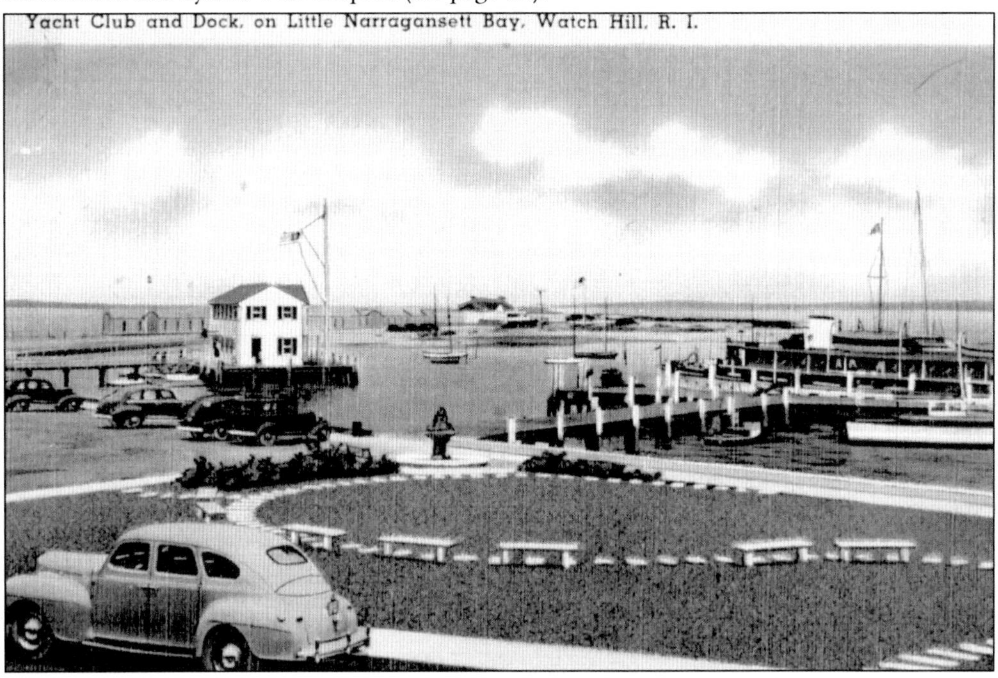

The racing fleet of 1913 consisted of a one design class of 12 sloop-rigged Swampscott Dories, 21 feet long, and also a handicap class of five sloops of various lengths. In the early 1920s, the yacht club added to its racing fleet. The Alden sloops replaced the Swampscott Dories. In 1923, the club added eleven jib-headed mainsail Herreshoff sloops to its racing fleet. These were a modification of the Buzzards Bay 15-footer called the Watch Hill Class.

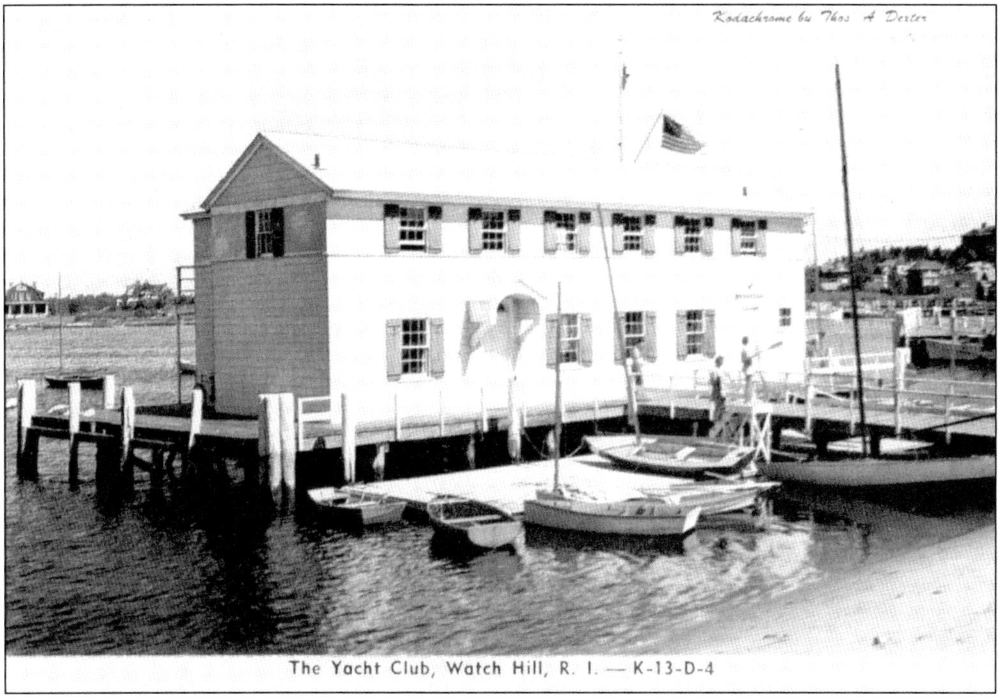

Work to replace the clubhouse piers started in late April 1973 and was completed on May 24. In 1984, renovations were made on the second floor of the clubhouse. The bar was moved to the street side, and the windows facing the harbor were altered to provide a spectacular view. Also in 1984, a new 22-foot launch was purchased.

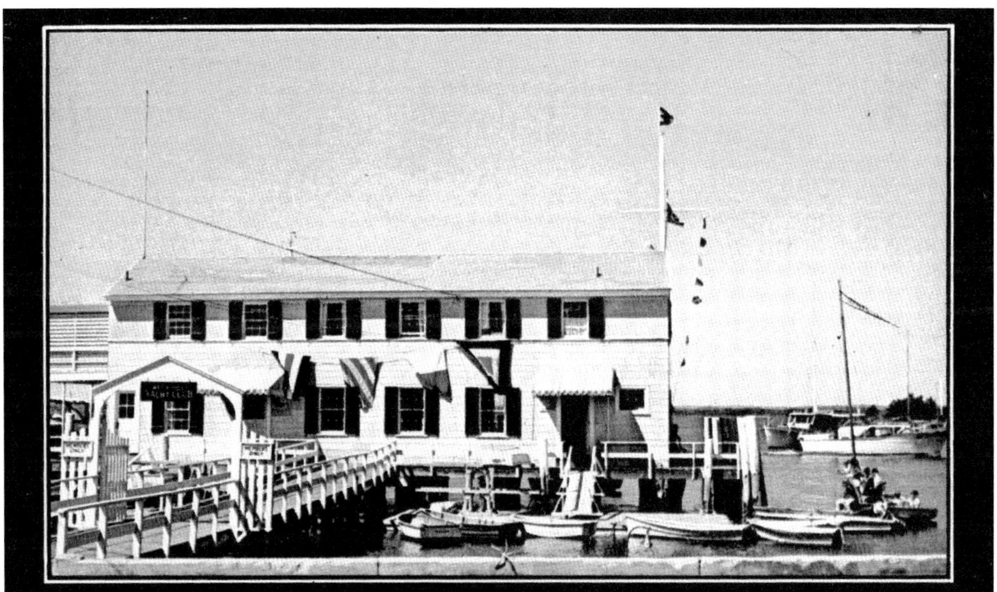

As of 1999, the Watch Hill Yacht Club's JY-15 fleet stood at 25 hulls with the addition of one boat that was found in the Boston area by a member and returned to the harbor. Another Herreshoff hull, the *Firefly*, was donated by the late Herman Muenchinger's family to the Herreshoff Museum in Bristol, Rhode Island.

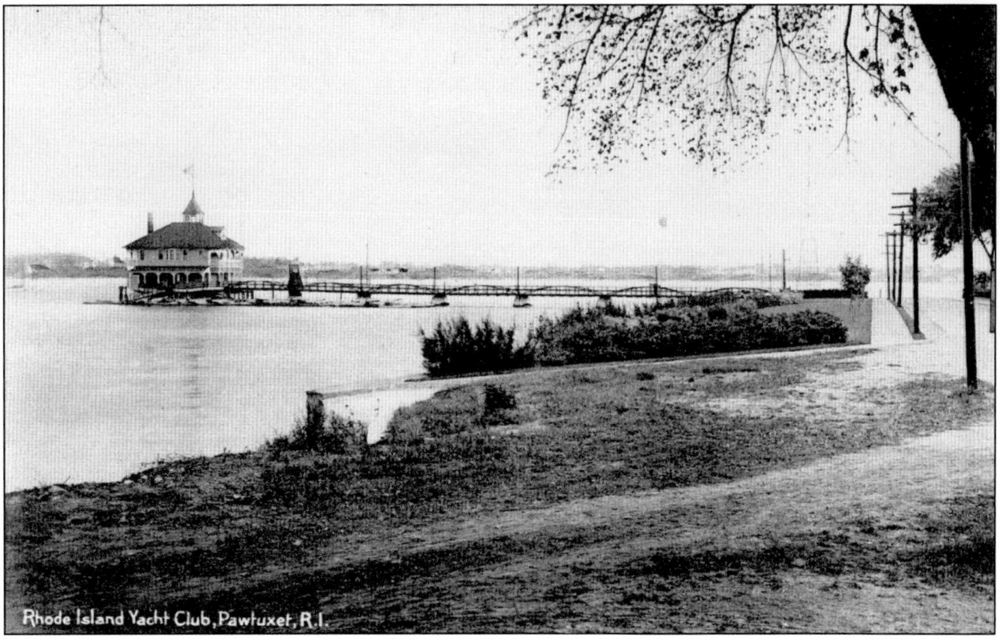

The Rhode Island Yacht Club was founded and chartered in 1875 as the Providence Yacht Club and incorporated on February 18, 1877. The club's credo is "for the purpose of encouraging yacht building, improvement in seamanship and the cultivation of naval science." For this purpose, the board of directors established an annual initiation fee of $5 with yearly dues of $10.

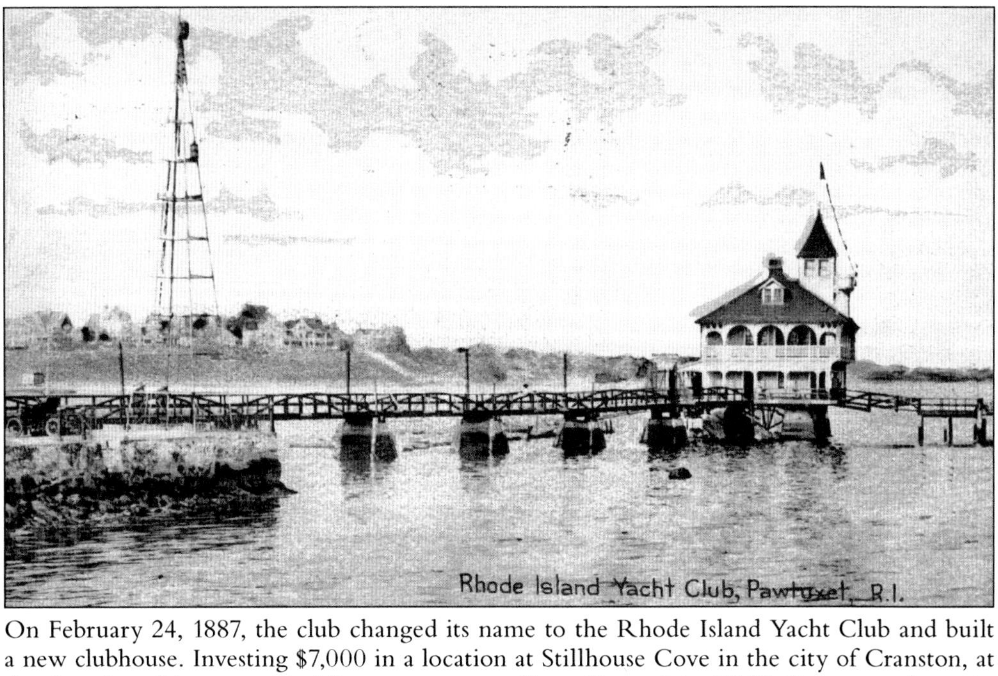

On February 24, 1887, the club changed its name to the Rhode Island Yacht Club and built a new clubhouse. Investing $7,000 in a location at Stillhouse Cove in the city of Cranston, at the site where Lieutenant Duddington, commanding officer of the HMS *Gaspee*, was brought ashore after the marauding British warship was burned by angry Americans as a prelude to the Revolutionary War.

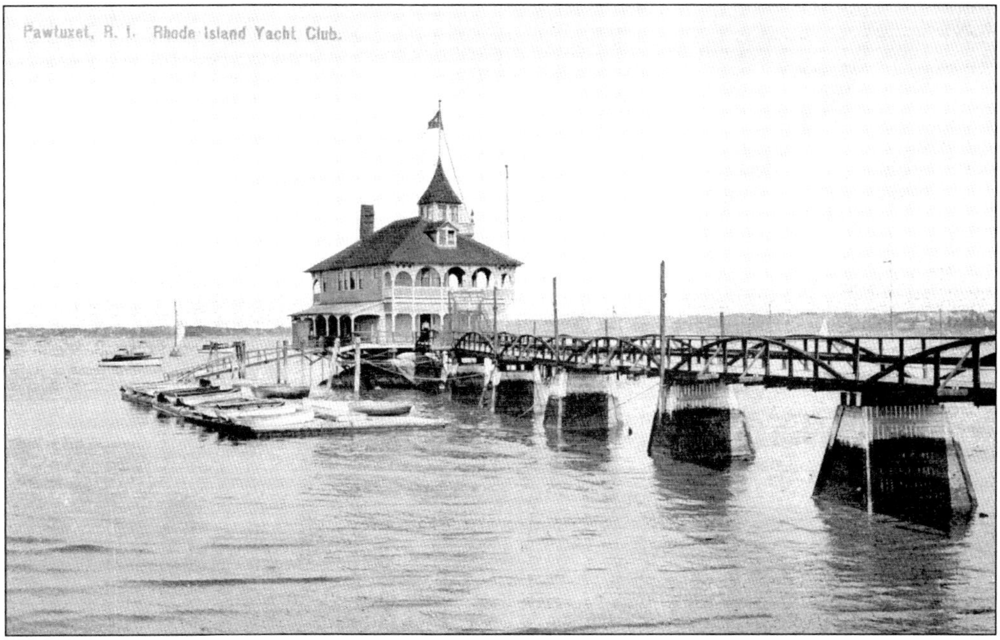

The club's yearbook, published in 1888, listed 427 members and 75 yachts. The membership roll read like a who's who in Rhode Island, along with its commodore, William Henry Low Jr., owner of the Low's Grand Opera House in Providence. In 1903, club member Arthur Austin purchased land at the foot of Ocean Avenue and created an imposing entrance to the bridge leading out to the clubhouse.

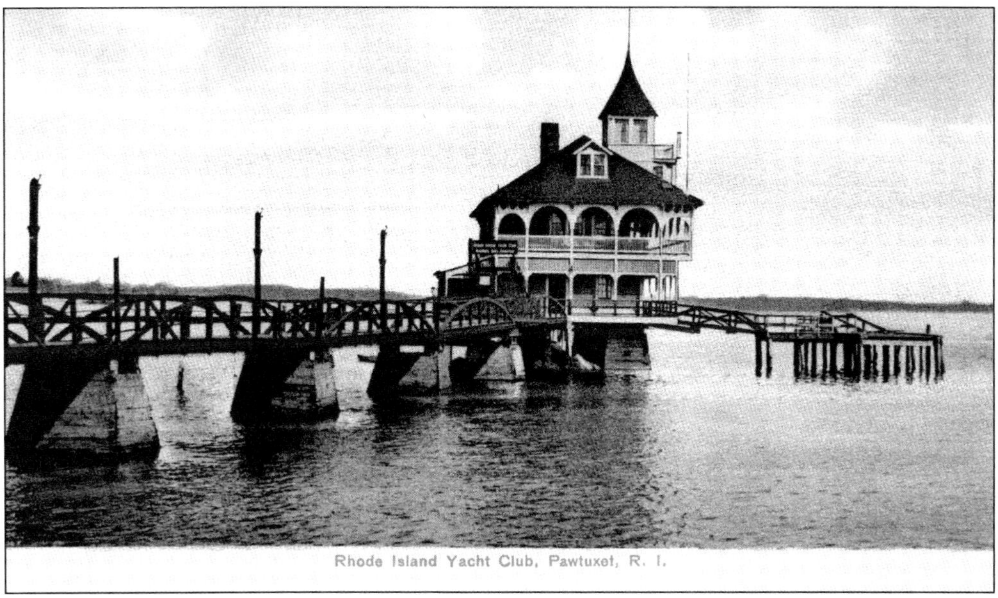

The 1938 hurricane and 30-foot tidal surge ripped the clubhouse from its piers, sweeping it out into the Providence River. Discouraged but not beaten, the members again built a new clubhouse on a wooden foundation on Great Rock and reopened the doors of the Rhode Island Yacht Club in 1940. In 1954, Hurricane Carol demolished all but the pilings of what was the short-lived second clubhouse on Great Rock.

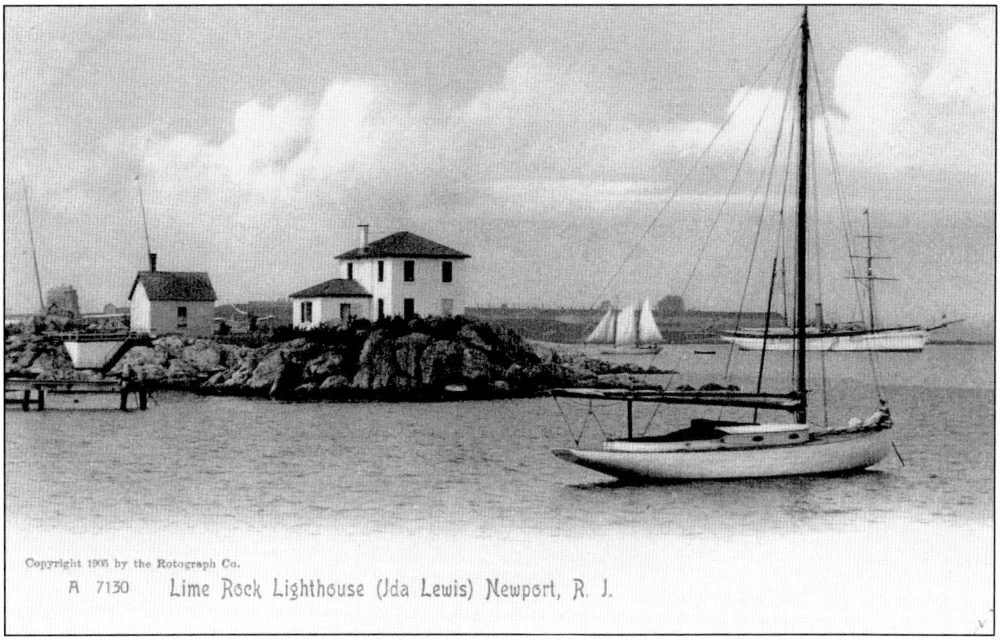

Idawalley Zorada Lewis was Newport Harbor's Lime Rock Lighthouse keeper from 1872 to 1911. In 1924, the Rhode Island general assembly officially changed the name of Lime Rock to Ida Lewis Rock. The lighthouse service changed the name of the Lime Rock Lighthouse to the Ida Lewis Lighthouse. In 1928, it became the clubhouse for the Ida Lewis Yacht Club.

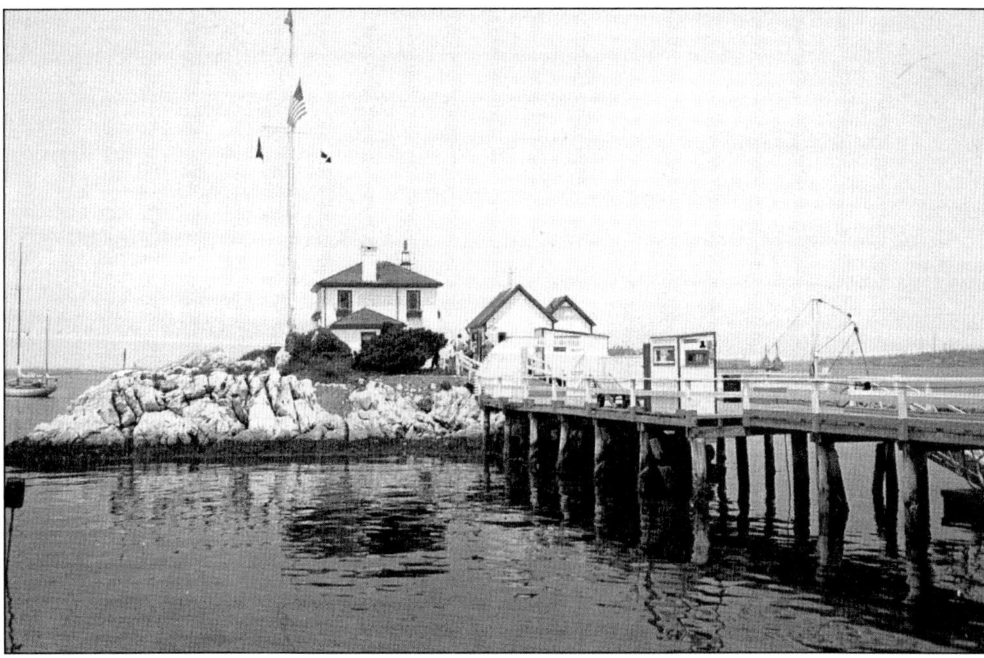

The Ida Lewis Yacht Club is located at the south side of the entrance to Newport's Brenton Cove. The club's burgee honors Lewis by being emblazoned with 18 white stars and a lighthouse against a red background representing the 18 lives saved by her.

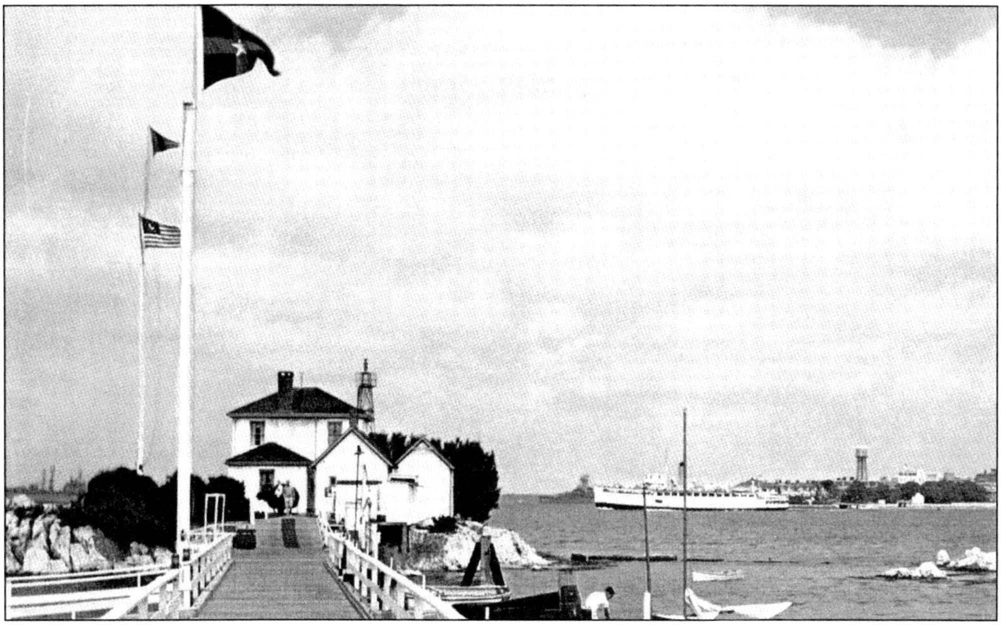

The club, however small and unpretentious, is known for its hospitality to visiting yachtsmen. Offshore races include the annual Twenty Hundred Club races to Cuttyhunk, and members take part in Narragansett Bay Yachting Association regattas.

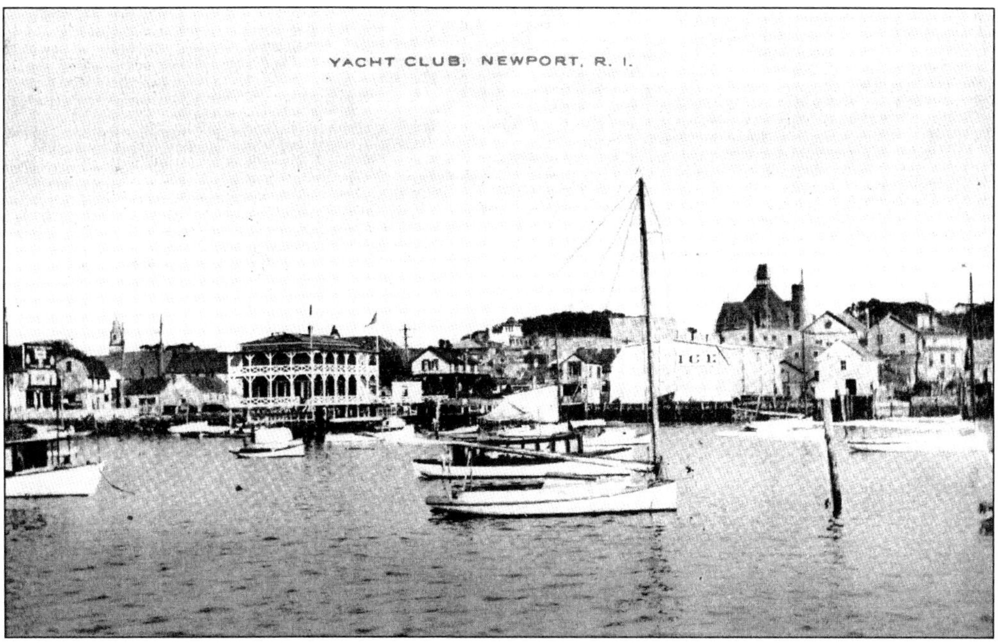

The Newport Yacht Club was organized in April 1894 and chartered in May of that year. At the first meeting, with nine men present, the objective of the club was stated: "This Club shall be known as the Newport Yacht Club and shall have for its objective the encouragement of yachting in and around Newport." This postcard is postmarked November 6, 1913.

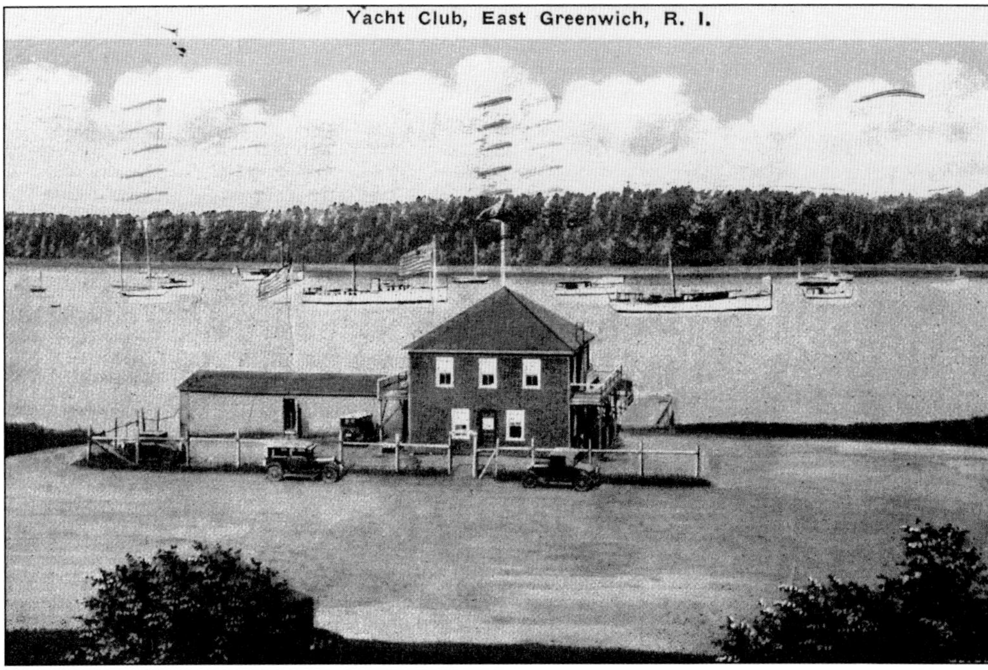

The first mention of establishing a yacht club in East Greenwich was in 1905, but it took another four years before it came to fruition. On Monday, October 4, 1909, a meeting was held to organize the club. In 1914, the initiation fee was $3 and dues were $5 per year, and they could be paid in two installments. In 1941, those figures were increased to $5 and $10.

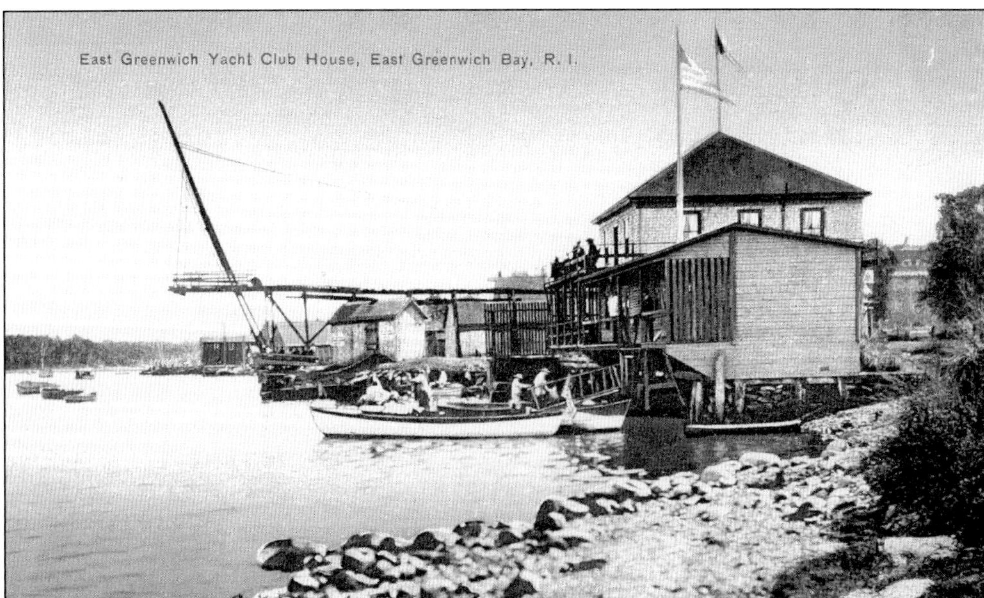

For more than 40 years, the activities of the club were pretty much seasonal, but the hurricane of 1954 changed everything. Out of the devastation of the storm came two names that will be forever intricately linked with the club: Bob Broz became the full-time steward and stayed for 32 years, and Al Waterman, his assistant, stayed for 10 more.

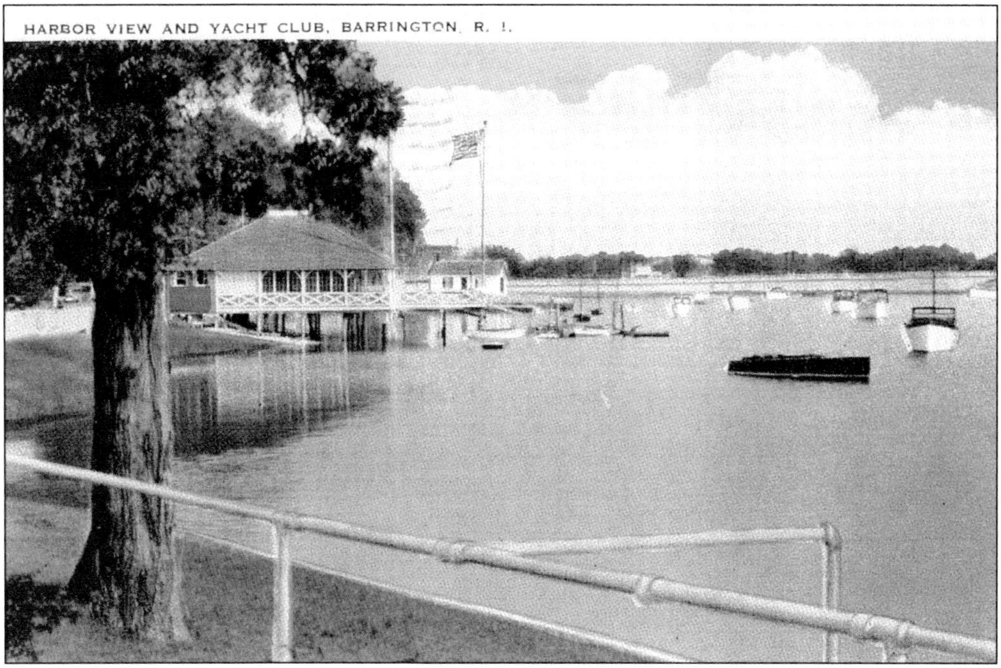

The Barrington Yacht Club was incorporated on March 25, 1908. Arthur L. Smith was the first elected commodore. The club must have been a success right from the start, as there were 218 members reported by August 1909; they all paid their $5 dues. On August 20, 1909, the original clubhouse was dedicated. Abbott Gardiner was hired as steward for $1 per day.

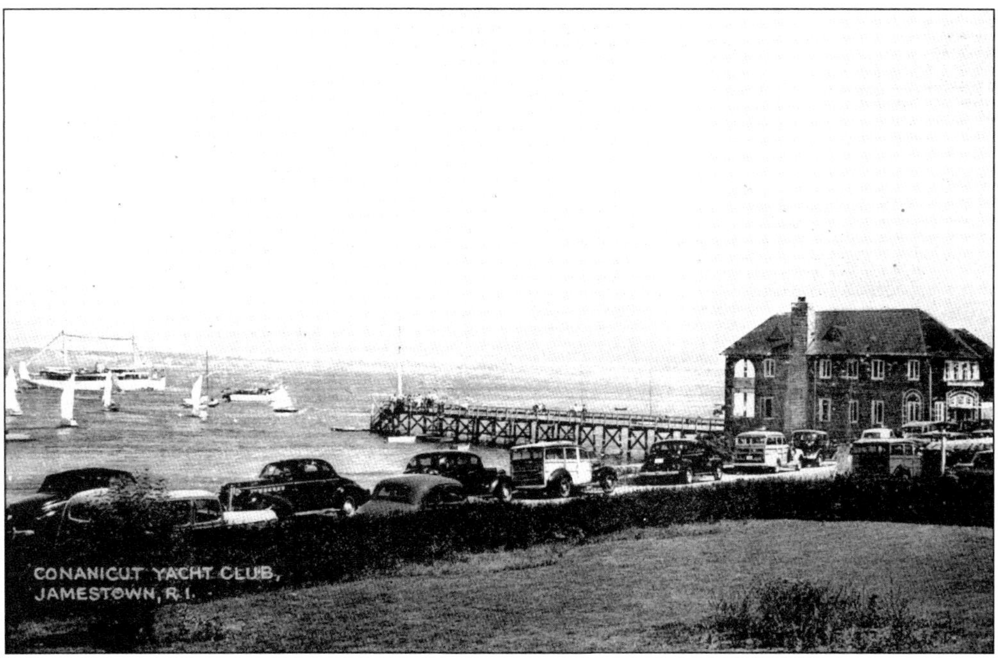

The Conanicut Yacht Club was established in 1891 as the Jamestown Yacht Club; in 1892, it adopted its present name. In 1916, the Conanicut Yacht Club merged with the Jamestown (Social) Club, which had enjoyed social entertainments since 1890.

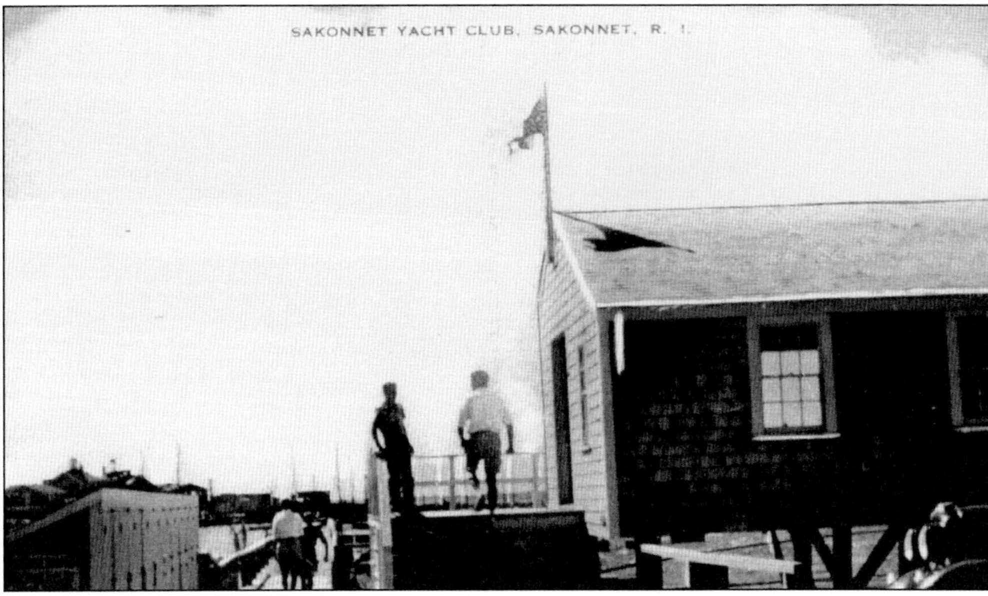

The Sakonnet Yacht Club (pictured around 1955) is a one-story, shingled, gable-roof building with a small ell set on pilings at the edge of Sakonnet Harbor's east shore. Established in 1939, the Sakonnet Yacht Club, like those in all other of Rhode Island's seaside communities, plays an important part in the town's recreational life.

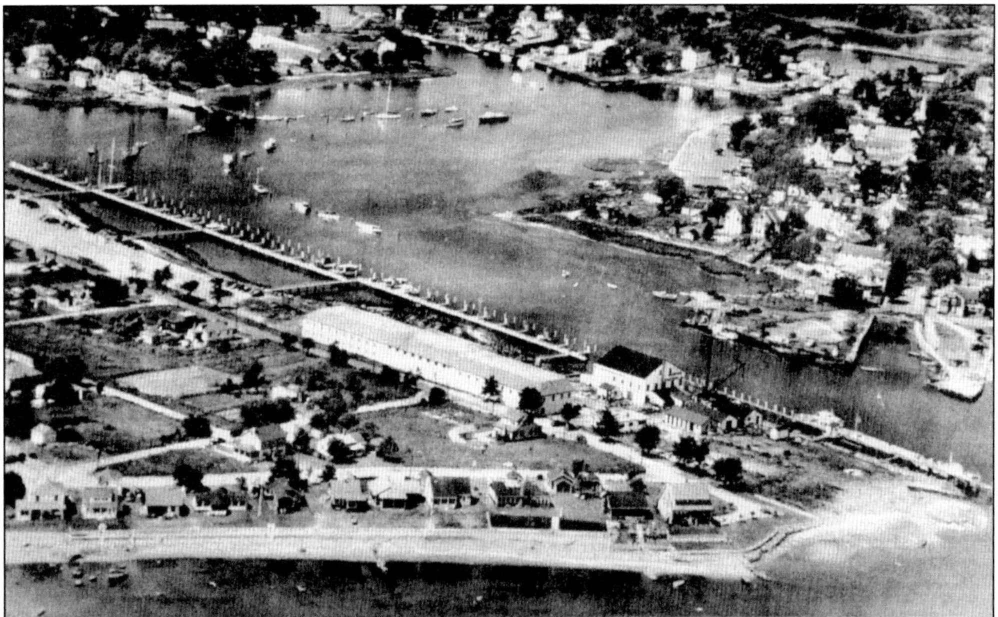

The first Wickford Yacht Club was organized in 1935; it remained in operation until waters of the 1938 hurricane inundated its clubhouse located in a stone building on Cornelius Island. After World War II, the second Wickford Yacht Club was formed by a group of Woodpussy Class sailors; when interest in Woodpussy Class sailing waned, so did interest in the club. The present Wickford Yacht Club formed in 1963. The current clubhouse was purchased in 1968.

Six

Life Saving Stations

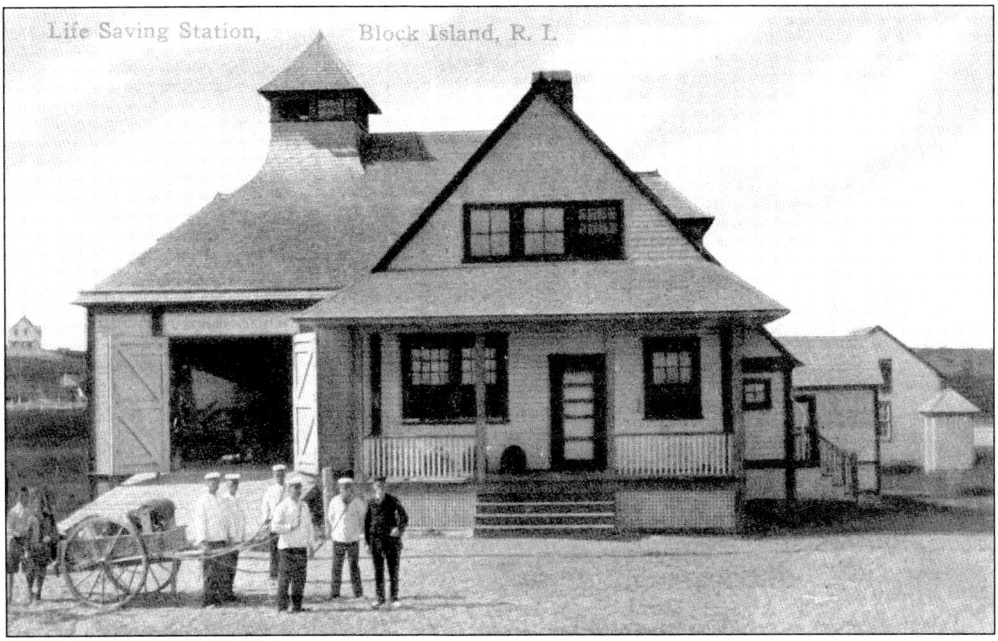

The United States Coast Guard is noted for many accomplishments, but foremost in the public's mind is the service's efforts in helping those "in peril upon the seas." Indeed, all of the various federal agencies that were brought together to form the modern-day United States Coast Guard dealt in some manner with assisting those who were in distress or in helping the prevention of loss of life at sea. Here several members of the Block Island Station of the United States Volunteer Life Saving Service (USVLSS) oblige the photographer by posing in front of their station building.

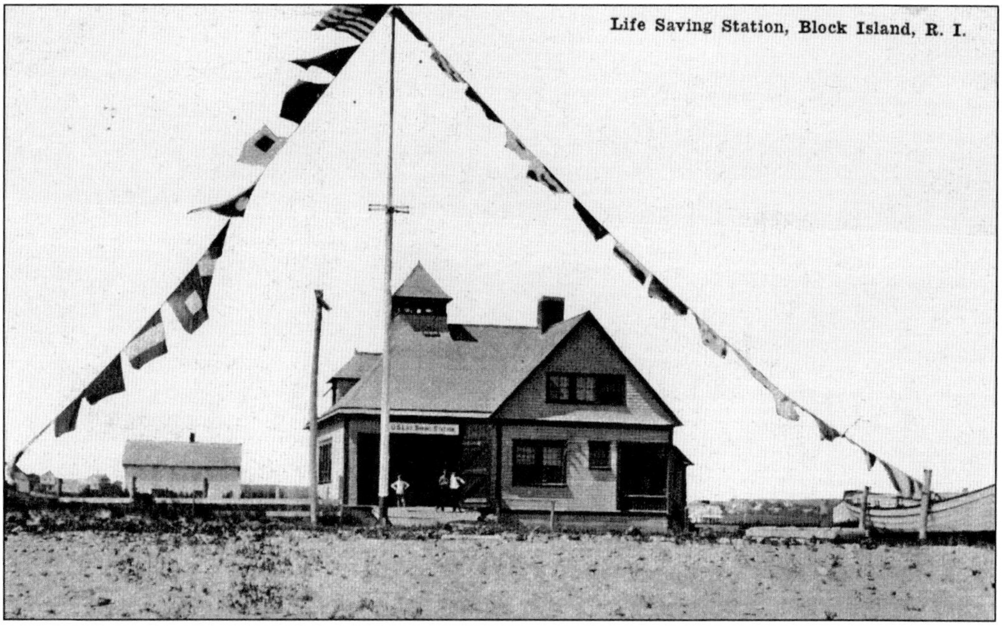

This is a beachside view of the Block Island USVLSS Station around 1910. In the 18th and 19th centuries, large sections of the United States' eastern seaboard were sparsely populated. The crew of any ship running aground could expect very little, if any, help. As maritime trade increased, so did the demand for assistance for those wrecked near the shore.

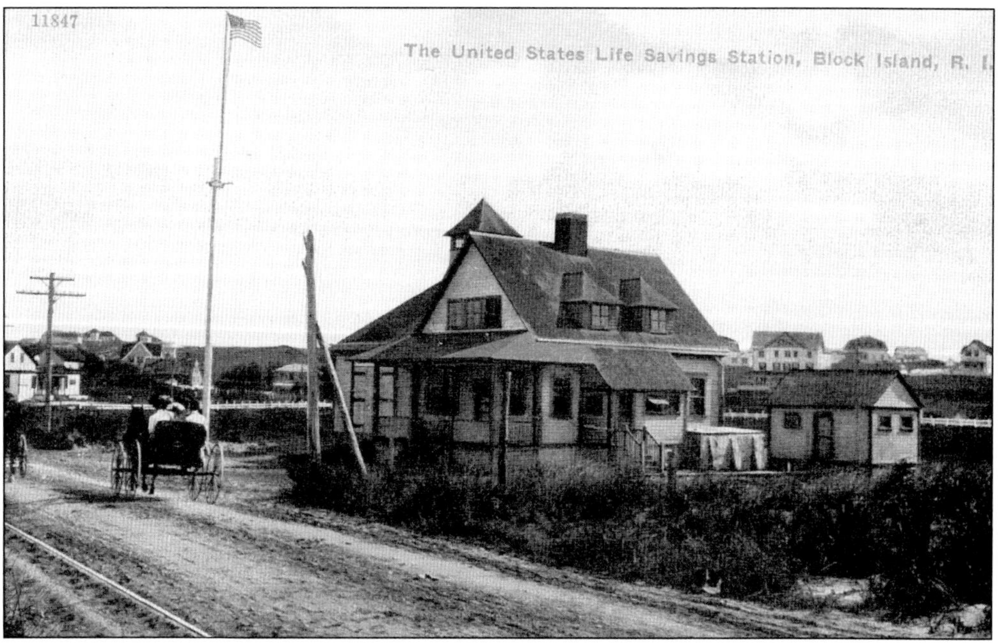

Here is another view of the same Block Island Station building. The concept of assistance to shipwrecked mariners from shore-based stations began with the volunteer lifesaving service, spearheaded by the Massachusetts Humane Society in 1786.

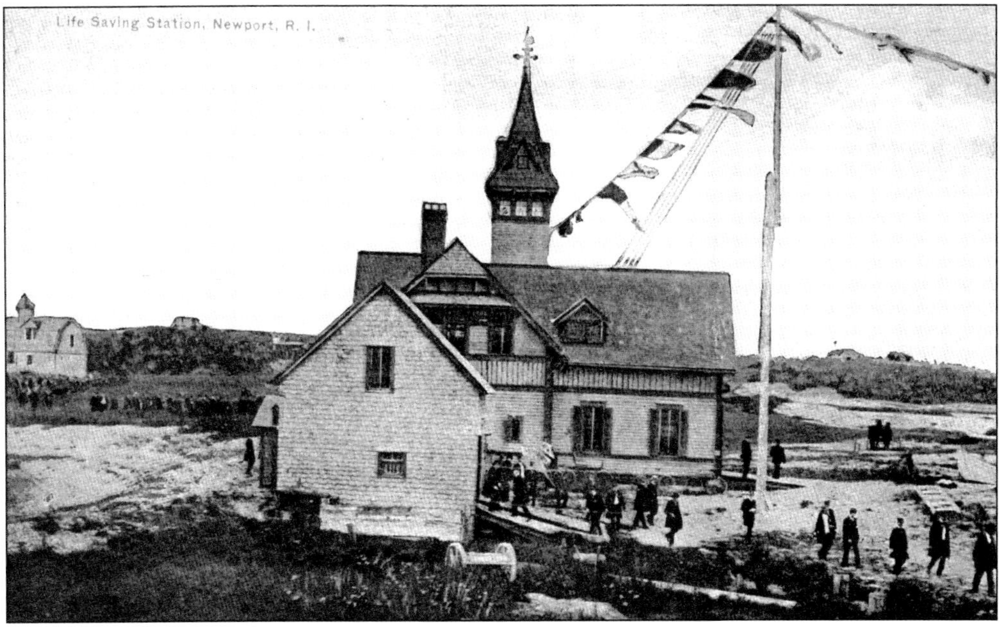

The Rhode Island branch of the USVLSS was organized in 1904, and the stations built in Newport were among the first built and manned. The greater part of the 73 drownings that occurred in Rhode Island in 1908 happened in inland waters, that is, not tidewaters.

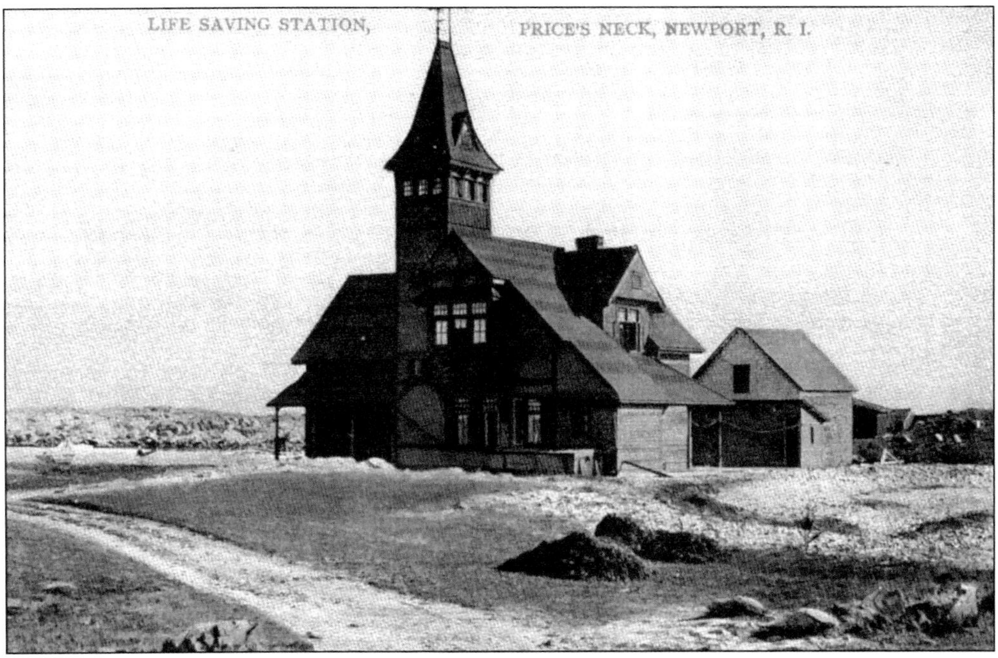

This is the Price's Neck at Newport Station around 1908. For the years 1904 through 1907, the Rhode Island branch of the USVLSS reported a total of 274 drownings and 141 rescues, this being the total for both inland waters and tidewater. The service reported that of the drownings in saltwater, a large portion were from circumstances unknown, which included a large percentage of suicides.

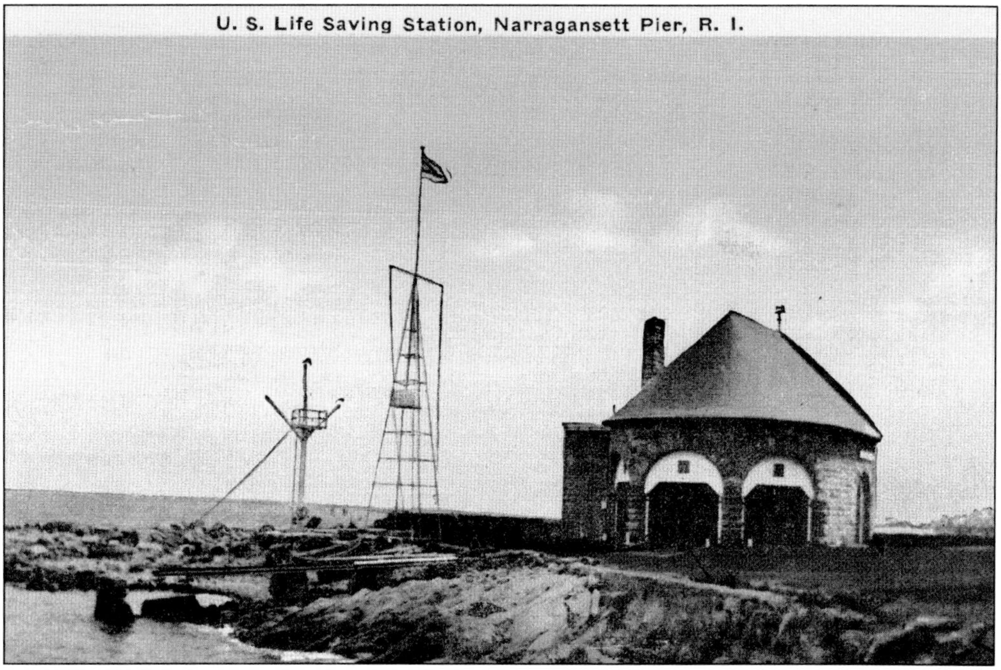

The stout stone-built USVLSS station at Narragansett Pier withstood many powerful hurricanes during which its neighbors suffered severe damage. It was recognized that only small boats stood a chance in assisting those close to the beach. A sailing ship trying to help near to the shore stood a good chance of also running aground, especially if there were heavy onshore winds.

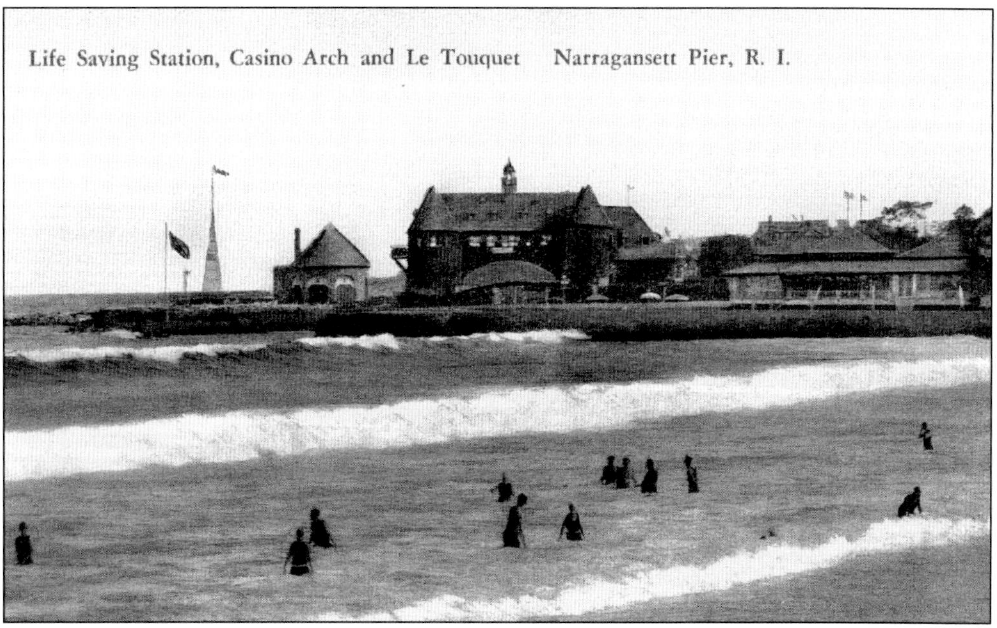

This and the next two postcard images chronicle changes in the skyline at Narragansett Pier. Generally, life saving stations were small, shedlike structures, holding rescue equipment that was to be used by volunteers in case of a wreck. The stations, however, were only near the approaches to busy ports and beaches; thus, large gaps of coastline remained without lifesaving equipment.

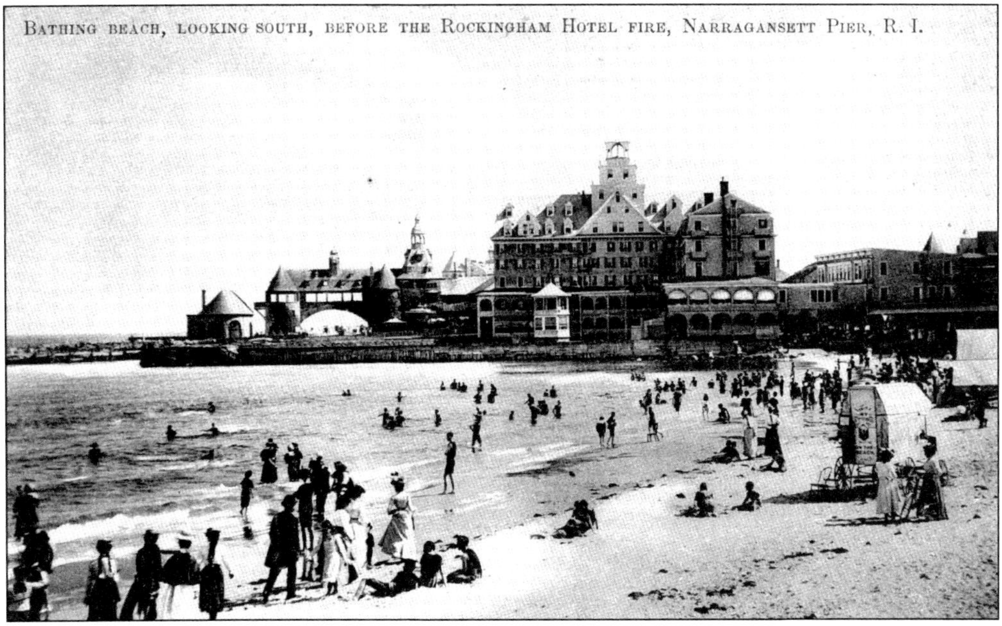

This is a view looking south from the Narragansett Pier bathing beach with the newly constructed Rockingham Hotel dominating the skyline. In 1848, the federal government entered the shore-based lifesaving business when Congress provided $10,000 for surfboats, rockets, carronades, and other necessary apparatus for the better preservation of life and property from shipwrecks on the nation's south East Coast.

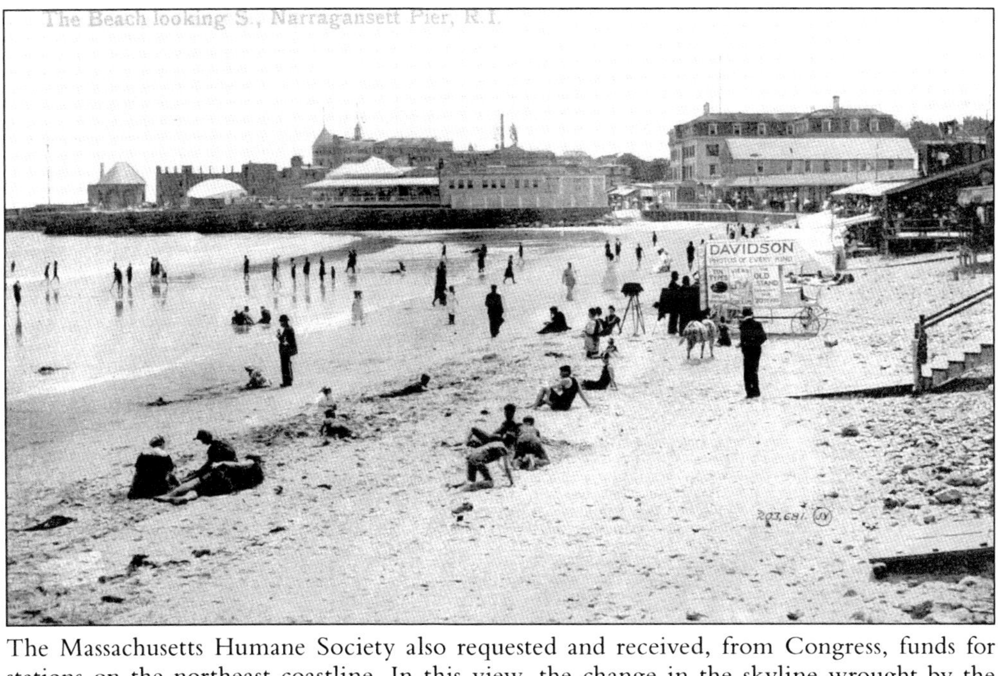

The Massachusetts Humane Society also requested and received, from Congress, funds for stations on the northeast coastline. In this view, the change in the skyline wrought by the hurricane of 1938 (the *Rockingham* was destroyed by fire) is shocking. Only the rugged little life saving station was unscathed by the storm.

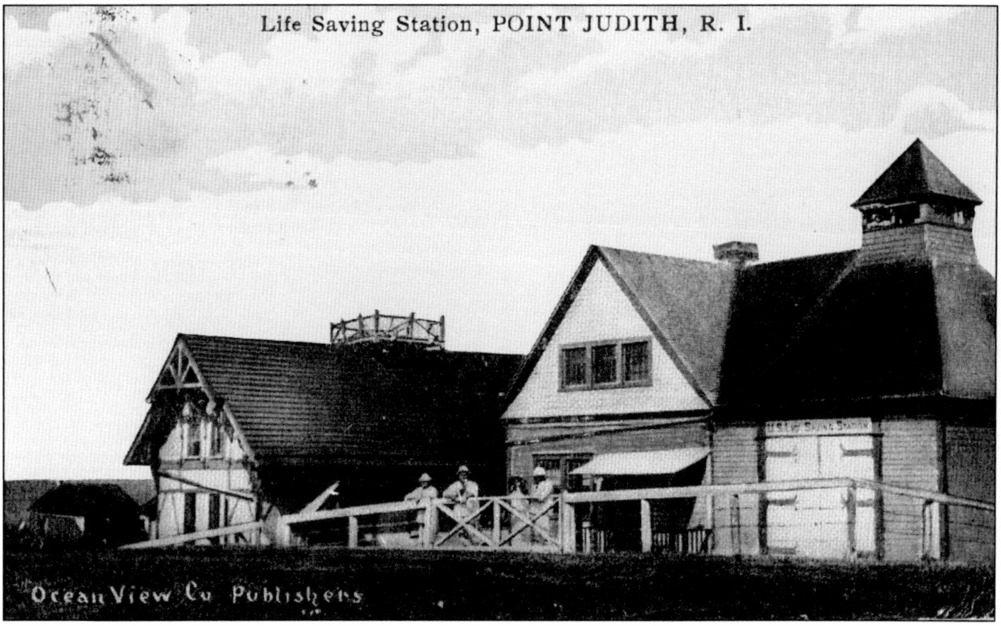

This is the Point Judith VLSS around 1916. Again, Congress appropriated funds for more stations. Some of the money was used to employ a full-time keeper at each station. Also included was money to hire two superintendents to supervise the stations. The problems, however, continued; the only person on duty was a keeper who received $200 a year, and if he discovered a vessel in distress, he had to collect a volunteer crew.

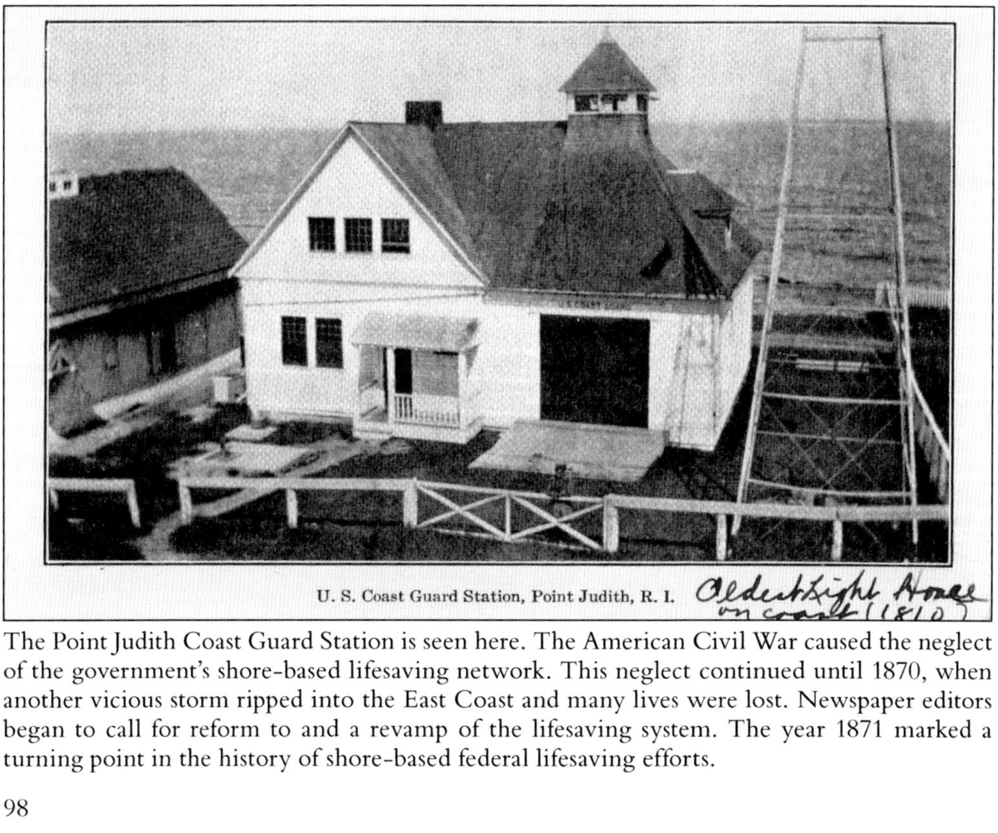

The Point Judith Coast Guard Station is seen here. The American Civil War caused the neglect of the government's shore-based lifesaving network. This neglect continued until 1870, when another vicious storm ripped into the East Coast and many lives were lost. Newspaper editors began to call for reform to and a revamp of the lifesaving system. The year 1871 marked a turning point in the history of shore-based federal lifesaving efforts.

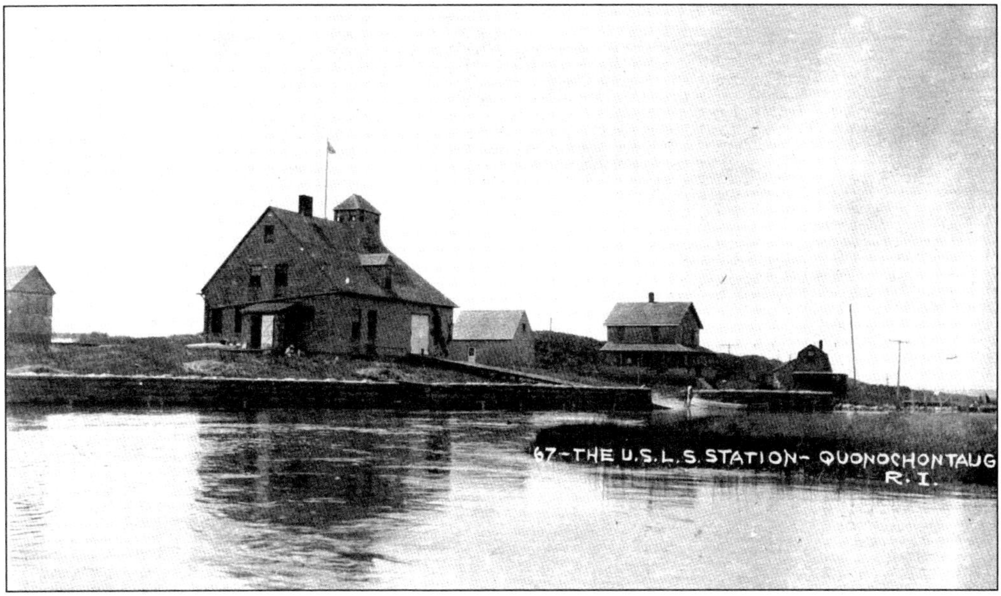

This is a *c.* 1916 real-photo postcard image of the USVLSS at Quonochontaug in Washington County, Rhode Island. The Quonochontaug Station was probably the most photographed for postcard use of all Rhode Island stations.

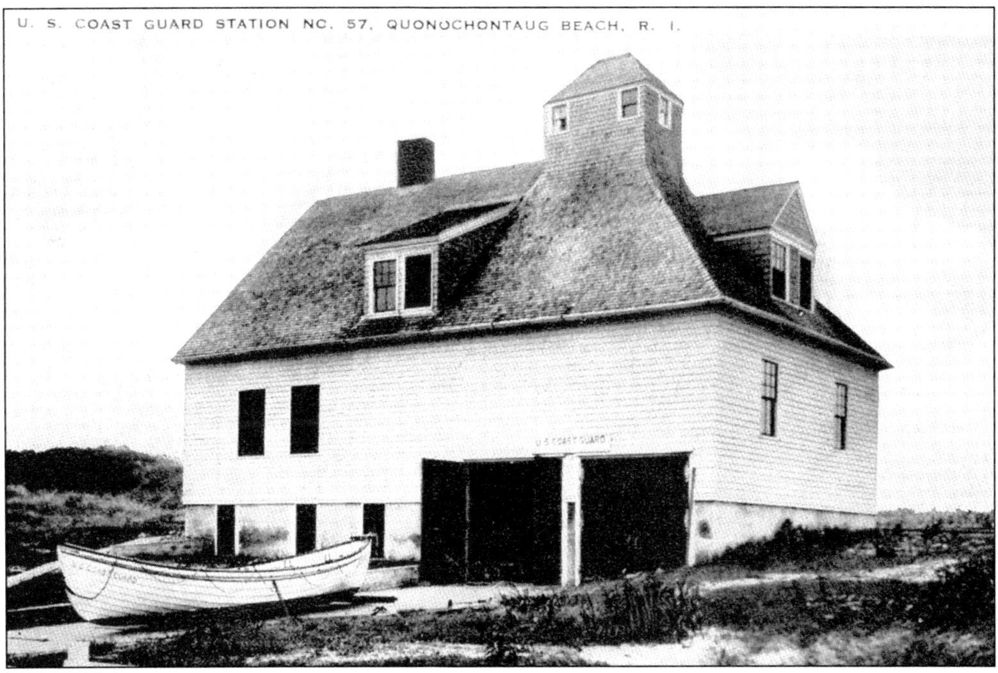

The volunteer life saving stations were to be administered by the U.S. Revenue Marine (later called the U.S. Revenue Cutter Service) within the Treasury Department. Actually, once the stations were built, including the Quonochontaug Station, they were run like a volunteer fire department but without anyone in charge or any inspection system to insure that men and equipment were up to standards. This is a postcard image from around 1925.

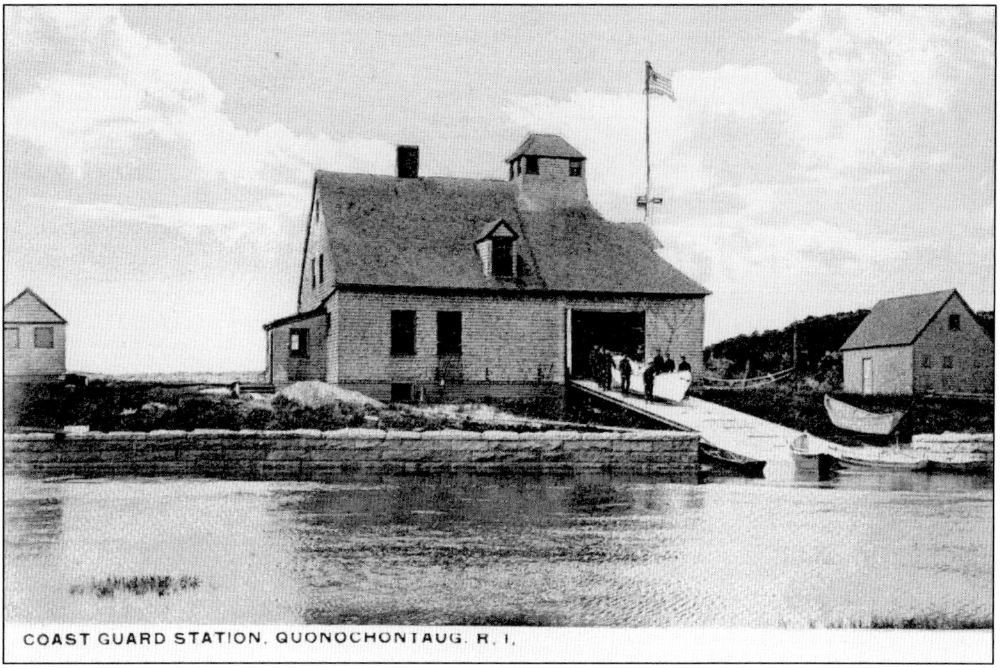

This is a *c.* 1919 view of the Quonochontaug Station volunteers launching their lifeboat. The lifesaving system managed to continue under this type of organization for the next six years. One town, not in Rhode Island however, used its lifeboat alternately as a trough for mixing mortar and a tub for scalding hogs.

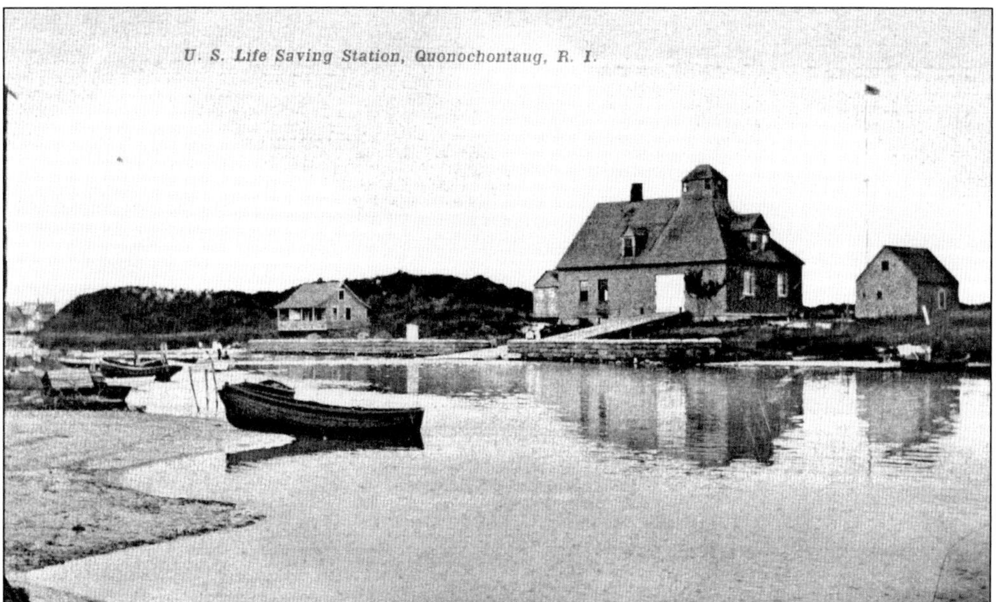

Here is low tide at the Quonochontaug salt pond around 1910. In 1878, the growing network of life saving stations was finally organized as a separate agency of the Treasury Department and named the U.S. Life-Saving Service. Congress created the U.S. Coast Guard in 1915.

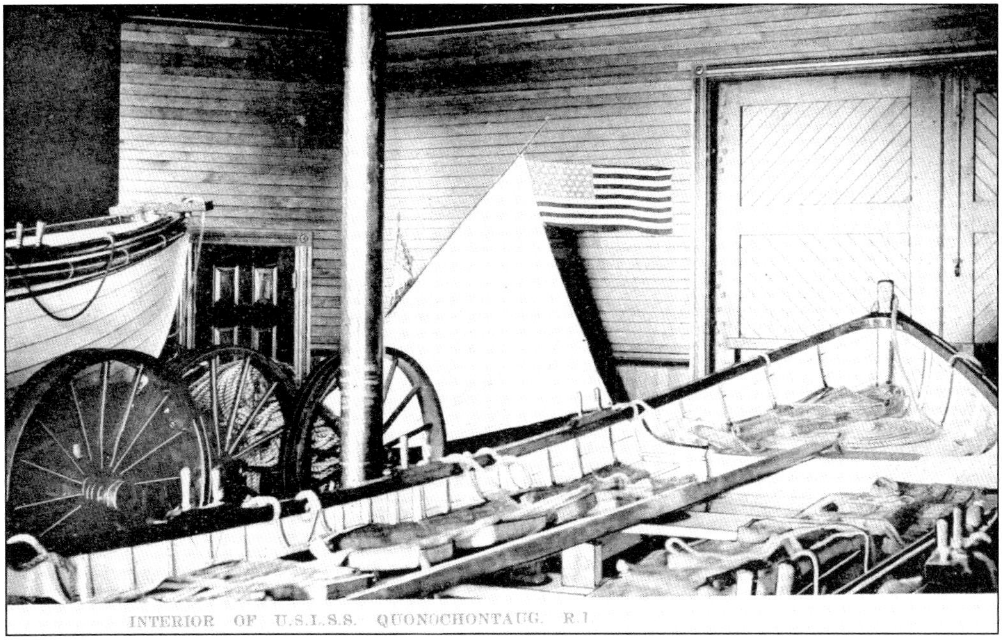

The service's reputation for honest, efficient, and nonpartisan administration, plus performance of duty, can be largely attributed to Sumner I. Kimball, general superintendent of the service.

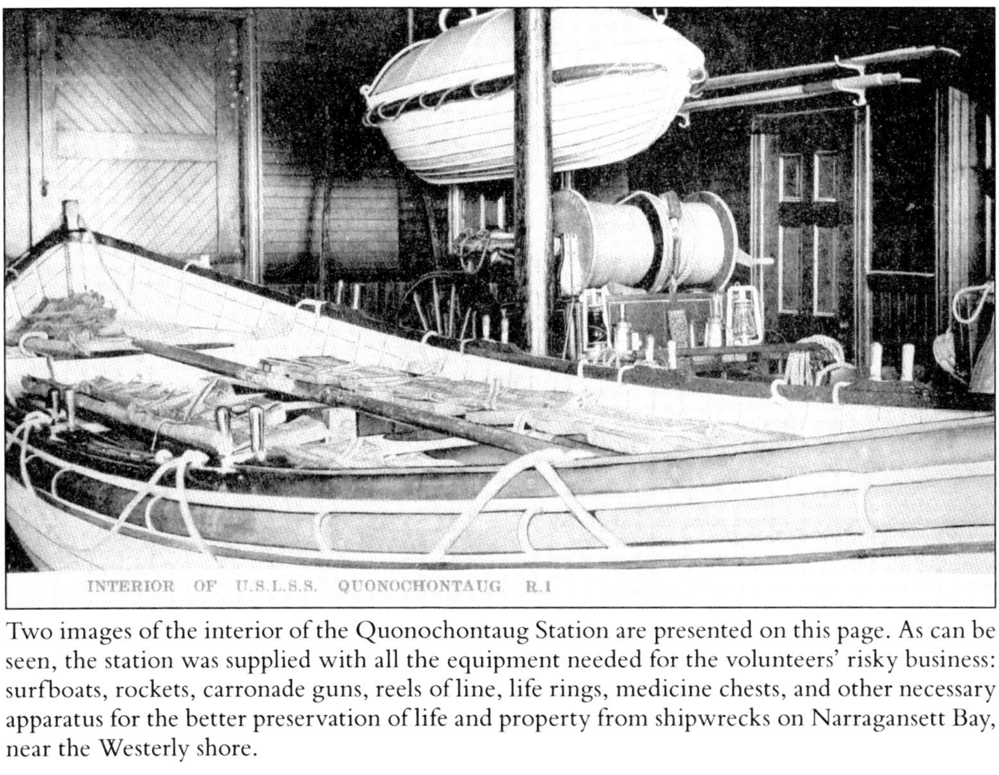

Two images of the interior of the Quonochontaug Station are presented on this page. As can be seen, the station was supplied with all the equipment needed for the volunteers' risky business: surfboats, rockets, carronade guns, reels of line, life rings, medicine chests, and other necessary apparatus for the better preservation of life and property from shipwrecks on Narragansett Bay, near the Westerly shore.

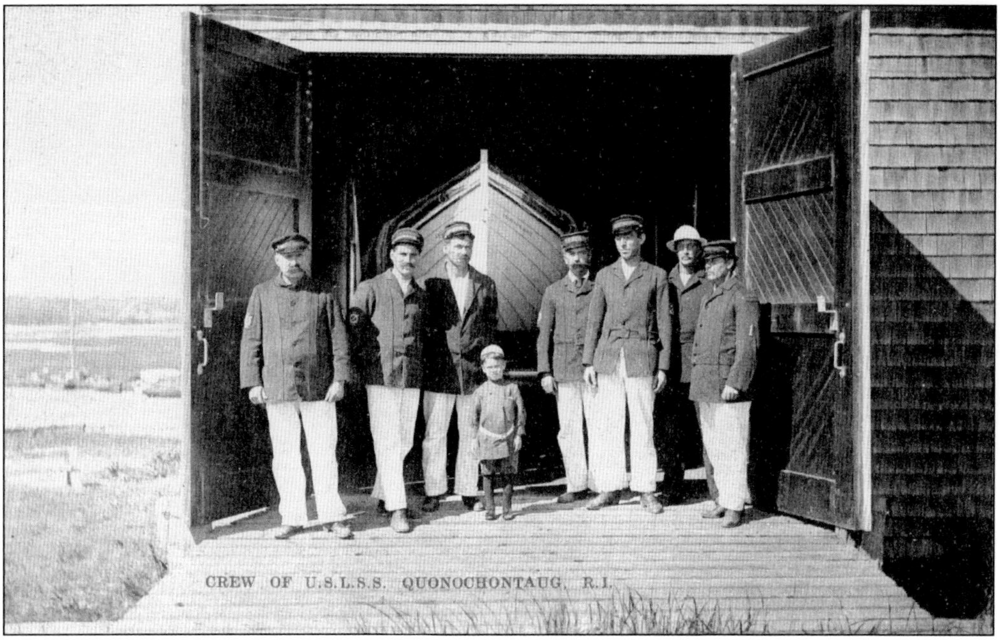

The proud and daring volunteers of the Quonochontaug Life Saving Station pose with their surfboat on the ramp of the station building.

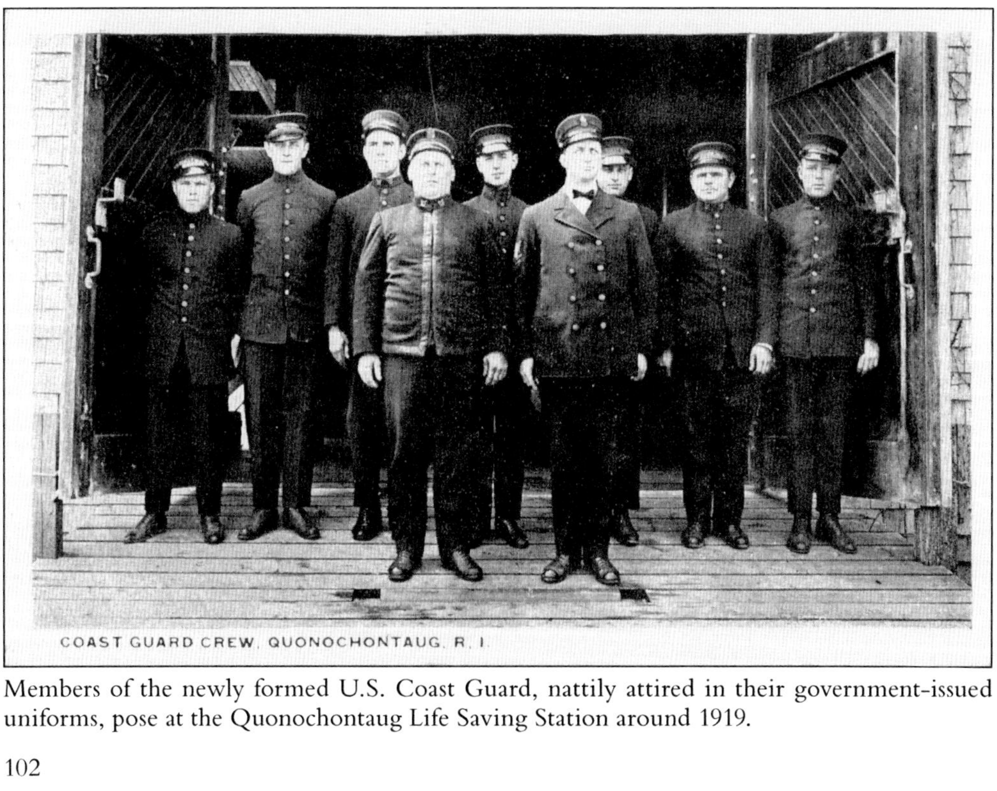

Members of the newly formed U.S. Coast Guard, nattily attired in their government-issued uniforms, pose at the Quonochontaug Life Saving Station around 1919.

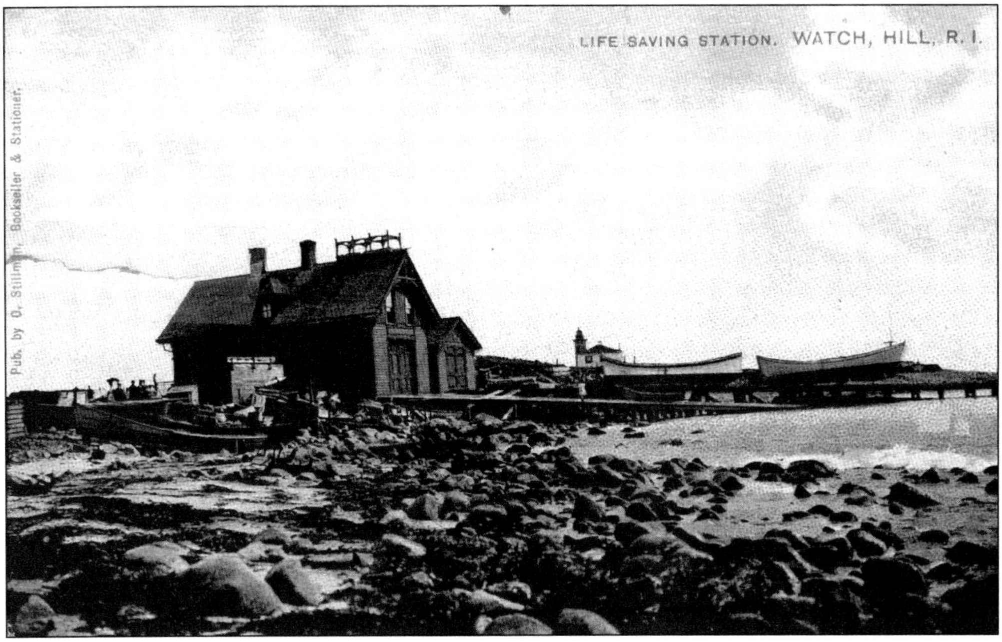

This is a view of the life saving station on the rocky Watch Hill (Westerly) shore, with surfboats on the ramp prepared for an emergency launching. Life saving stations were manned by full-time crews during the period when wrecks were most likely to occur. On the East Coast, this was usually from November to April and was called the "active season."

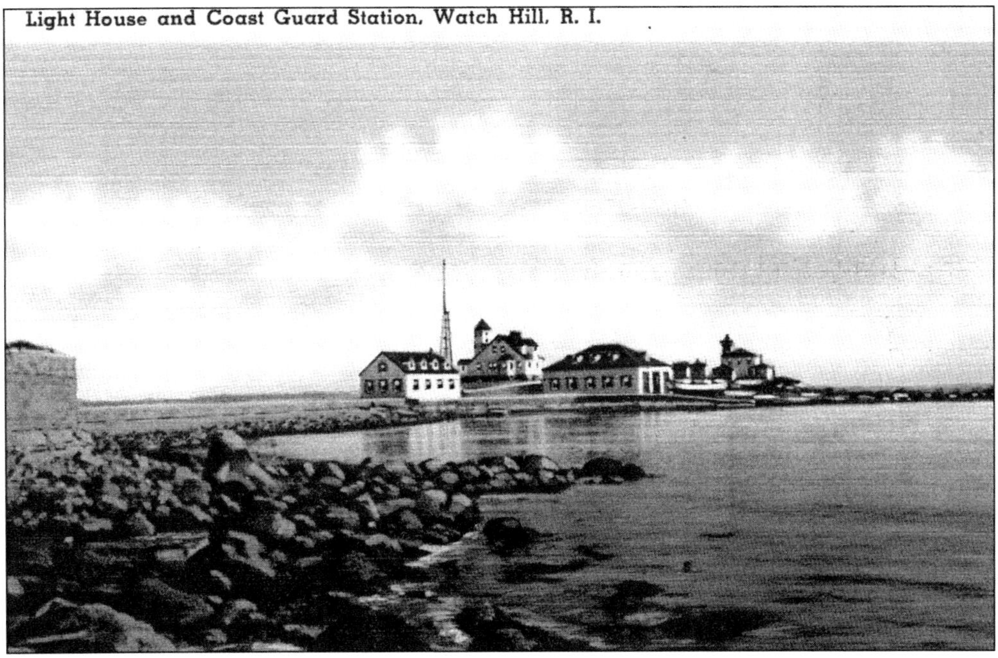

This is another view of the Watch Hill Station with the Watch Hill Lighthouse in the background. By the start of the 20th century, the active season was year-round. Most stations were in isolated areas, and crewmen had to be able to perform open beach launchings. That is, they were required to launch their boats from the beach directly into the surf.

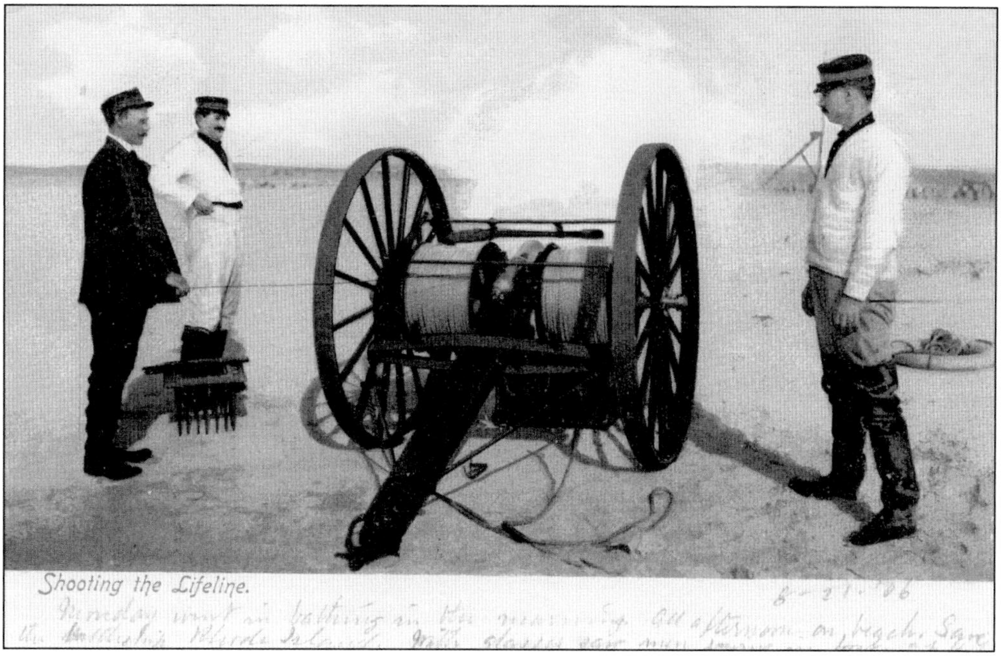

A crew of volunteers practice shooting the lifeline from their carronade gun. Before the beginning of the 20th century, there were very few recreational boaters, and most assistance cases came from ships engaged in commerce.

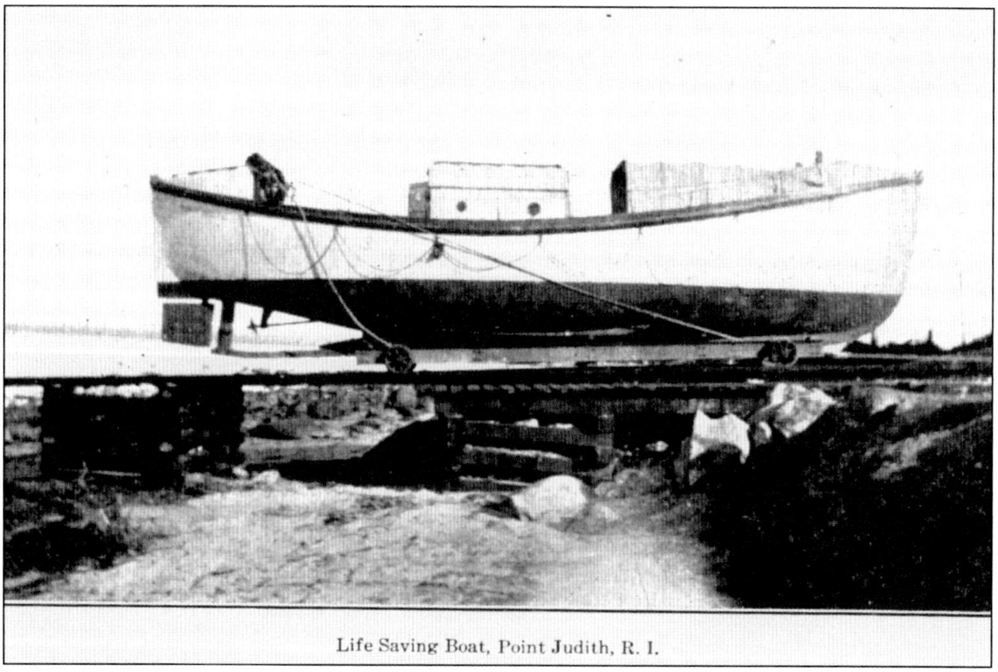

Here is an example of the Point Judith Station's fully prepared surfboat. Deep water, combined with piers and other waterfront structures, allowed the launching of heavy lifeboats directly into the water by marine railways on inclined ramps.

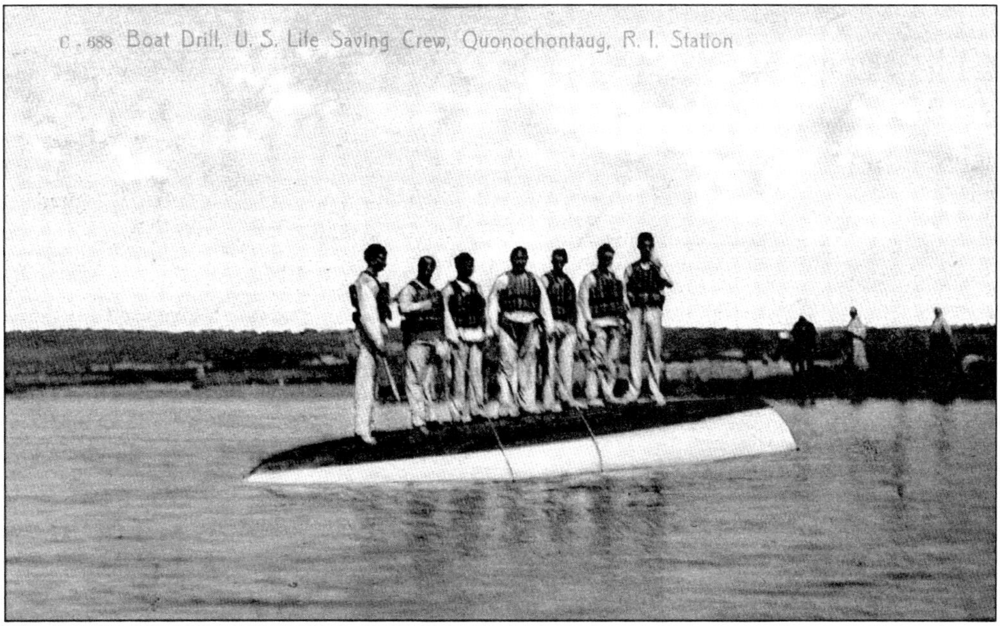

In this *c.* 1908 postcard image, the Quonochontaug volunteers practice the capsized boat drill. The U.S. Life-Saving Service had two means of rescuing people onboard ships stranded near shore: by boat and by a strong line stretched from the beach to the wrecked vessel.

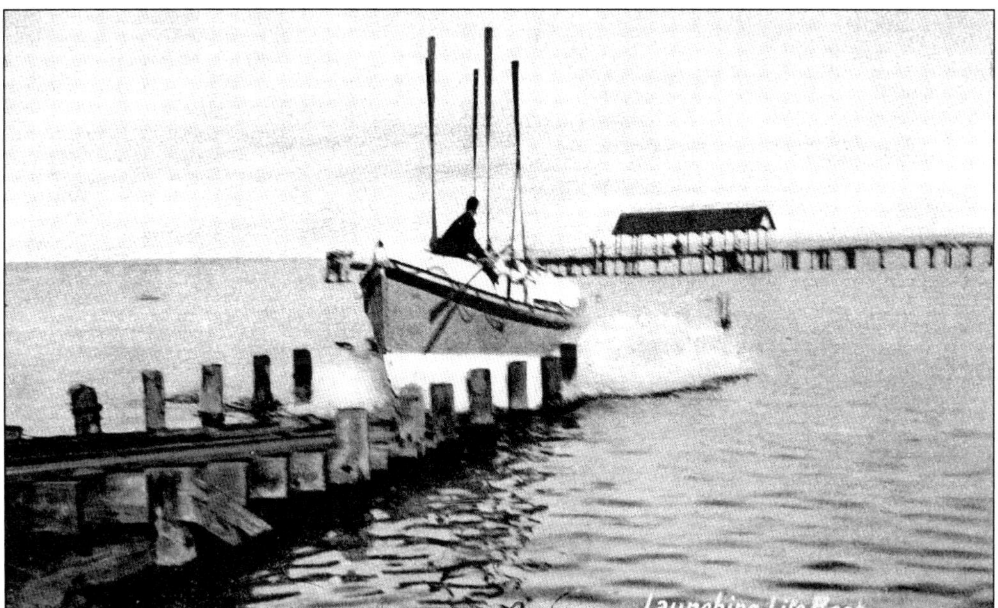

The Watch Hill volunteers are in the act of launching their surfboat. The service's boats were usually 700 to 1,000 pounds or a two- to four-ton self-bailing, self-righting surfboat pulled by six surfmen with 12- to 18-foot oars. The surfboat could be pulled on a cart by crewmen, or horses, to a site near a wreck and then launched into the surf.

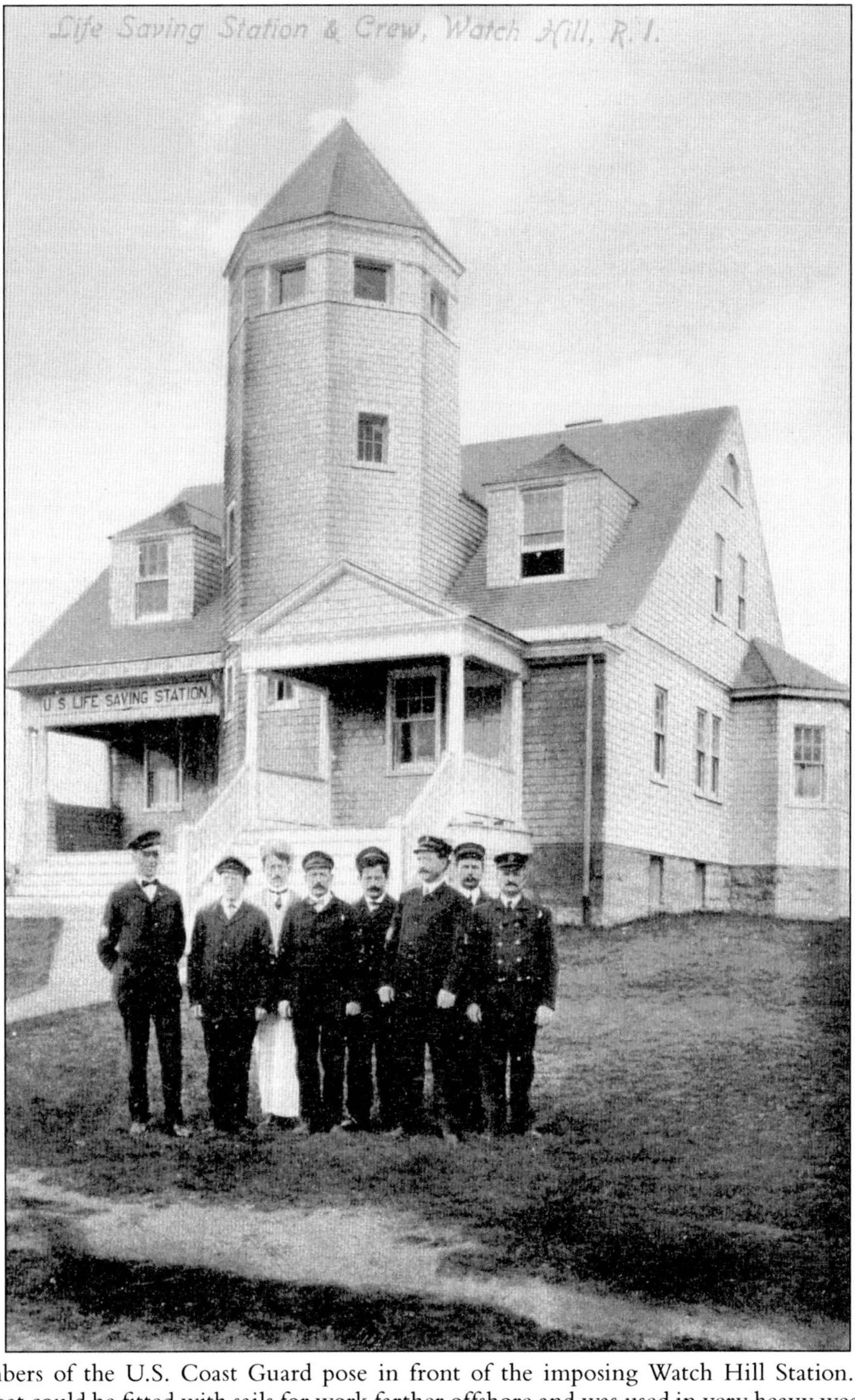

Members of the U.S. Coast Guard pose in front of the imposing Watch Hill Station. The lifeboat could be fitted with sails for work farther offshore and was used in very heavy weather. Some crews, at first, viewed the lifeboat with skepticism because of its great weight and bulk. After repeated successes, the skepticism soon changed, for the boat enabled the crews to provide assistance when the most powerful tugs and steam craft refused to go out of the harbor.

Seven

NARRAGANSETT BAY LIGHTS

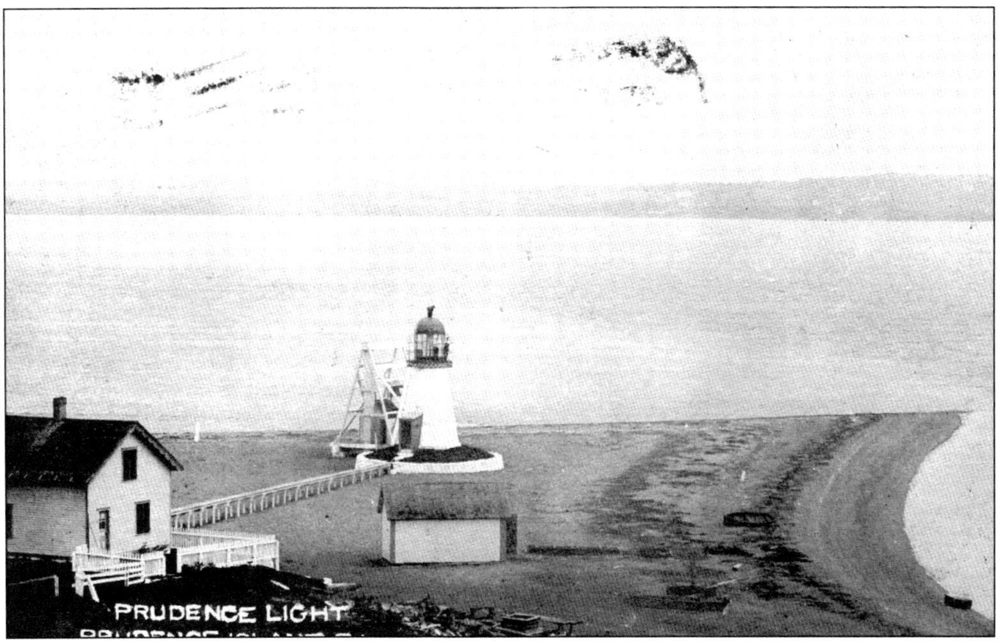

This is a *c.* 1907 real-photo postcard view of the Sandy Point Light on Prudence Island in Portsmouth. This is Rhode Island's oldest surviving lighthouse and an unusual example of a small early-19th-century light tower. The light was built in 1823 and relocated from Goat Island near Newport in 1851. Different sources give different dates of removal from Goat Island (see page 109).

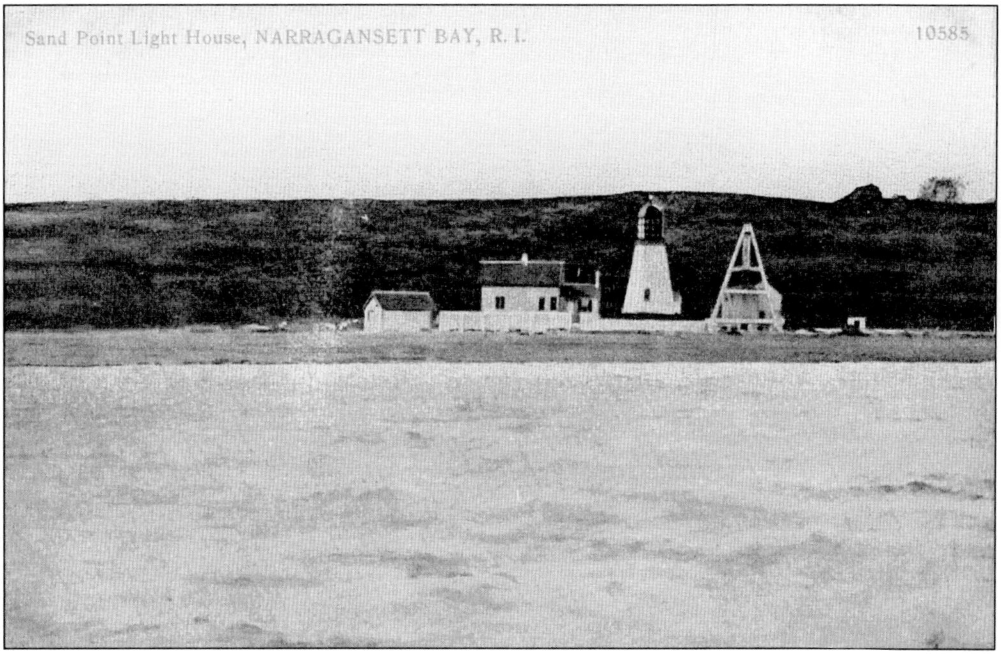

The tower is octagonal granite with a very rare 19th-century "birdcage" lantern. The lighthouse is painted white, the lantern black. The keeper's house was destroyed by the hurricane of 1938.

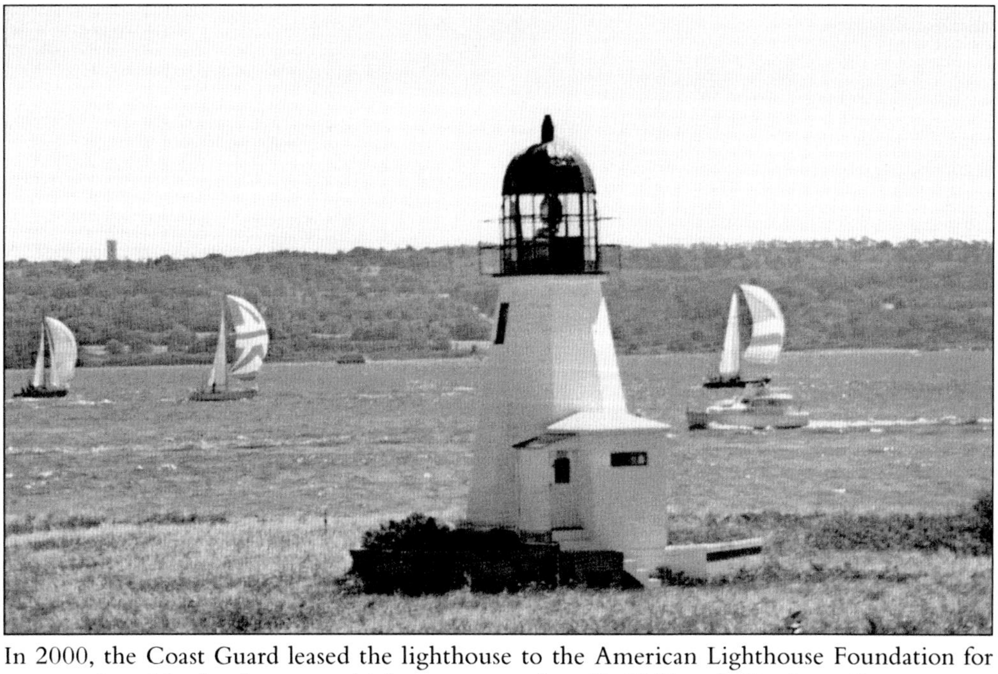

In 2000, the Coast Guard leased the lighthouse to the American Lighthouse Foundation for preservation. After local protests, this lease was transferred in 2001 to the Prudence Conservancy. In 2002, conservancy members refurbished the lighthouse, repairing the foundation and painting the tower and lantern.

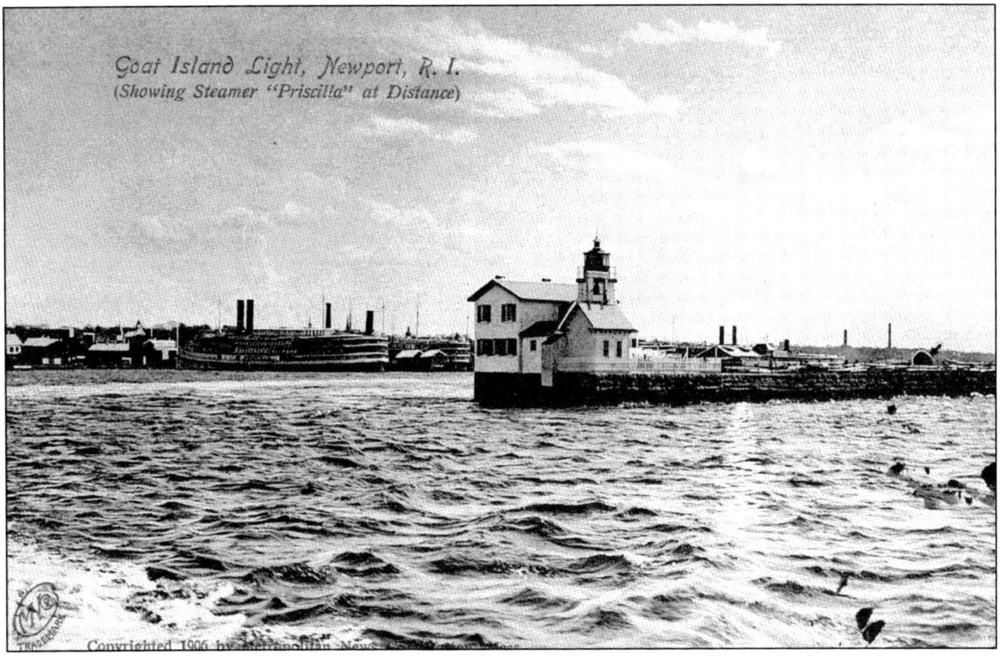

The Goat Island Light in Newport Harbor is seen here around 1909. The sound steamer *Priscilla* is in the background. The octagonal granite tower with lantern and gallery was built in 1842. The light is still active; it has a focal plane of 33 feet and projects a continuous green light 35 feet.

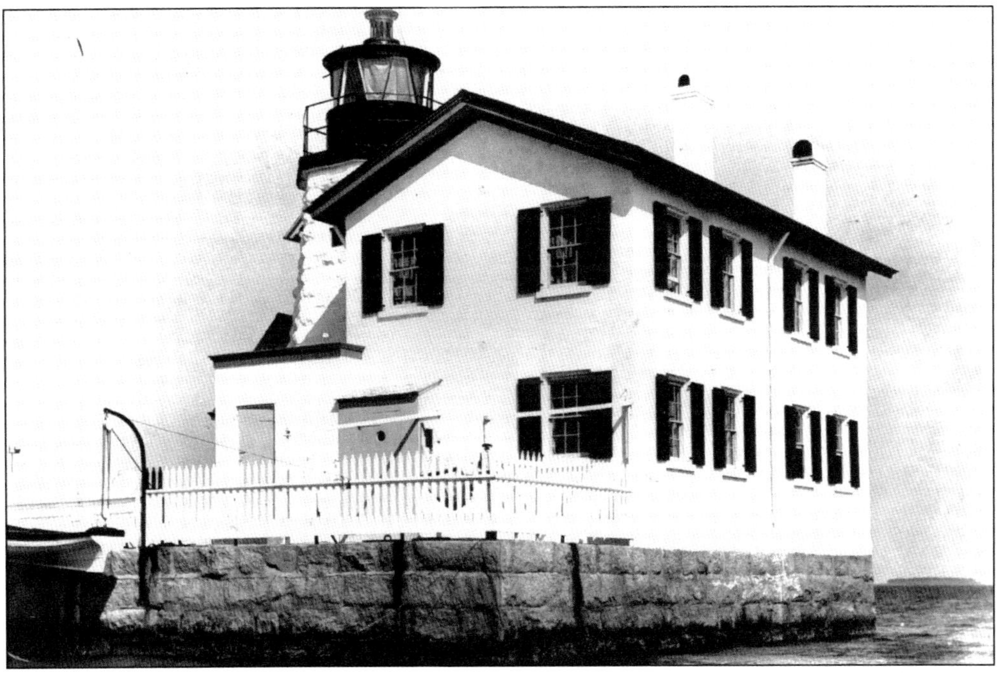

This is the Goat Island lighthouse keeper's house, which was demolished in 1923 after being damaged when a submarine ran aground on the island. The tower now stands on a granite foundation, part of the breakwater on which it was originally built. See *Building the Mosquito Fleet*, Arcadia Publishing, 2001, page 149.

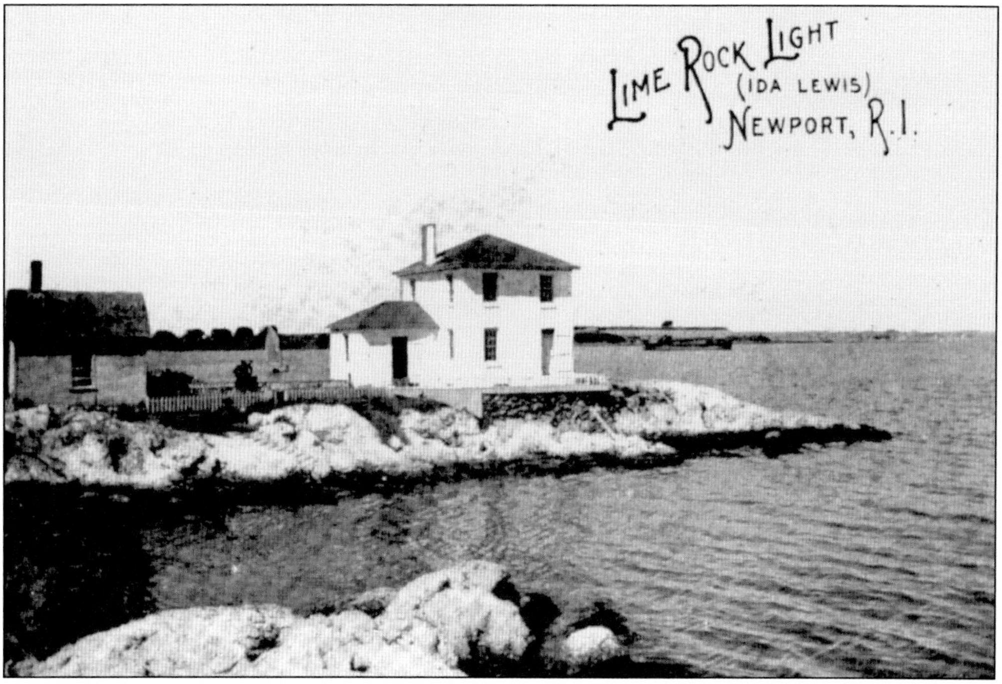

The original Lime Rick Light was built in 1854. Out of respect for longtime keeper Ida Lewis, who died in 1911, the light's name was officially changed to Ida Lewis Light. The light has been inactive since 1927. A lantern mounted on one corner of the two-story granite and brick keeper's house is lighted as a decorative light during holidays.

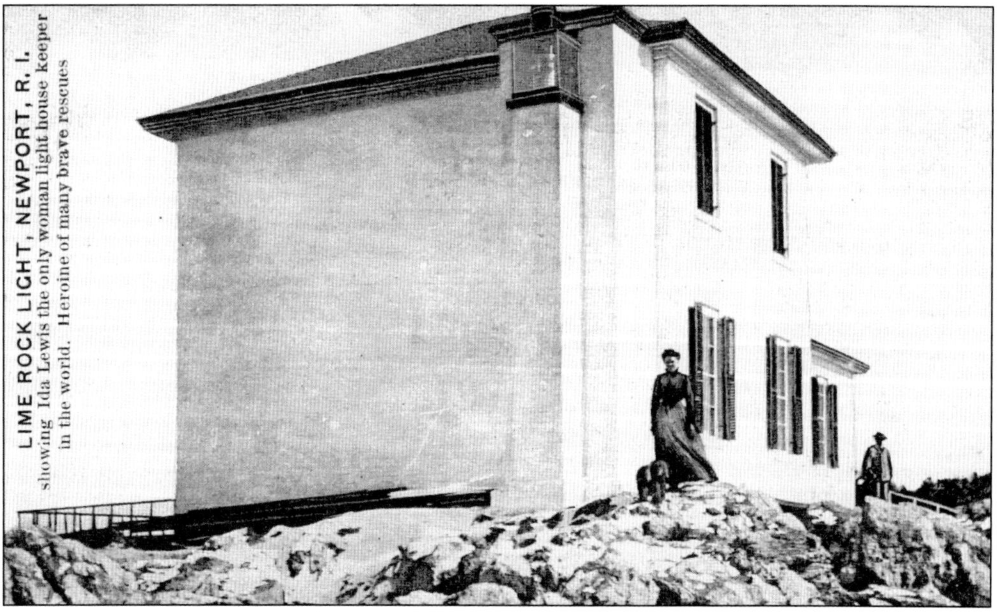

The tiny lighthouse, famous for its legendary keeper Ida Lewis (1857–1911), is now home of the Ida Lewis Yacht Club. The building, including modern additions, is now part of the yacht club. The island has been connected to the mainland by a causeway. For more on this subject, see pages 88–89.

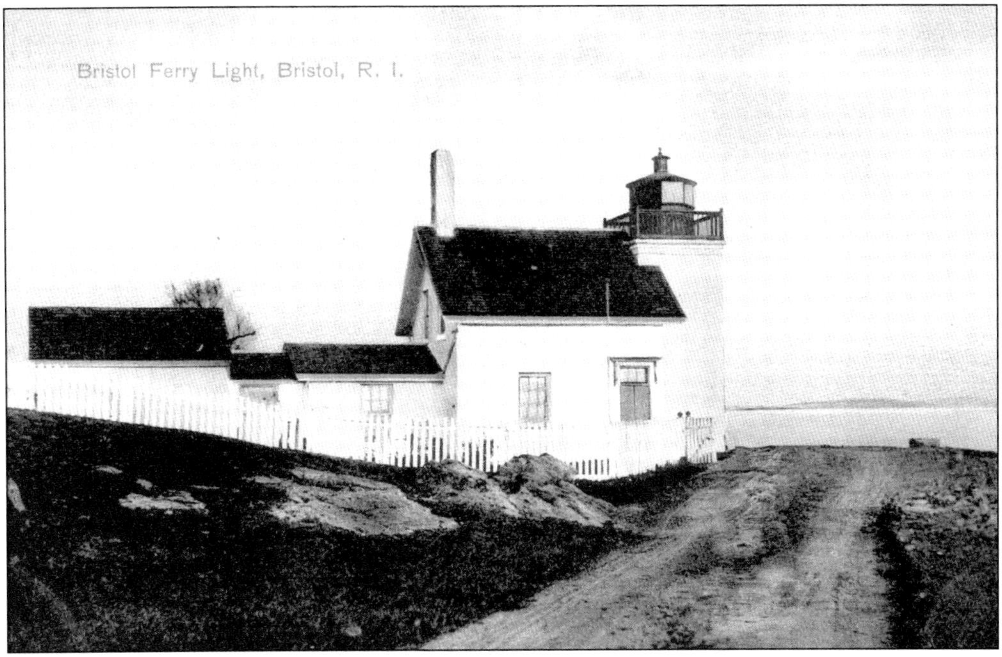

Built in 1855, the Bristol Ferry Light has been inactive since 1927. The square cylindrical brick tower with lantern and gallery is 34 feet high; it is attached to the original one-and-a-half-story keeper's house. For more information on this lighthouse, see Postcard History Series: *Bristol*, Arcadia Publishing, 2005.

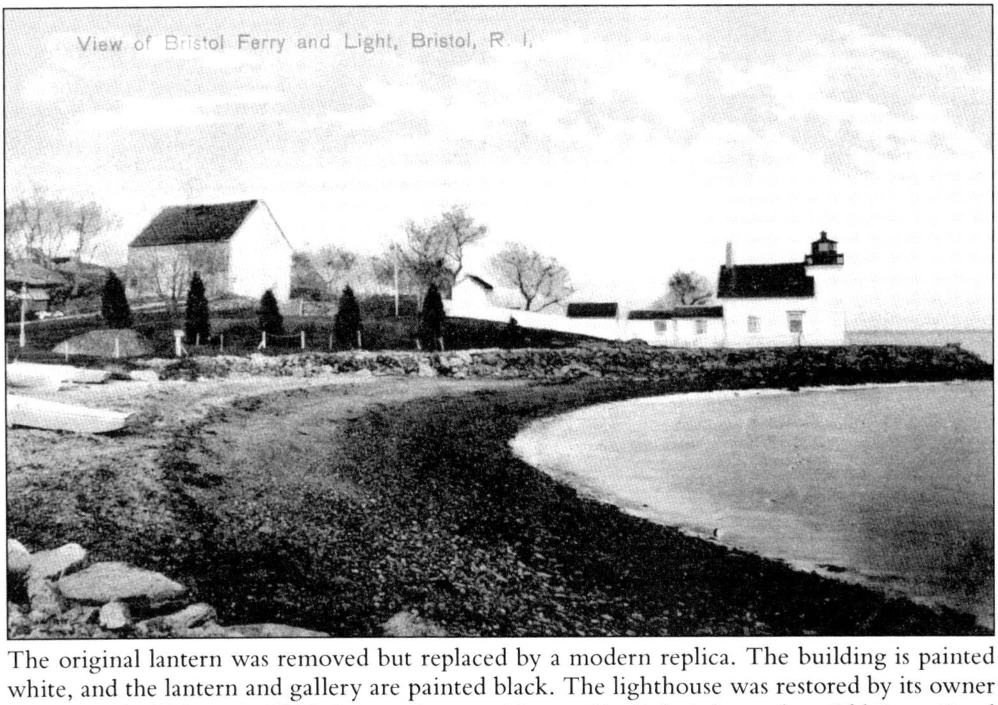

The original lantern was removed but replaced by a modern replica. The building is painted white, and the lantern and gallery are painted black. The lighthouse was restored by its owner in 1992 and sold in early 2000; it is used as a residence. The light is located on Old Ferry Road in the shadow of the north end of the Mount Hope Bridge (Route 114) in Bristol.

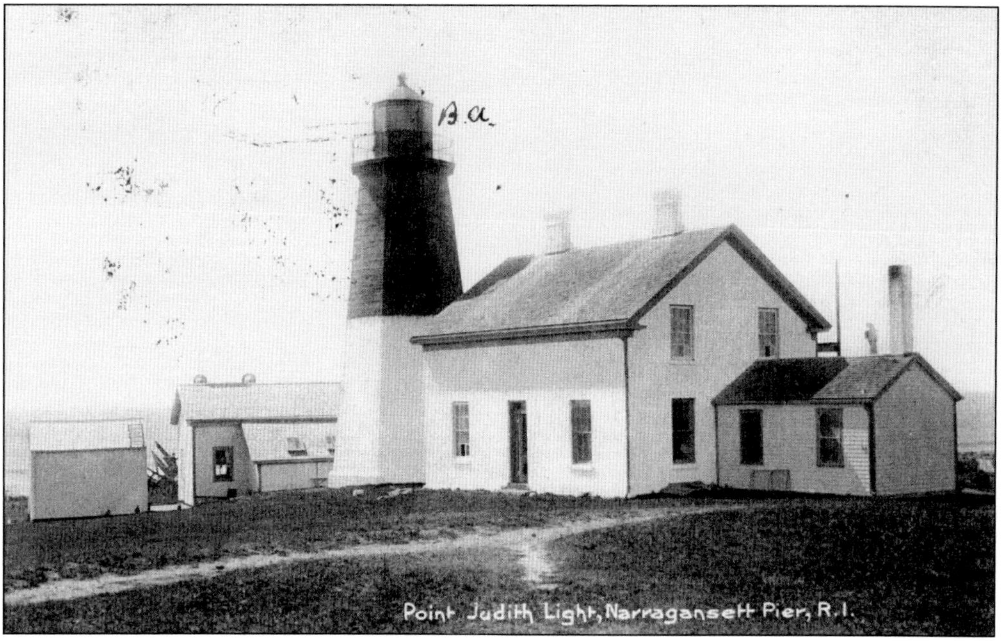

Built in 1857, the Point Judith Lighthouse, located on Watch Hill Point at the end of Lighthouse Road in Westerly, is a 45-foot square cylindrical unpainted granite tower with lantern and gallery, attached to a one-and-one-half-story brick keeper's house. This image is from around 1906.

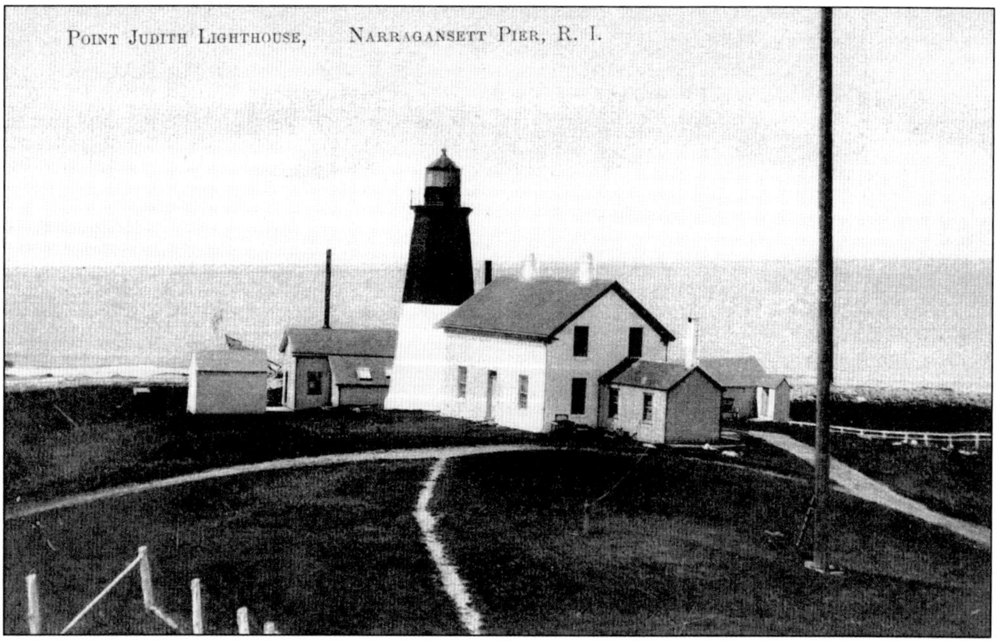

The Point Judith Light keeper's house was demolished in 1954; the oil house (1917) and fog signal building (1923) survived. A $200,000 Coast Guard restoration saved the lighthouse during 2000. The lantern and lens were refurbished, glass replaced, and the brownstone tower repaired. It is now an active U.S. Coast Guard station. This postcard image is from around 1909.

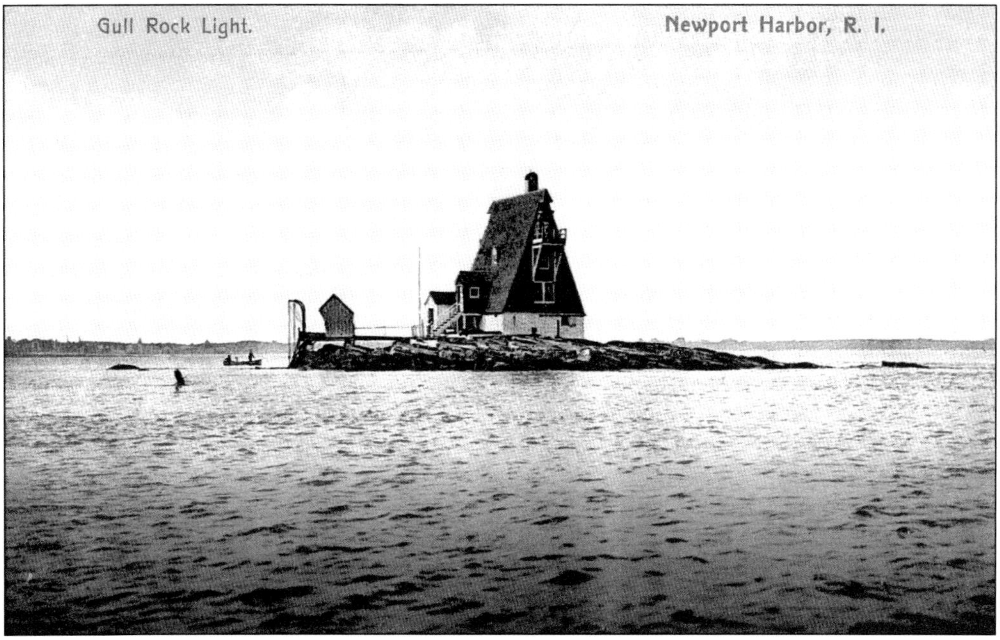

This unusual shaped lighthouse called Gull Rock Light has been inactive since 1928. The A-frame keeper's house, which had two lights mounted at the peak ends of the roof, was demolished in 1970. The small outhouse-shaped oil house survives on the tiny island almost directly under the Newport Bridge (Route 138) between Jamestown and Newport.

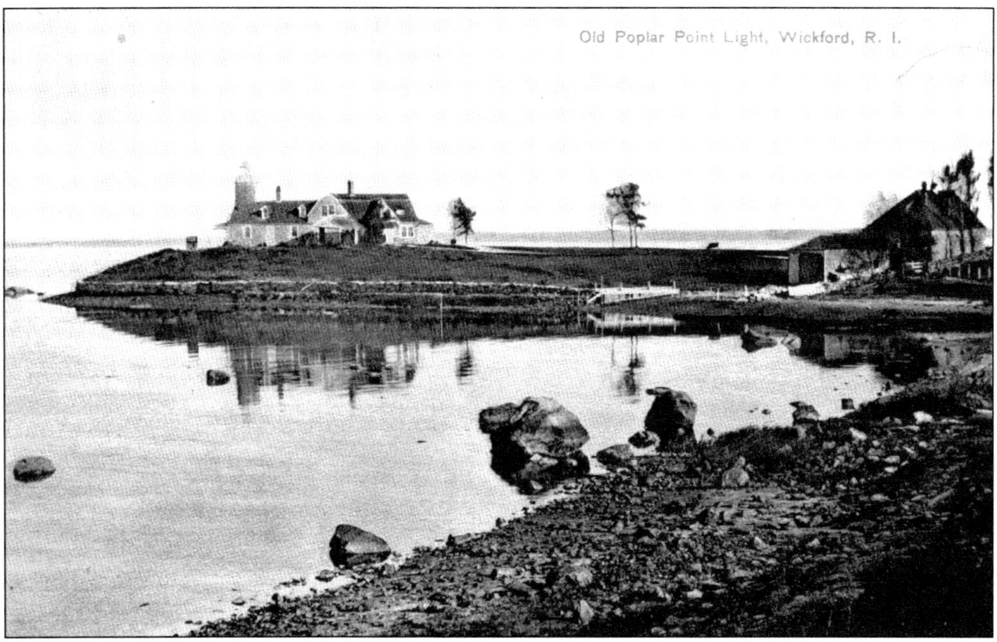

The Poplar Point Light is located at the entrance to Wickford Harbor in North Kingstown; it has been inactive since 1882. The 45-foot octagonal wood tower with lantern and gallery is attached to the one-and-a-half-story wood keeper's house. It has been a private residence since 1894. The well-preserved light tower is the oldest wooden light tower in the nation.

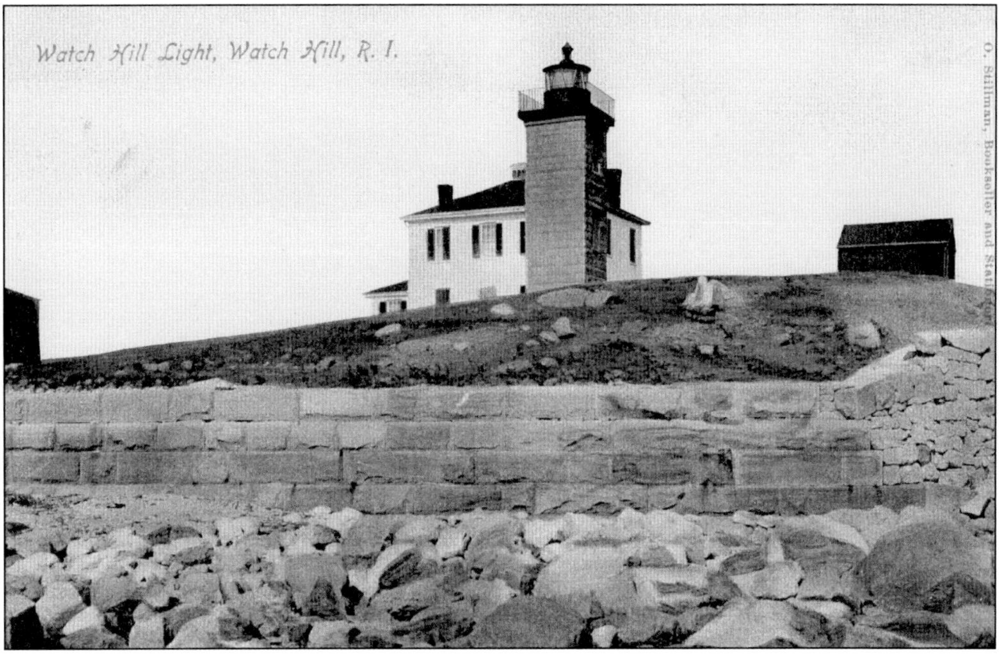

The Watch Hill Light has been active since 1857. The 45-foot square cylindrical unpainted granite tower with lantern and gallery is attached to a two-story brick keeper's house.

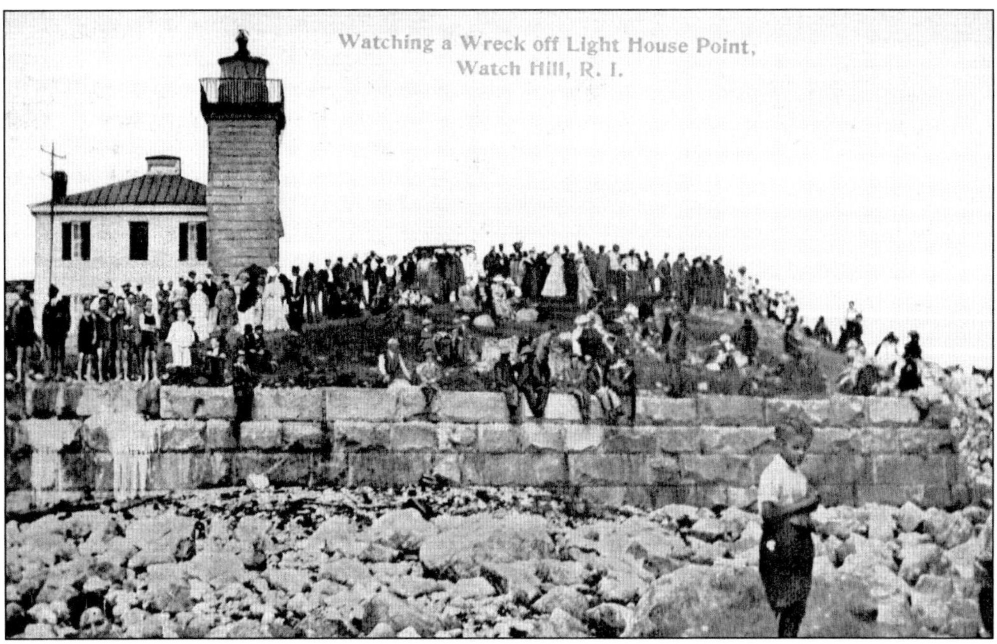

The light station was established in 1807. It is a very well-preserved light, located on Watch Hill Point at the end of Lighthouse Road in Westerly. There is a small museum in the oil house.

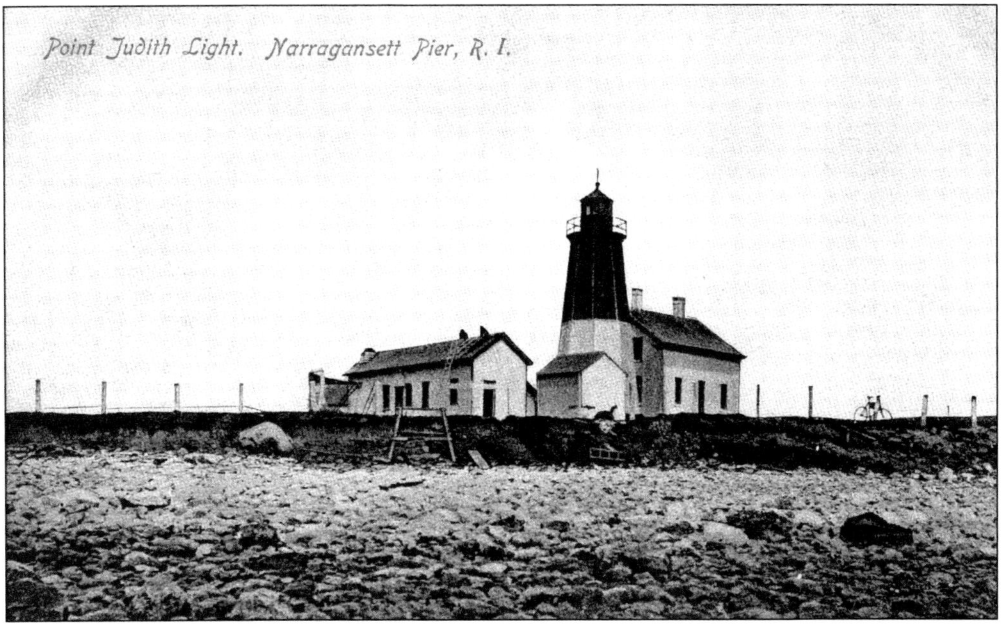

The Point Judith Light Station was established in 1810. The 51-foot octagonal brownstone tower, with lantern and gallery, and the original four-degree Fresnel lens are still in use. This is an active Coast Guard station, located at the end of Route 108 in Narragansett.

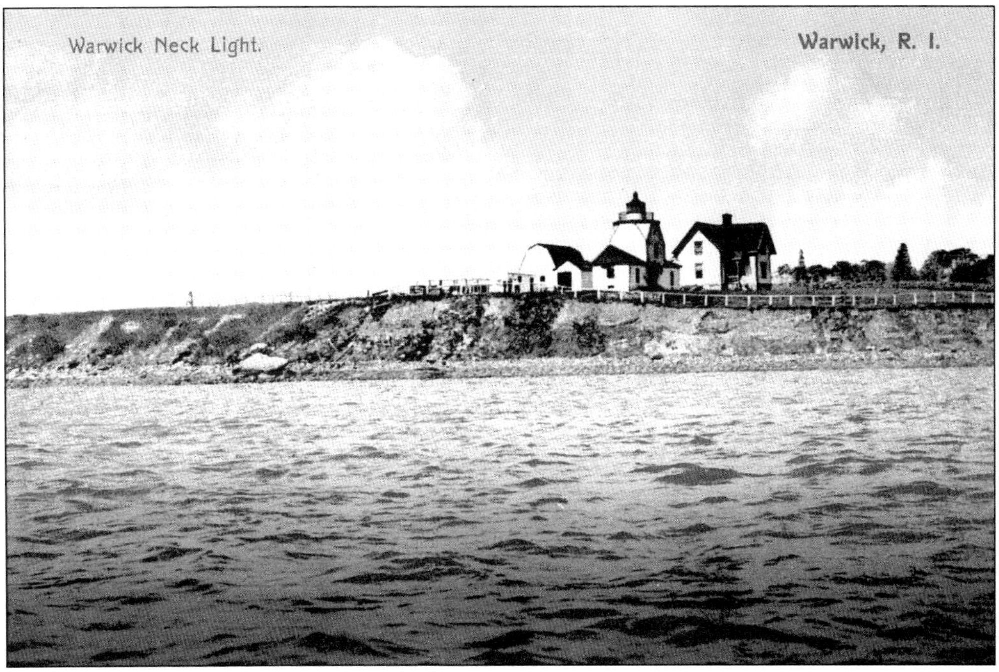

The Warwick Neck Light Station was established in 1826. The steel tower with lantern and gallery is 51 feet high; the one-and-a-half-story wood Victorian-era keeper's house (1889) is used as Coast Guard housing. All the buildings are painted white, the lantern black, and roofs red. After the 1938 hurricane, the lighthouse was relocated 50 feet inland (1939) to escape beach erosion.

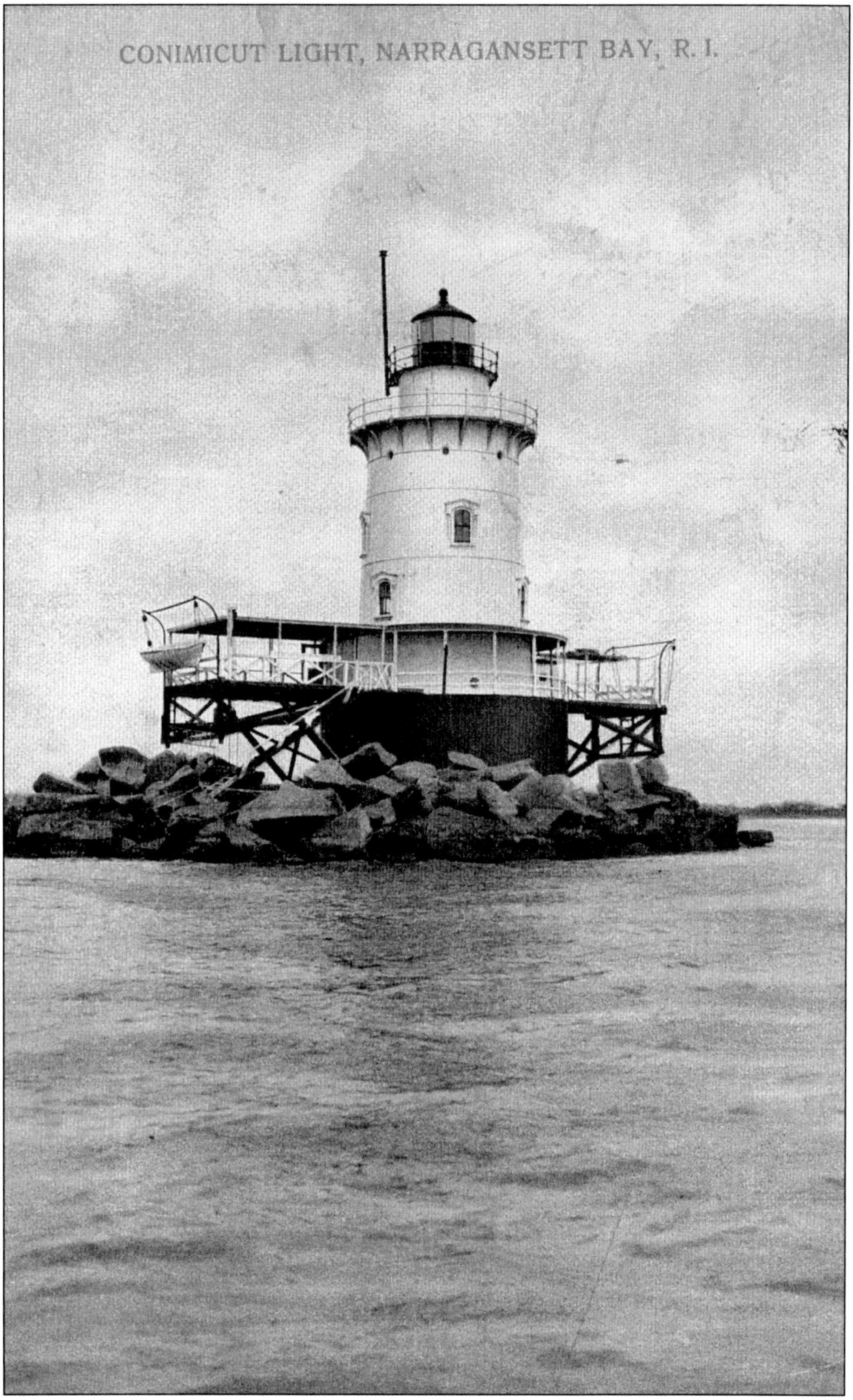

The first Conimicut Point Lighthouse was a granite tower built in 1866. In 1883, the old granite tower was torn down and a new cast-iron, sparkplug-style light was built.

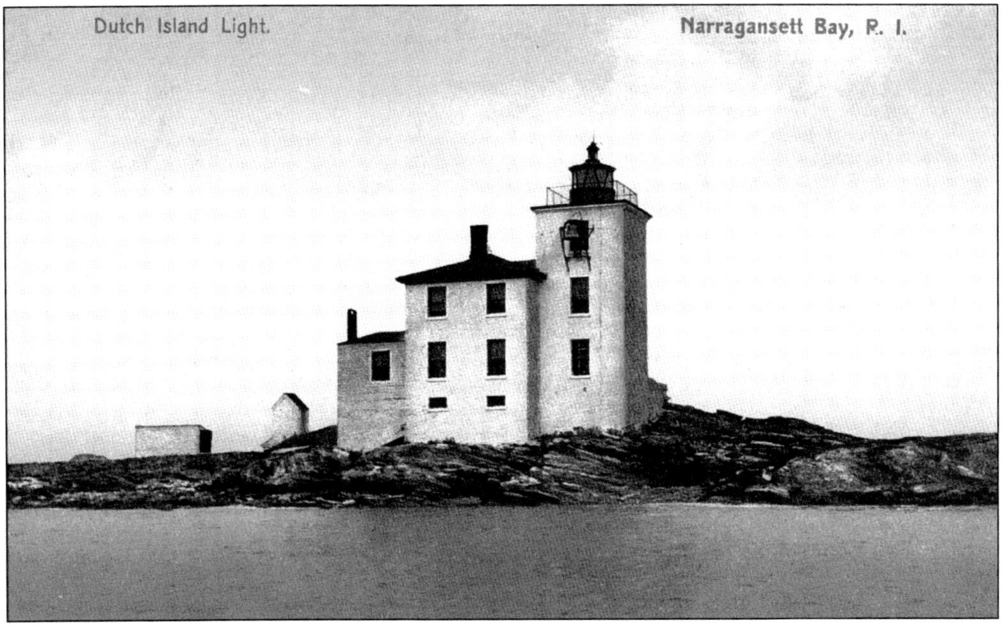

The 1857 Dutch Island Light has been inactive since 1947. The 42-foot square cylindrical brick tower had an attached keeper's house. Gravely endangered by neglect, vandalism, and decay, the keeper's house was demolished in the early 1960s. The site is located on Dutch Island, a wildlife management area in the middle of Narragansett Bay between Jamestown and Saunderstown. It is visible from Fort Getty Recreation Area in Jamestown.

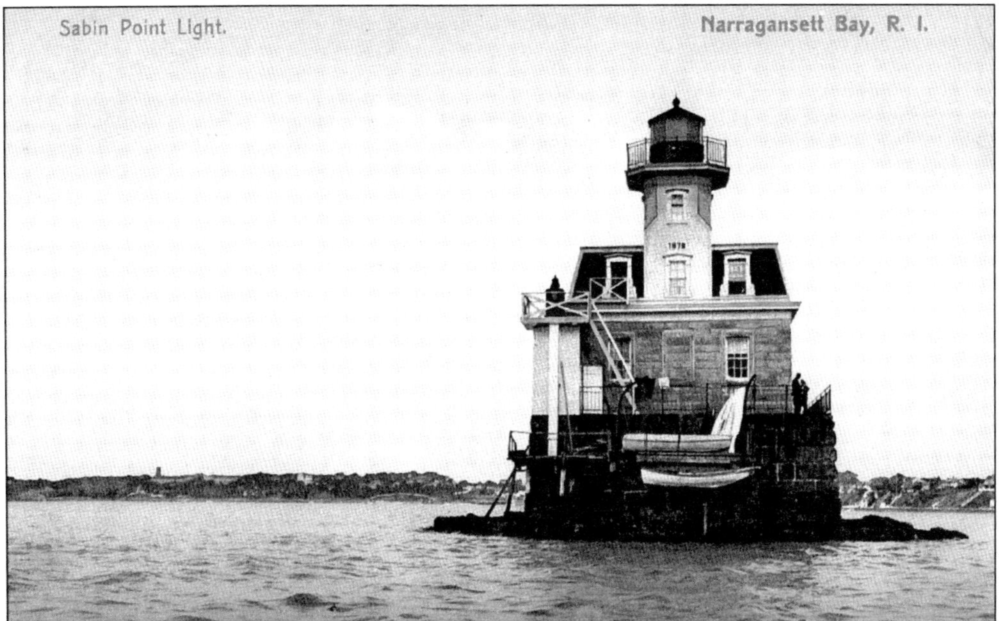

The Sabin Point Light was first lighted in November 1872. It was demolished in 1968. It was located in the Providence River about a quarter of a mile from shore. The lighthouse was very similar in appearance to several others built in the same period, including Pomham Rocks Light just to the north. The octagonal tower was built into the stone of the keeper's house.

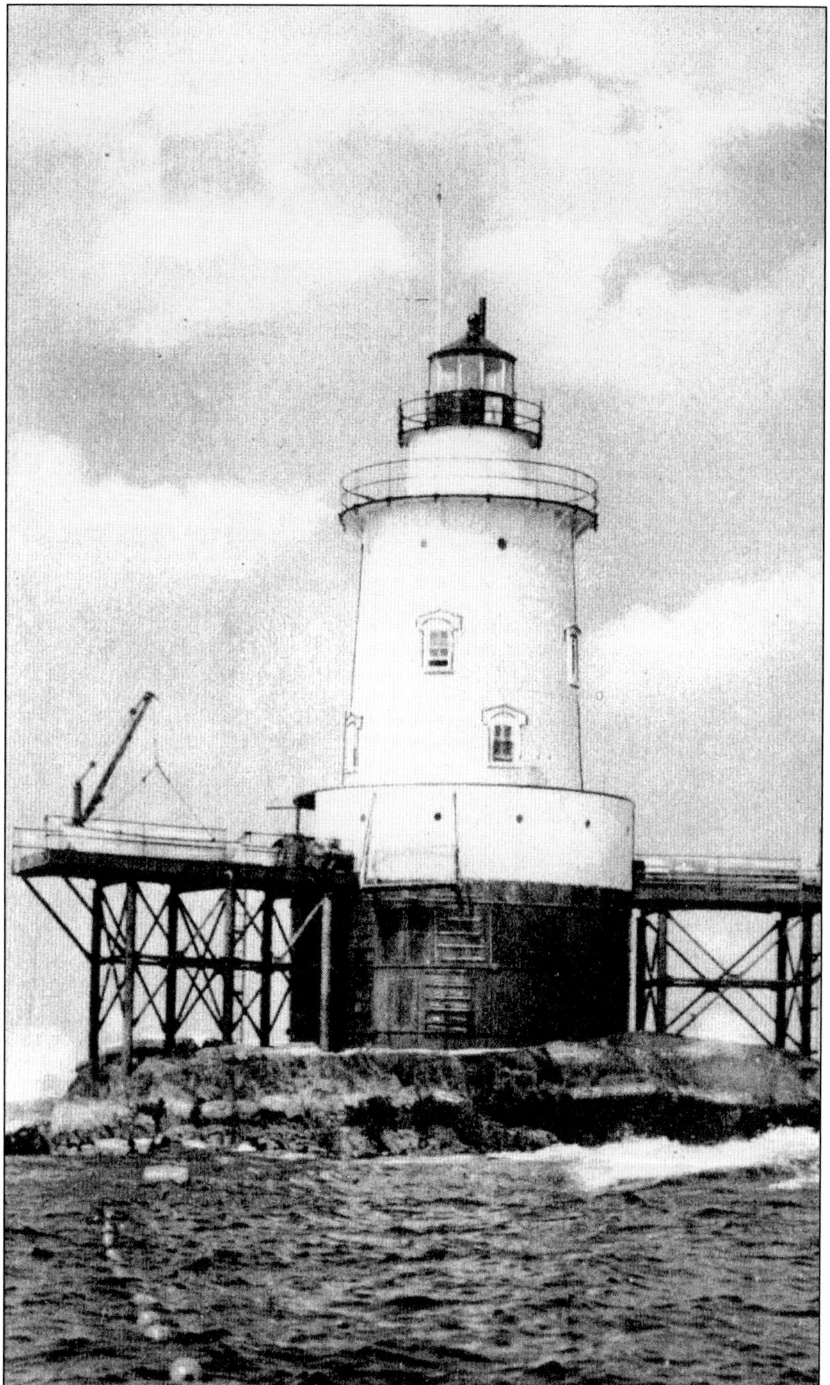

Now reactivated, the Sakonnet Point Light (1884) was inactive from 1955 to 1997. The 66-foot cast-iron, sparkplug-shaped, brick-lined tower with a lantern, and double galleries above and a lower gallery, incorporates a three-story keeper's quarters, mounted on a concrete caisson. Saved from destruction and restored by private efforts and local fund-raising, the light is located 800 yards off Sakonnet Point in Little Compton.

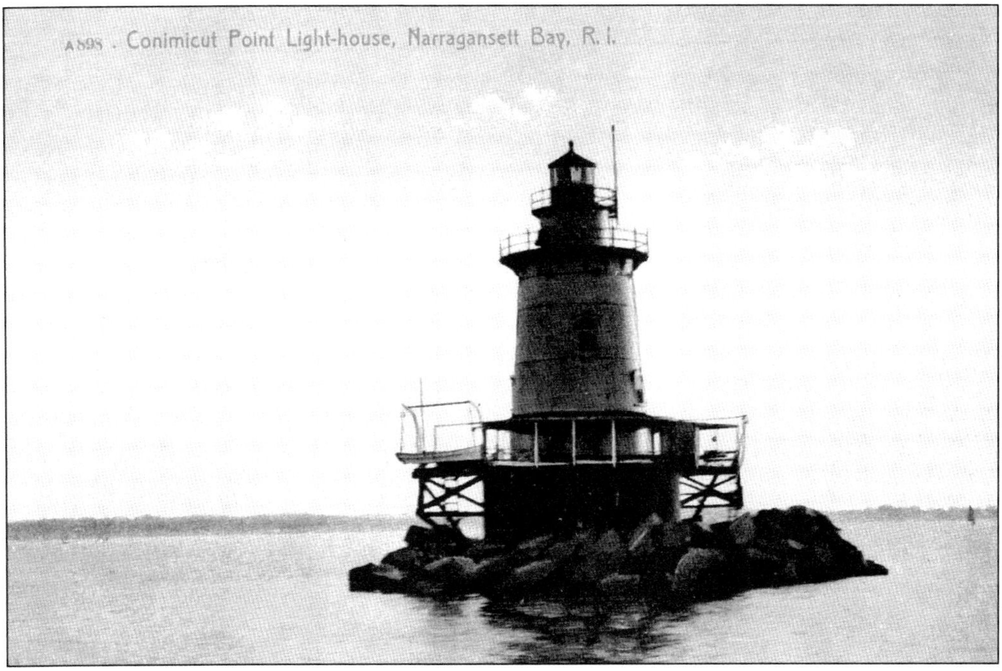

The active Conimicut Point Lighthouse is a 58-foot cast-iron, sparkplug-shaped tower that incorporates a three-story keeper's quarters, with a lantern, two upper galleries, and a lower gallery mounted on a granite caisson. This postcard image was taken around 1907.

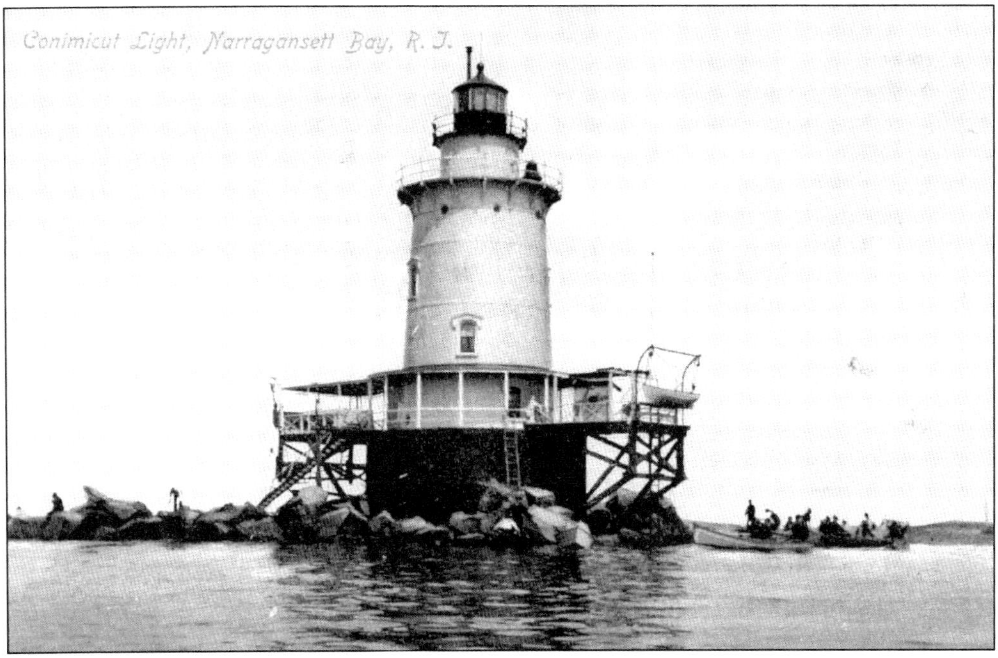

The Conimicut Point Lighthouse is painted white with black trim and the lantern black; the foghorn makes two blasts every 30 seconds. Ownership of the lighthouse was transferred to the City of Warwick on September 30, 2004.

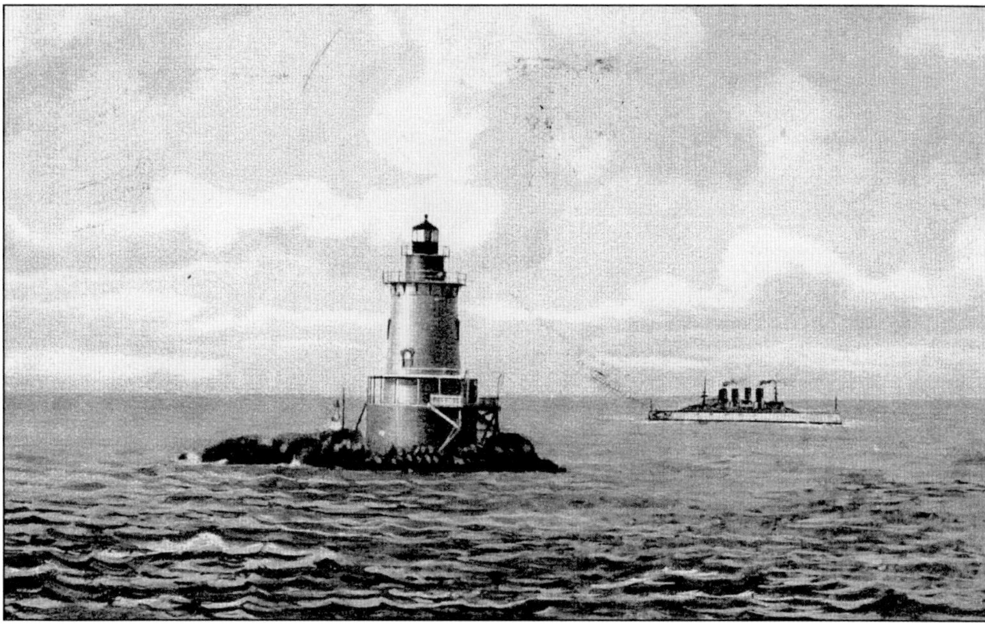

There are plans to restore the Conimicut Point Lighthouse tower and hopes of eventually offering tours. The structure is located on a dangerous shoal near the mouth of the Providence River. Views from Conimicut Point Park in Warwick can be seen. This postcard image was taken around 1909.

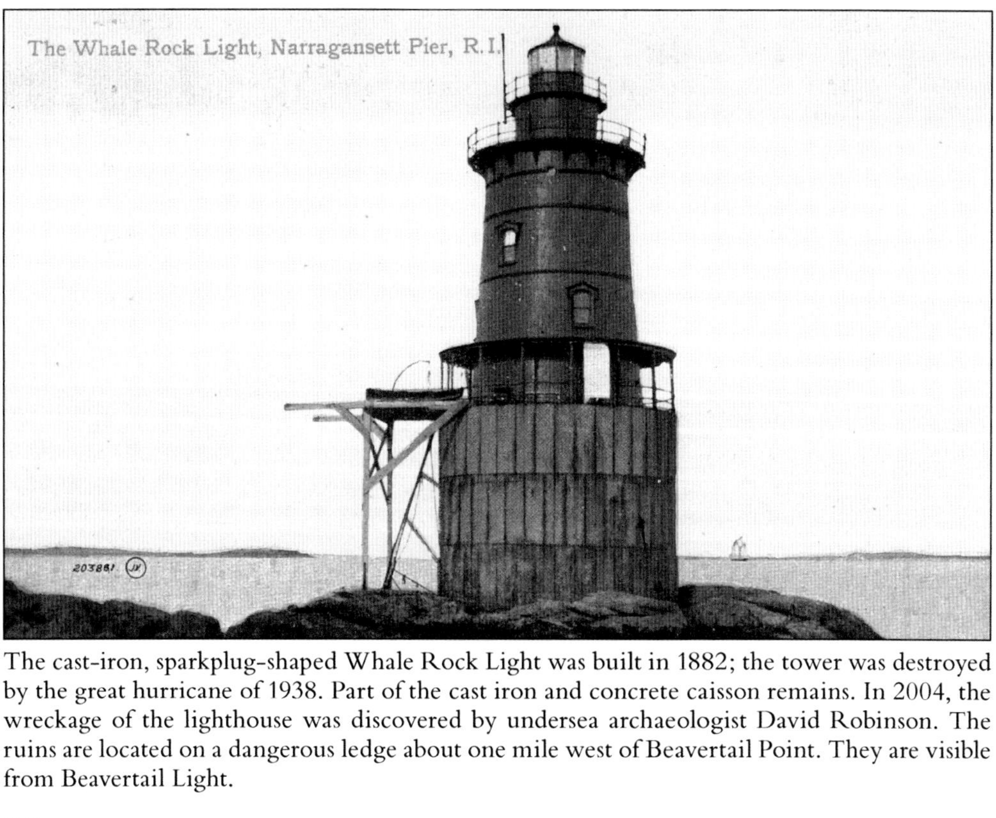

The cast-iron, sparkplug-shaped Whale Rock Light was built in 1882; the tower was destroyed by the great hurricane of 1938. Part of the cast iron and concrete caisson remains. In 2004, the wreckage of the lighthouse was discovered by undersea archaeologist David Robinson. The ruins are located on a dangerous ledge about one mile west of Beavertail Point. They are visible from Beavertail Light.

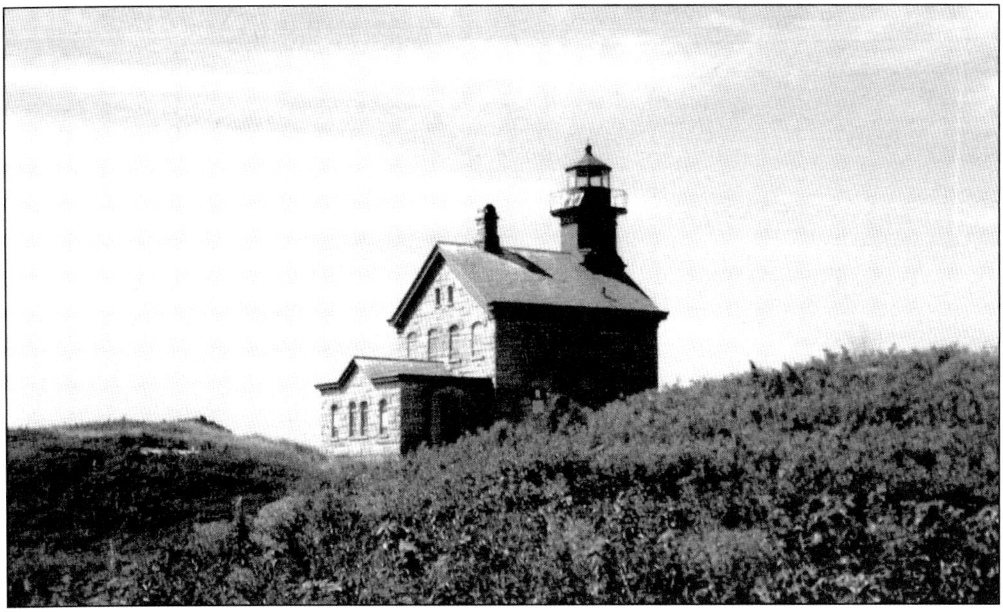

Block Island's North Lighthouse was built in 1868; it was inactive from 1973 to 1989. It has since been reactivated. The Victorian-era building has an octagonal cylindrical granite tower with lantern and gallery, attached "schoolhouse" style to the front of a two-story granite keeper's house. The light tower and lantern are painted red; the rest of the building is unpainted granite.

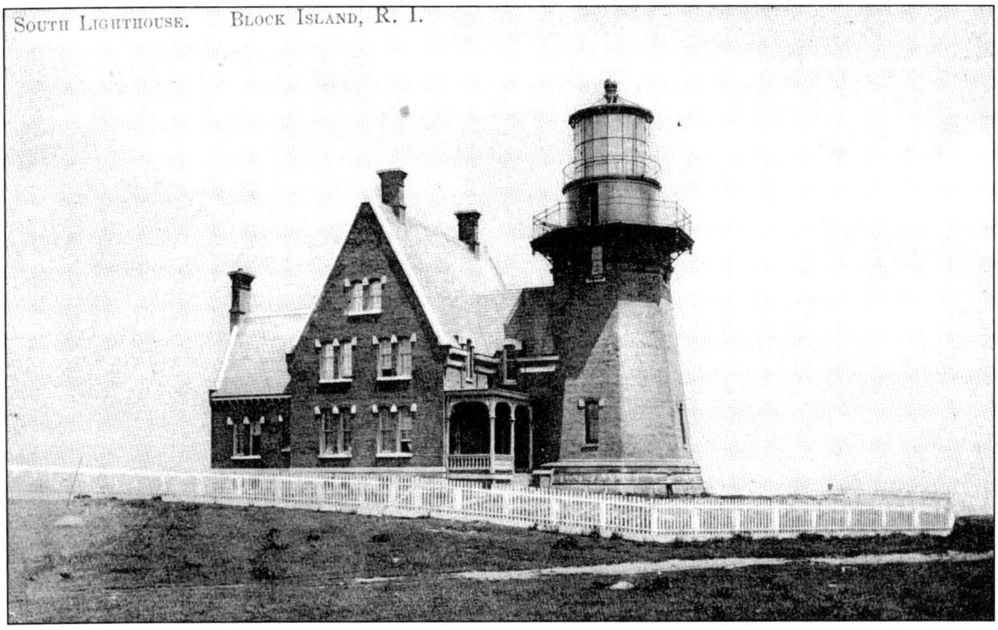

A *c.* 1919 view of Block Island's reactivated Southeast Lighthouse, built in 1875, is seen here. The 52-foot octagonal cylindrical brick tower with lantern and double gallery is attached to a massive two-and-a-half-story brick Gothic keeper's house. This impressive building is recognized as a national historic landmark. The entire four-million-pound structure was relocated 360 feet back in 1993 to escape erosion of the bluffs.

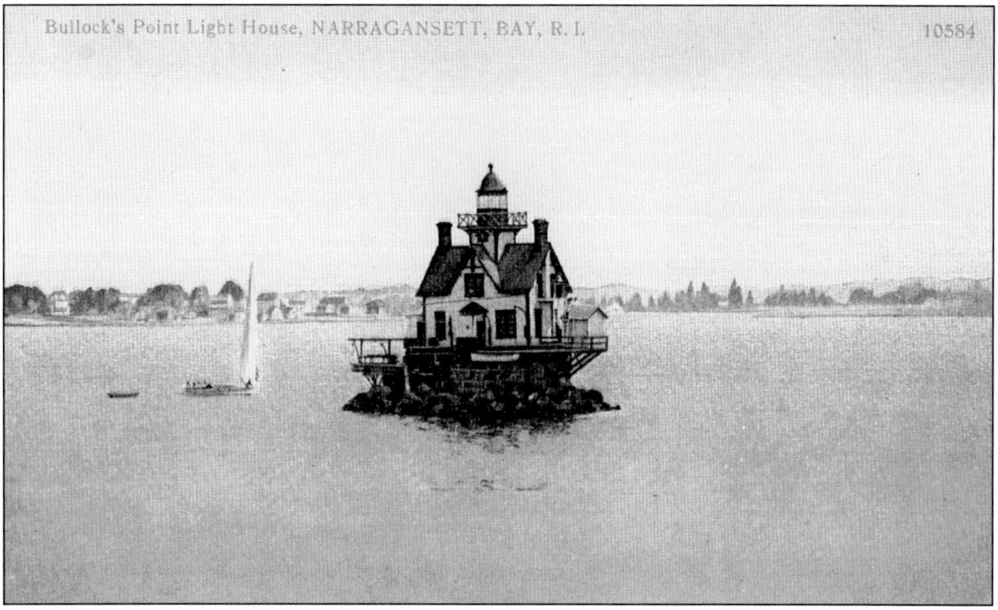

The Bullock's Point Lighthouse was built in 1876. It became inactive in 1938 when the lighthouse was heavily damaged by the great hurricane of that year; it was demolished around 1940. An active white light, occulting every four seconds, is on a skeletal tower mounted atop the stone crib that supported the building. It is located off Bullock's Point about two miles north of Nyatt Point.

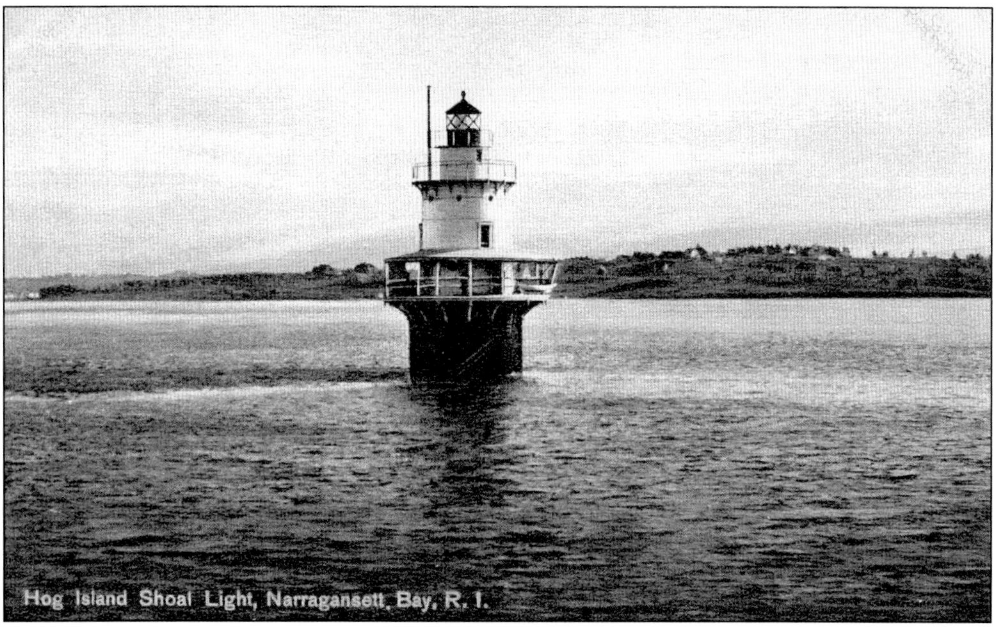

The Hog Island Shoal Light is a 60-foot cast-iron, sparkplug-shaped tower, incorporating a two-story keeper's quarters, with a lantern, two upper galleries, and a lower gallery mounted on a granite caisson. The Coast Guard renovated and repaired the tower in 1995. In 2004, the lighthouse became available for transfer under the National Historic Lighthouse Preservation Act of 2000; the only application received was rejected.

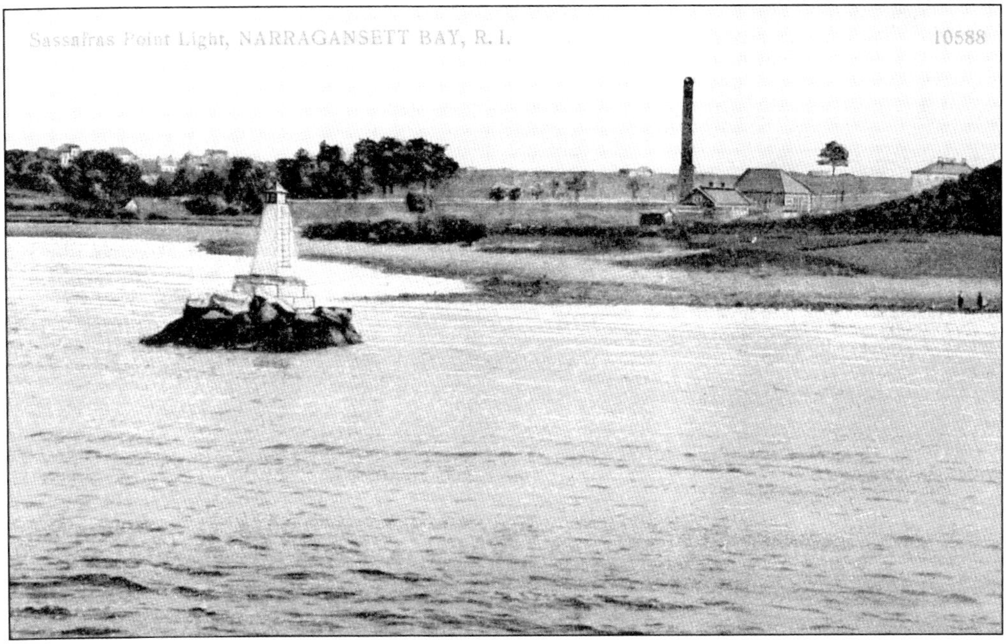

The Sassafras Point Light was built in 1872. The small hexagonal tower had a fixed red light 25 feet above sea level. Because the keeper had no dwelling on the light, he had to row the half mile from shore to care for the beacon.

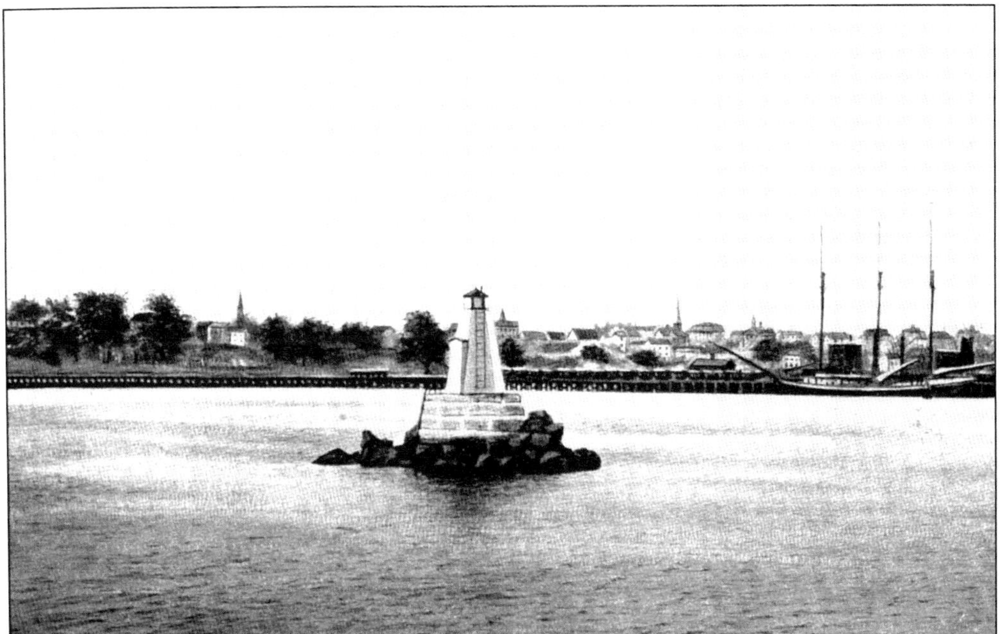

Sassafras Point, on the west side of the Providence River, took its name from the profusion of that variety of tree growing there. The Sassafras Point Light was removed in July 1912 to facilitate widening of the channel.

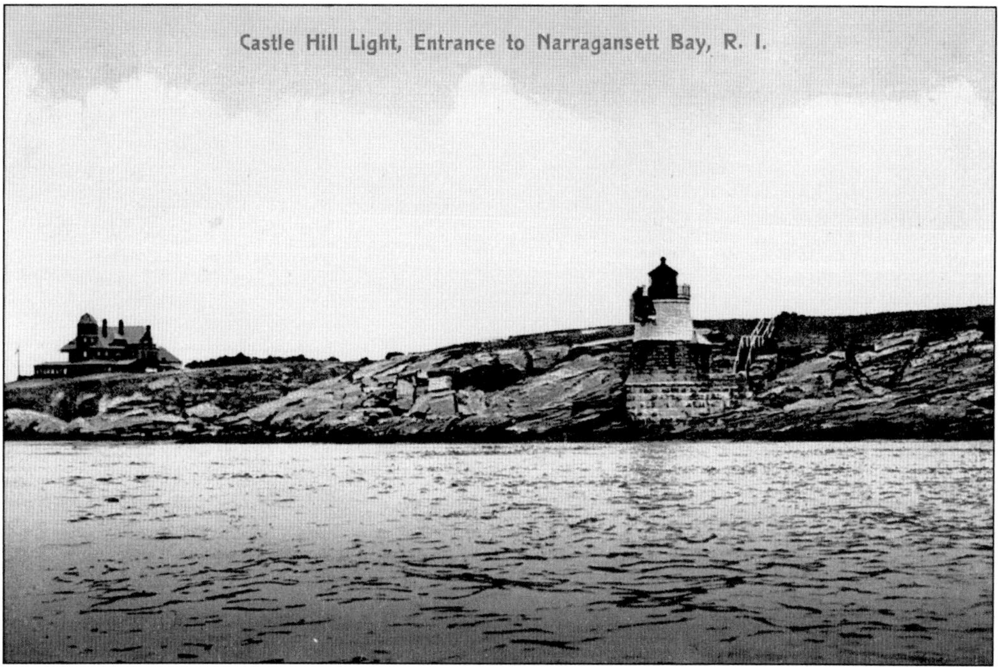

The Castle Hill Light at the entrance to Newport Harbor was built in 1890. This active light is 34 feet above sea level. It has a granite tower with lantern and gallery. The upper half of tower is painted white, the lower half is unpainted, and the lantern is painted black. The two-story brick keeper's house stands near Castle Hill Cove, a few hundred feet from the lighthouse. This postcard image was taken around 1915.

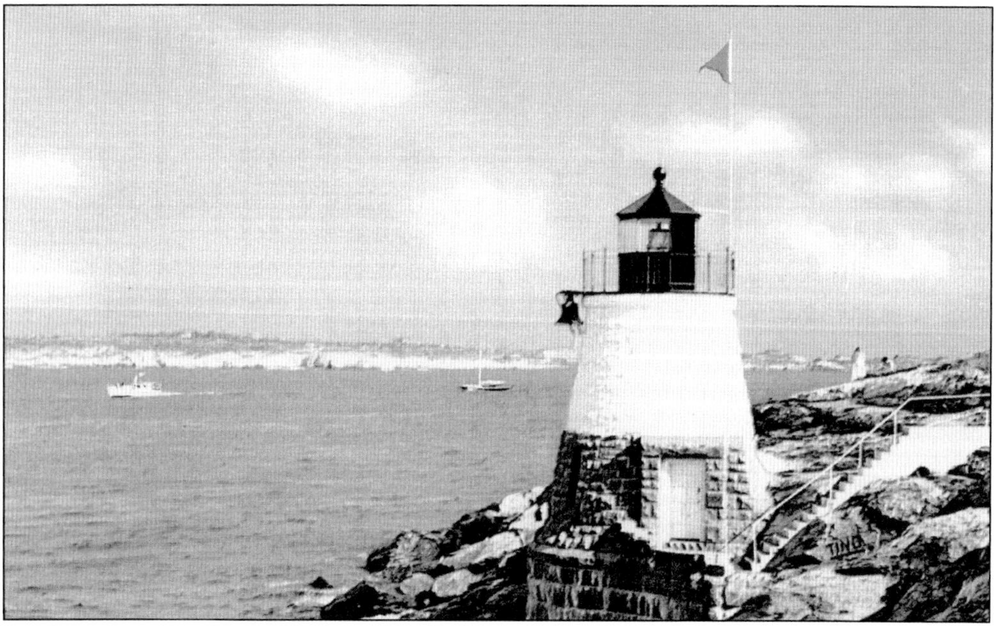

The Castle Hill Light is located at Castle Hill Point at the southwestern end of Newport. The lighthouse is accessible by a short walk from the nearby Castle Hill Cove Marina. This postcard image was taken around 1965.

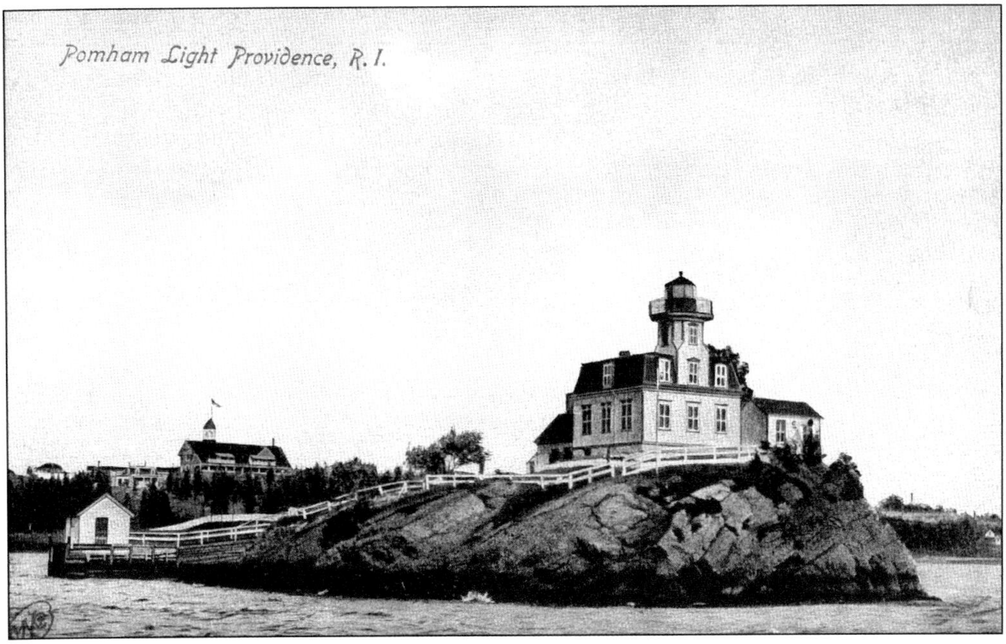

The Pomham Rock Light was built in 1871; it has been inactive since 1974. The octagonal cylindrical wood tower with lantern and gallery is 40 feet high, mounted on a two-story Empire-style wood keeper's house. Formerly occupied by caretakers, the building is currently vacant.

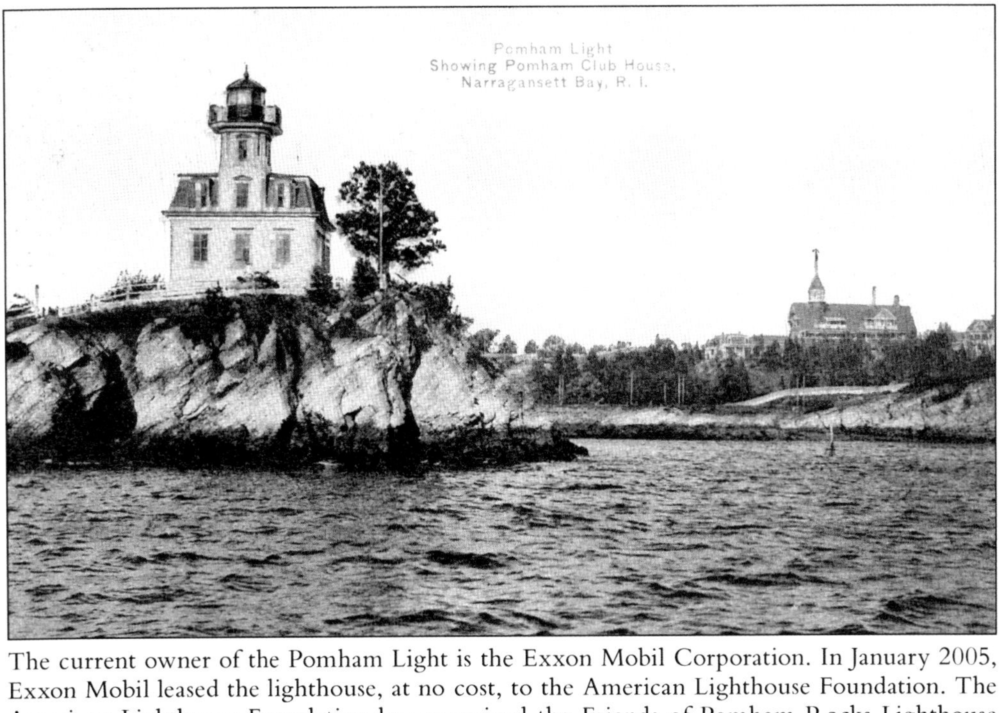

The current owner of the Pomham Light is the Exxon Mobil Corporation. In January 2005, Exxon Mobil leased the lighthouse, at no cost, to the American Lighthouse Foundation. The American Lighthouse Foundation has organized the Friends of Pomham Rocks Lighthouse to work for restoration and reactivation of the lighthouse. Restoration work by the Abcore Restoration Company was underway in the summer of 2005.

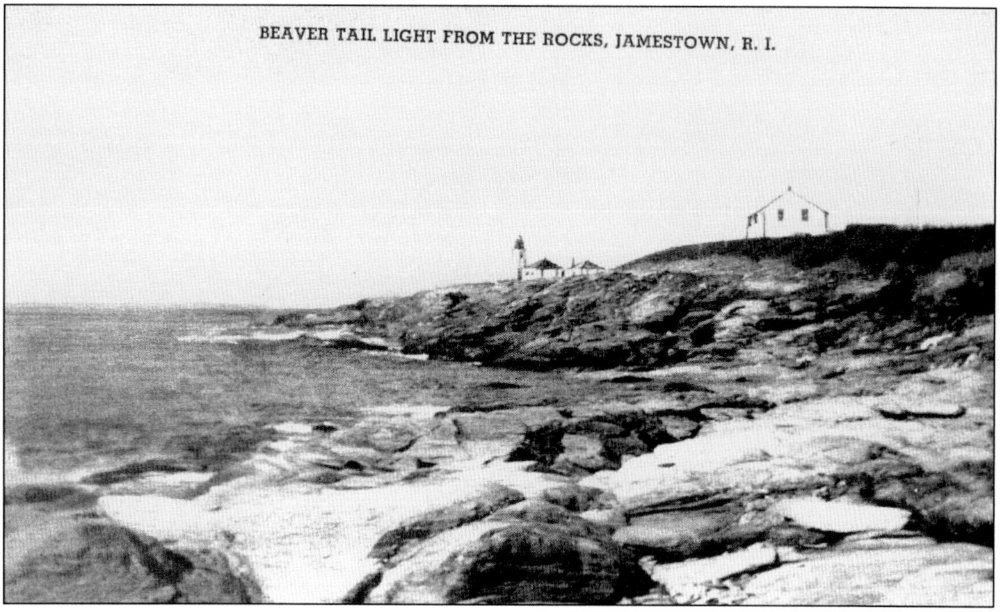

The Beavertail Light Station was established in 1749. The 45-foot square cylindrical granite tower with lantern and double gallery is attached to a two-story stucco-clad brick keeper's house that was built in 1856. The tower is unpainted granite, the lantern and watch room are painted black, and the keeper's house is white with red roofs. The assistant keeper's house, built in 1898, contains a museum.

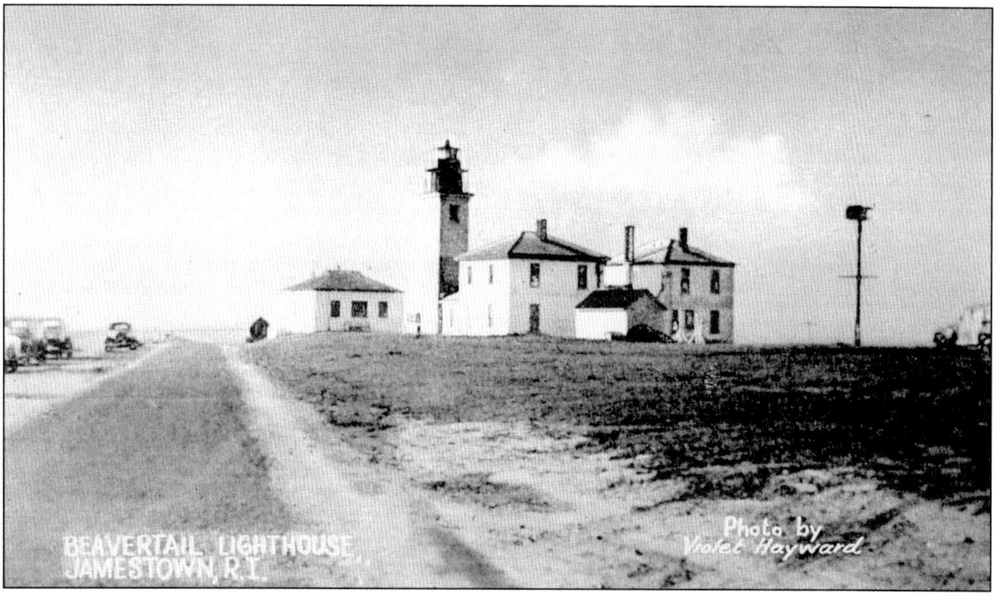

This is the nation's third-oldest light station. The foundations of the 1749 lighthouse remain visible. The Beavertail Lighthouse Museum Association works for preservation of the light station. In late 2004, the lighthouse became available for transfer under the National Lighthouse Preservation Act; the Beavertail Lighthouse Museum Association is coordinating an application for ownership. The site is located on Beavertail Point on the southern tip of Jamestown on Conanicut Island.

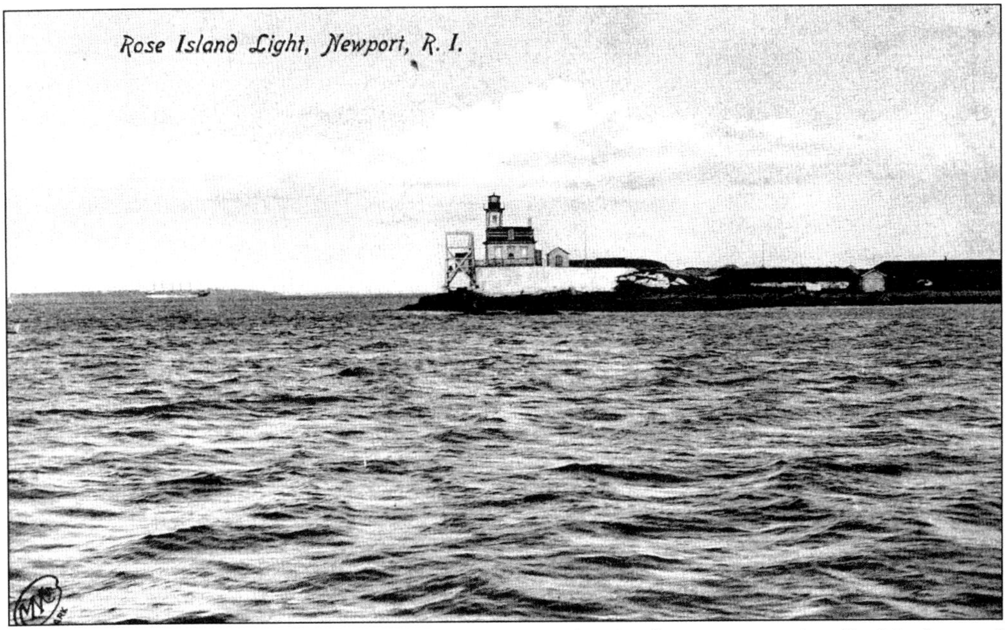

The Rose Island Lighthouse was built in 1870. The 35-foot octagonal cylindrical wood tower with lantern and gallery is mounted on a two-story Empire-style wood keeper's house. Beginning in 1992, the lighthouse has been carefully restored to its 1912 appearance. The first floor of the building is a museum, and the second floor has two guest rooms available year-round for one-week stays by volunteer caretakers.

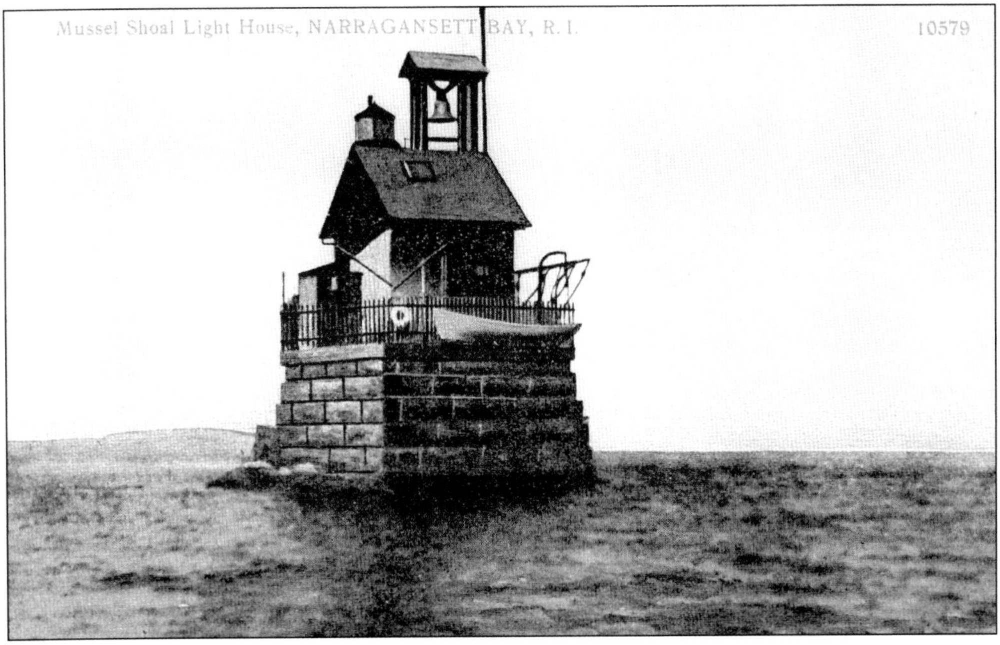

The Mussel Shoal Light Station, off Bristol Ferry at the entrance to Mount Hope Bay, was established in 1873. The 20-foot skeletal tower is on a concrete pad resting on the ruins of a granite pier. The modern light replaces an 1879 lighthouse that stood on the same pier until destroyed by the hurricane of 1938. This postcard image was taken around 1900.

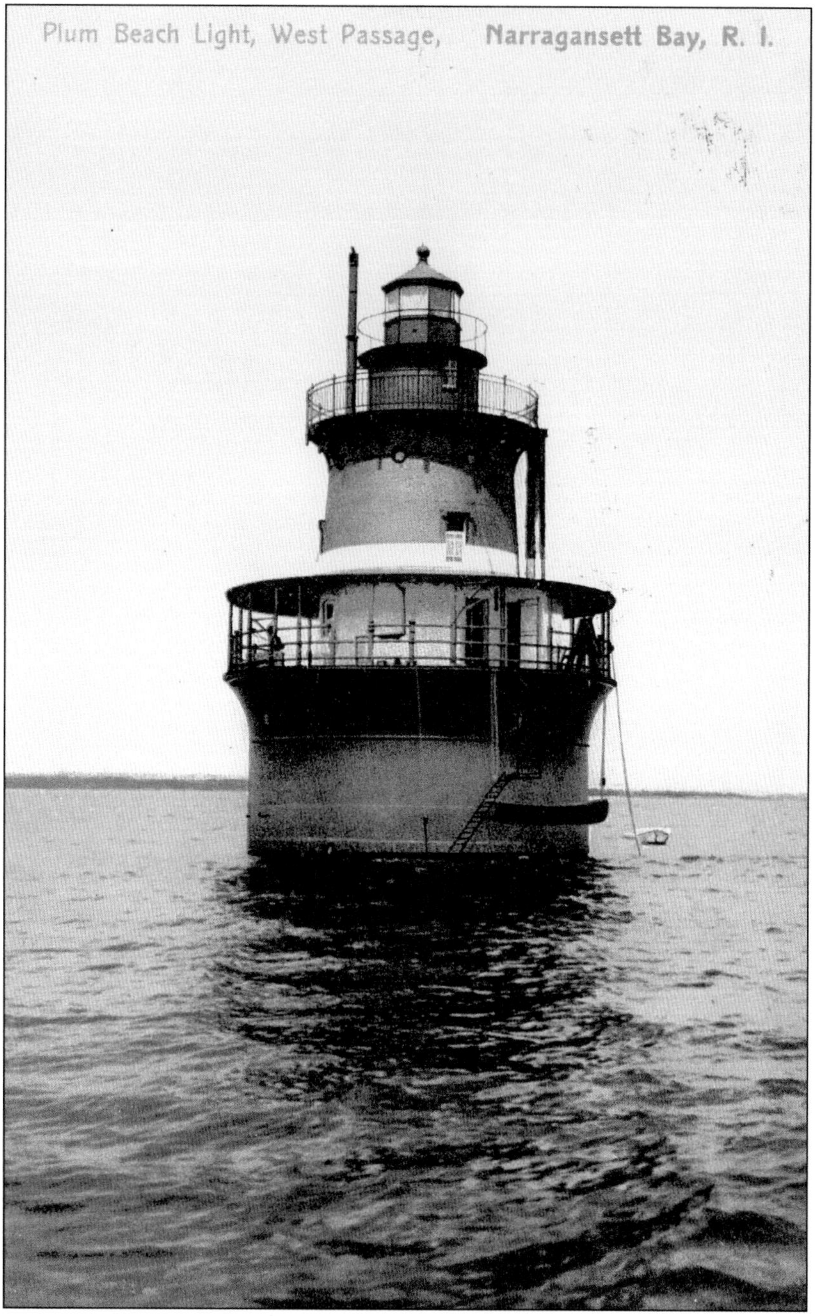

The Plum Beach Light in the West Passage of Narragansett Bay was built in 1899. The reactivated light, now privately maintained, is a 53-foot cast-iron sparkplug tower with lantern, double galleries above, and a lower gallery, incorporating a three-story keeper's quarters, and mounted on a cast-iron caisson. Previously abandoned and rusting, the lighthouse spent years on the Lighthouse Digest Doomsday List. A long dispute over ownership was settled in favor of the State of Rhode Island in 1998. In 1999, the Friends of Plum Beach Lighthouse received ownership and a $500,000 grant for restoration. The restoration project was carried out during the summer and fall of 2003.